What Do Dreams Do?

What Do Dreams Do?

SUE LLEWELLYN

University of Manchester, UK

OXFORD

UNIVERSITY PRESS

OXFORD

UNIVERSITY PRESS

Great Clarendon Street, Oxford, OX2 6DP,
United Kingdom

Oxford University Press is a department of the University of Oxford.
It furthers the University's objective of excellence in research, scholarship,
and education by publishing worldwide. Oxford is a registered trade mark of
Oxford University Press in the UK and in certain other countries

© Oxford University Press 2020

The moral rights of the author have been asserted

First Edition published in 2020

Impression: 1

Published in the United States of America by Oxford University Press
198 Madison Avenue, New York, NY 10016, United States of America

British Library Cataloguing in Publication Data

Data available

Library of Congress Control Number: 2020944550

ISBN 978–0–19–881895–3

Printed and bound by
CPI Group (UK) Ltd, Croydon, CR0 4YY

Acknowledgements

This book has benefited greatly from comments and suggestions from many people. My particular thanks go to György Buzsáki, John Dawson, Martin Desseilles, Matthew Erdelyi, Allan Hobson, Caroline Horton, Penny Lewis, Tom Llewellyn, Josie Malinowski, Tore Nielsen, Carlyle Smith, and ChunLei Yang. I'd also like to thank Becky Ritchie for the dream illustrations and the liena image, Tina Wulff for the figures and diagrams, and Sam Price for the book cover.

Contents

Prologue: What Do Dreams Do?

What do dreams do? If asked, I suspect many people would answer 'Not a lot!' I believe people dismiss their dreams for three reasons.

First, to our minds, when awake, dreams don't seem to make sense. We use words like 'strange', 'odd', 'bizarre' or 'weird'—'I had a really funny dream last night ...' In *A Midsummer Night's Dream* Shakespeare has Bottom say 'I have had a dream, past the wit of man to say what dream it was'. Like Bottom, we don't know what to make of our dreams.

Second, to our minds, when awake, we don't feel we own dreams. They seem more like things that happen to us rather than narratives we generate. The way we talk about dreams demonstrates this—like Bottom, we speak of *having* a dream rather than *creating* one.

Third, although we experience a dream as a real, on-going involvement in a series of situations, when we wake up we say it was *just* a dream. We tend to distance ourselves from dreams, thinking and talking about them as 'unreal'. Assuming they, 'don't mean, do or yield much'. Again, in *A Midsummer Night's Dream*, Shakespeare has Puck say 'And this weak and idle theme, No more yielding but a dream'. The ironic comment 'Dream on' suggests disconnection between dreams and reality. Dreams are ephemeral, leading us nowhere. 'It's just a dream' describes a hopelessly ill-conceived project. A plan we already know we will never achieve.

But some people don't dismiss their dreams. Some still believe a dream is a revelation or 'message' from an external source. Ancient societies—the Sumerians may be the first—believed dreams were sent by the gods; they employed dream priests to interpret them. After Freud, some think dreams come from the unconscious. Interpreting dreams to understand their hidden meanings has widespread intellectual currency and underpins psychoanalysis. Chapter 9 looks at dream meanings. Chapter 12 compares and contrasts my dream theory with Freud's. There are people who research dreams. I am one of them! Despite this research, overall, I think it's fair to say, now, in the second decade of the 21st century, many, if not most, people dismiss their dreams, believing they dissolve and vanish on waking and have little, if any, impact on their lives.

This book presents an entirely different picture. I think, originally, we dreamed to survive. So we should take dreams seriously! Chapter 4 tells the 'backstory' of dreaming, in the sense of the evolutionary, basic survival reason for dreaming. I argue other important functions of dreaming are linked to basic survival: dream to remember; dream to decide; dream to predict; and dream to create. All of these derive from making associations between experiences and dreaming is our most associative state. When we make associations between things we are finding a pattern. Chapter 2 explains my theory of dreaming as complex, non-obvious pattern identification.

We shouldn't dismiss our dreams but, paradoxically, we don't need to puzzle over what dreams mean to benefit from them. Most dreamwork happens unconsciously. Our dreams influence our memories, decisions, expectations, and actions without us realizing it. Being in a dream-like state of mind also makes you more creative, which can merge into being crazy. Dreams do a lot. This book tells you how.

1

What Is a Dream?

Introduction

Here I cover current knowledge about what dreams are, along with features of sleep that are relevant to later chapters. I start with rapid eye movement (REM) sleep. If you are familiar with sleep and dreams, you could skip this chapter.

Dreams and REM Sleep

Until fairly recently people thought of sleep as what happens when you get tired—as a passive period of unconsciousness for rest and restoration. This view changed when Eugene Aserinsky and Nathaniel Kleitman discovered REM sleep in 1952. They noticed, during this sleep stage, both eyes moved in tandem, darting rapidly from side to side, hence the name 'REM'. In contrast, the muscles in the rest of the body (apart from vital organs) are paralysed. Also, when Aserinsky and Kleitman awakened people from REM sleep, they almost always reported vivid and elaborate dreams. For example:

> I am trying to organize a group for departure. I find one member at the foot of a hill, near some water. I urge him to go up the hill to a rendezvous point for de-parture. Suddenly, or perhaps always, he is in a red car, which runs along beside me up the hill. The peculiar thing is that the front of the car, including the driver, is underground. Yet its trajectory is smooth and the ground is unbroken! As we climb, the car moves ahead of me and I make a strong but vain attempt to keep up with its progress. The car then crosses from left to right and runs, still half under-ground into a wall. I wonder if the driver will have hurt his head in the crash. The scene changes. I am in a locker room and approach my son Ian who has been hurt. At first his legs appear to have been amputated at the knees and I feel dread. But, as I approach, what I took to be stumps are his blood-smeared kneecaps (very bright red blood-like the car-and he is smiling- not crying). I am relieved and wake up.[1]

These vivid dreams show that people are conscious during REM—this discovery blew away the idea that all of sleep is passive unconsciousness.

What Do Dreams Do? Sue Llewellyn, Oxford University Press (2020). © Oxford University Press.
DOI: 10.1093/oso/9780198818953.001.0001.

REM dreams usually involve the dreamer in many different actions—we are almost always moving about. The muscular paralysis during REM sleep prevents dreamers acting out what is going on in their dreams. After Aserinsky and Kleitman's discovery, it was thought for some time that all dreaming happened during REM sleep. Then researchers found people reported dreams outside of REM sleep, in sleep stages now called non-REM (henceforth, NREM). But these NREM dreams were shorter, more thought-like and less associative, less vivid, less elaborately narrative, less bizarre and less emotional than REM dreams. For example, one dreamer reported, 'I was thinking of problems about my examination ... I had the image of the open book ... nothing else.'[2] Another NREM report was somewhat closer to a REM one: 'I think I was talking with some people about whether or not a certain manufacturer had a specific kind of brace designed for some crippled leg. It seemed hard to find. It wasn't too clear, that's all I recall. I think there was some visual imagery.'[3]

If you think of consciousness as different states existing along a continuum, in NREM dreams people seem to be in a state of mind in-between REM dreaming and waking consciousness.

In this book I concentrate on REM dreams because there is evidence that REM sleep is more important for complex pattern identification. To identify non-obvious patterns, elements have to be extracted from memories of experiences and then integrated into a visual narrative. This means that memories have to be reorganized during sleep. Several studies support the conclusion that this process of reorganizing, extracting, and integrating memory elements to identify complex patterns occurs during REM sleep.[4] REM dreams may visualize these patterns in a series of scenes that make up a narrative, but NREM dreams may also have functions. I discuss NREM dreams in this chapter, but this book focuses primarily on REM dreams, so, in the later chapters, 'dreams' refers specifically to REM dreams unless otherwise stated.

REM Sleep and Dreams vs NREM Sleep and Dreams

Whether NREM dreams should be considered as *dreams* is a matter of some heated debate. This controversy is, at least in part, a definitional one. There is no agreed definition of dreaming.[5] If you take a broad, inclusive definition of dreams, for example, 'a dream is conscious mental activity during sleep', then NREM occurrences are definitely dreams. On the other hand, definitions that focus on dream content, such as 'vivid, bizarre, emotional, highly associative mental experiences which develop in a story-like manner during sleep and are embodied, but out of volitional control', may exclude NREM dreams.

There are physiological differences between the brain states that underlie REM and NREM sleep that will make the subjective dream experiences different in the two states.[6] These physiological differences show up in the way brain cells (neurons) transfer information (send messages) and in the specific brain areas that are active (i.e. sending messages), or inactive, during REM and NREM sleep and dreams.

First, neuronal communication of information underlies all our sensations, thoughts, feelings, actions, memories, and dreams; it takes two forms—electrical and chemical. Both forms enable neurons to 'talk to each other'. Electrical communication is through brainwaves and occurs within the neuron. Most people think of a brainwave as a sudden, bright idea, but brainwaves convey all ideas. Brainwaves during NREM sleep are slow and deep, about two to four per second, i.e. they are low frequency, whereas those during REM sleep are fast and occur at a rate of about 60 per second, i.e. they are high frequency. As regards brainwaves, those during REM sleep and dreams are actually quite like those that occur in wakefulness, which is why REM is sometimes called 'paradoxical' sleep (from now on I will refer to wakefulness as simply 'wake' so that sleep and wake have some equivalence as complementary brain/mind states).

Typically, neurons do not touch each other. Electrical brainwaves cannot 'leap' across the tiny gaps that separate them. So across these tiny gaps, called synapses, electrical communication is replaced by chemical communication that occurs through neurotransmitters—chemical 'messengers' that move between one neuron and another. Through the drug industry, the names of some of these messengers have become well known. For example, serotonin, the 'feel-good' neurotransmitter, is boosted by anti-depressive drugs like Prozac. REM sleep, NREM sleep, and wake differ in their chemical messengers.[7] For example, serotonin is shut off in REM sleep. In NREM sleep serotonin is at about half its level in wake. From the perspective of brain chemistry, we could say REM and wake differ, with NREM being in-between.

Second, brain activation differs in NREM and REM sleep. During NREM, brain activation is diminished compared with levels in wake, but it would be wrong to assume that little of any consequence happens, as will be explained in later chapters. During REM, some brain regions are as active, or even more active, than in wake; other areas are deactivated. The visual, associative parts of the brain are hyperactive during REM, as are the emotional processing regions and ones that enable conscious experience of the self. Brain structures involved in memories of experiences are highly activated. Motor areas are also hyperactive, giving rise to the embodied movement that characterizes REM dreams. On the other hand, regions that enable control over thought and actions aren't active during REM (which is why REM dream narratives develop outside of volition), nor are those that allow sustained concentration. Brain areas that underlie 'reality-testing' are inactive. In consequence, when impossible events happen in REM dreams they aren't questioned, nor do dreamers realize they are dreaming.

These brain differences in REM and NREM sleep mean that differences in their corresponding mind states would be anticipated too. In consequence, REM and

NREM dreams would be expected to differ, and their functions may vary too. As will become clear, this is my own view.

An issue here is the relationship between the mind and the brain. In this book I will use the shorthand 'mind/brain' and avoid a lengthy digression on their relationship. For readers who are interested, a good source is 'How are the mind and brain related?'[8] For the purposes of this book, the expression mind/brain means that if the mind constructs a REM dream, underlying brain processes enable dream construction to happen. As Allan Hobson, a well-known American dream researcher, writes 'Therefore, if we detect a dream form, we can seek a corresponding brain form.'[9]

Similarly, while awake, if I'm giving a research presentation I really have to concentrate and not allow my mind/brain to become distracted. My mind/brain is in concentration form. In contrast, if I'm on a bus on the way into work my mind/brain may be diverted and daydreaming prevails. Just as your mind/brain can assume different forms in waking hours, it takes various forms during sleep, but during sleep these different forms occur in a distinct sequence of stages. So far I have distinguished REM and NREM, but the latter has some clear subdivisions into stages 1, 2, and 3. During sleep, when we aren't responding to the external world, complex stages play out across the night.

Different Sleep and Dream Stages Across the Night

On falling asleep you pass through NREM stage 1, a brief period of drowsiness, followed by stage 2, a period of light sleep. During this NREM stage 2 light sleep, brainwaves incorporate sleep spindles—these are intermittent, short bursts of fast brainwaves that start out shallow, get deeper, and then go shallow again, like a spindle, hence the name. Sleep spindles come in two varieties, fast and slow, and may be related to dreams (see Chapter 5). After this first period of light NREM stage 2 sleep, you enter NREM stage 3, more commonly known as 'slow-wave' sleep, when slow and deep brainwaves occur. This first period of slow-wave sleep lasts about an hour. It would be very difficult to wake you during this and subsequent stages of slow-wave sleep. Also, if you are awakened during slow-wave sleep in the early part of the night, you are very unlikely to report any conscious experience.[10] After the first slow-wave sleep stage and another brief period of NREM stage 2 light sleep, comes the first REM period, which lasts about 10 minutes, and then the cycle repeats every 90–100 minutes. If you go to bed at 11pm and wake at 7am, you will have progressed through five sleep cycles. Across these cycles, periods of slow-wave sleep get shorter. The last cycle generally has no slow-wave sleep, whereas periods of REM get longer—in the last cycle REM sleep lasts about an hour. So, in the first half of the night, slow-wave sleep predominates, followed by REM domination in the second half of the night. About 45–55% of a night's sleep consists of stage 2 NREM with its characteristic, intermittent sleep spindles (see Figure 1.1). You will notice that on the night depicted in Figure 1.1 the sleeper awoke briefly during the night at the end of cycle 3. For interested readers, several websites and books give a fuller account of these different sleep stages.[11]

What can we say about dreaming during these different sleep stages? A recent study calculated that 96.4% of awakenings from REM sleep came with a dream report.[12] But 50% of people awakened from NREM sleep recall some mental activity; whether this qualifies as dreaming is a definitional issue—with a restricted definition of vivid, bizarre dreaming (as given on p. 2), many NREM reports don't qualify.[13] Also, people experienced in dream research were able to discriminate between REM and NREM dream reports with a high degree of accuracy (90–95%) without knowing which stage of sleep the dream was from, indicating there are distinct differences between REM and NREM dreams.[14]

However, differences between REM and NREM dreams are complicated by the sleep stage in which they occur. Late-night/early-morning NREM dreams are more like REM dreams: they become less thought-like and more visual. i.e. hallucinatory.[15] Two explanations have been proposed for this. Late-night NREM dreams could be generated by the presence of some aspect of REM brain physiology in NREM sleep—this possibility has been termed covert REM sleep processes during NREM.[16] Or dreams recalled from late-night NREM sleep, especially early in the NREM period, could be related to dreams remembered from the previous REM period. As the two explanations aren't mutually exclusive, both may contribute to late-night NREM dreams being more like REM dreams.

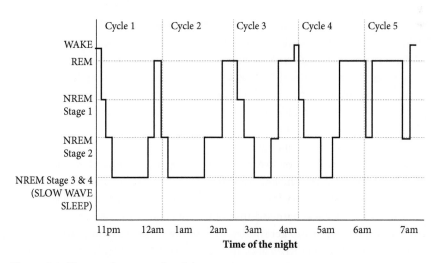

Figure 1.1 Sleep cycles across the night.

Comparing naps that consist of only REM or NREM sleep eliminates the possibility of prior REM dreams influencing the content of NREM dreams. A study of such naps concluded that dreaming (when defined as any conscious experience during sleep) can happen during NREM sleep, but some REM sleep mechanisms intrude into NREM sleep in the morning (when there is the most REM sleep) and generate REM-like (more vivid, bizarre, and emotional) NREM dreams.[17]

Another study found that during dreams (defined inclusively as conscious experience during any stage of sleep) brainwaves in a region at the back of the brain (called a 'hot zone' by the researchers) had a local decrease in low-frequency brainwaves (slow waves), along with a local increase in fast and frequent brainwaves (similar to those occurring during REM sleep), even though some slow-wave activity was still taking place in other parts of the brain.[18] This study, like the nap study, showed that vivid, fully developed dreaming happens in NREM sleep when physiological markers (i.e. the brainwave profile) for REM sleep is present. The study also demonstrated that brainwaves within slow-wave sleep aren't all slow— there can be local variation. Another study by the same group of researchers showed that dreaming in NREM sleep occurred not only in the presence of decreased slow waves, but was also preceded by fast spindles that occurred towards the back of the brain.[19]

Research on dream content across several sleep stages shows some continuity across the night, for example through repeating themes.[20] The content of late-night NREM dreams may be influenced by prior REM dreams. So both explanations of why late-night NREM dreams are more like REM dreams may be correct.

Dreams in NREM Sleep Onset: Stage 1

So far we haven't looked at any conscious experiences we may have in NREM sleep stage 1—the drowsy sleep that happens at sleep onset. These conscious experiences haven't generally been considered as dreams, although recent investigations have dubbed them 'microdreams'.[21] Traditionally, conscious experiences at sleep onset are termed hypnagogic hallucinations because, unlike fully developed dreams, they tend to be short, static, occupy only the centre of the visual field, and don't involve the dreamer as an active participant.[22] If hallucinations happen when waking up, at the border between sleeping and wake, they are called hypnopompic. Like dreams these hallucinations are usually visual rather than auditory (i.e. auditory hallucinations are such things as hearing voices when no-one is speaking or music when none is being played). In one survey, 39% of people reported hallucinations; of these 25% were hypnagogic and 7% hypnopompic; in more than half the cases they weren't linked to any mental or physical disorder.[23]

Lucid Dreams

Occasionally, during REM dreaming,[24] the brain can spontaneously transition into a state that is more like wake, termed lucid dreaming. We shouldn't be surprised by this, given that REM dreams are similar to wake in many ways. During dream lucidity, the brain regions that are normally inactive during REM sleep become partially reactivated so the dreamer becomes aware they are dreaming. For example:

> I was standing on a paved road in the desert in the American West, somewhere like Arizona. It was very hot and dry and a warm wind was blowing. I was talking to my boyfriend, with whom I have been having some difficulties. We were just talking and suddenly I felt my hairpiece falling out and causing my hair to really blow around. I caught the hairpiece before it fell and noticed it was my pink one, the one I always wear to bed. When I realized this, I looked at my boyfriend and said, 'Oh! This means I'm dreaming!'[25]

This awareness is the hallmark of lucid dreaming. Sometimes awareness is accompanied by the ability to direct the dream narrative. (Normally, dreams are out of volitional control.) Some people find the ability to direct the dream plot enjoyable. With control over dream content, sex and flying are the most popular choices.[26] Unfortunately for those engaged in sex or flying, lucid dreams aren't usually maintained for long—the dreamer either wakes up or reverts back to REM dreaming.

About 55% of people report at least one lucid dream in their lifetime; for around 23% of the population lucid dreaming happens once a month or more.[27] Dream lucidity can be trained. Also those who meditate have more lucid dreams.[28] The ability to control dream content can be therapeutic. During a nightmare the dreamer can redirect the plot to a more pleasant outcome. However, recent research has linked spontaneous, as opposed to trained, lucid dreaming to mental health conditions.[29]

Daydreaming

The very name suggests it: the idea of dream-like states occurring during wake is commonly accepted. During daydreaming your mind/brain wanders in an unconstrained manner, making associations between past experiences in a similar way to dreaming while asleep. For example,

> I am daydreaming about walking the streets of London and, due to some memory of or fondness for British barber poles with their red and white stripes, this includes visualizing such a pole at the entrance to a barber shop; the colour and name of this pole give rise, by means of association, to the image of the Polish flag

and hence to some thought about Poland; because of some long-standing desire to visit that country, I stop my daydream about London and begin to occupy myself instead with a daydream about visiting Poland, starting off with the thought of this country; this again may remind me of my Polish friend at school whom I have not heard of for years, since she entered art school; and I may thus begin to daydream about her subsequent life and about meeting her again.[30]

Because this mind-wandering in wake occurs in the absence of tasks requiring concentration, the network of brain regions involved is often called the default network.[31] One way of thinking about this network is as a psychological baseline—what your mind/brain does when it's not doing anything else, or, at any rate, anything very demanding. In the presence of tasks requiring logic, focus, and concentration the default network gives way to the executive network, which supports cognitive control and the achievement of goals. But to think of the default mode as a network during which the mind wanders to no particular purpose would be wrong. During daydreaming, people retrieve personal memories, picture their futures, and dwell on significant others.[32] Imaging techniques, which show regional brain activation during different states of mind, demonstrate REM dreaming is an intensified form of default mind-wandering.[33] During daydreaming there may be short periods when the mind/brain is actually dreaming, just as it does in sleep.[34]

Briefly. . .

To summarize the current thinking about what dreams are: everyone recognizes they happen in REM sleep. Also consensus reigns about conscious experiences occurring during NREM sleep, but whether these conscious experiences are dreams is, I suggest, a definitional issue. It's becoming clearer that some aspects of REM-type brain activity are required for conscious experiences to happen in NREM. So-called NREM dreams may happen because of REM-type brain activity in NREM sleep.

If conscious experiences occur in NREM stage 1, they are generally termed hallucinations rather than dreams. Lucid dreams and daydreaming may be two sides of the same coin. During lucid dreams, wake-like control of dream content is sometimes possible, while in daydreaming the mind/brain wanders like it does in dreaming. One clear difference, however, is that spontaneous lucid dreaming is rare. In contrast, one survey found people spend half their waking hours daydreaming.[35] If the daydreaming half of wake is combined with quarter of sleep spent dreaming, consciousness is mostly dreaming! Maybe it's worth thinking about what dreaming does.

Next

The next chapter explains my own theory about what dreams do.

Notes

1. Dream example (p. 24) from Hobson, J. A. (2002). *Dreaming: An Introduction to the Science of Sleep*. Oxford University Press, New York.
2. Dream example (p. 1013) from Occhionero, M., & Cicogna, P. C. (2011). Autoscopic phenomena and one's own body representation in dreams. *Consciousness and cognition, 20*(4), 1009–1015.
3. Dream example (p. 557) from Kales, A., Hoedemaker, F. S., Jacobson, A., Kales, J. D., Paulson, M. J., & Wilson, T. E. (1967). Mentation during sleep: REM and NREM recall reports. *Perceptual and Motor Skills, 24*(2), 555–560.
4. Peigneux, P., Laureys, S., Fuchs, S., Destrebecqz, A., Collette, F., Delbeuck, X., ... & Luxen, A. (2003). Learned material content and acquisition level modulate cerebral reactivation during posttraining rapid-eye-movements sleep. *Neuroimage, 20*(1), 125–134; Barsky, M. M., Tucker, M. A., & Stickgold, R. (2015). REM sleep enhancement of probabilistic classification learning is sensitive to subsequent interference. *Neurobiology of Learning and Memory, 122*, 63–68; Landmann, N., Kuhn, M., Maier, J. G., Spiegelhalder, K., Baglioni, C., Frase, L., ... & Nissen, C. (2015). REM sleep and memory reorganization: potential relevance for psychiatry and psychotherapy. *Neurobiology of Learning and Memory, 122*, 28–40; Djonlagic, I., Rosenfeld, A., Shohamy, D., Myers, C., Gluck, M., & Stickgold, R. (2009). Sleep enhances category learning. *Learning & Memory, 16*(12), 751–755.
5. Pagel, J. F., Blagrove, M., Levin, R., States, B., Stickgold, B., & White, S. (2001). Definitions of dream: a paradigm for comparing field descriptive specific studies of dream. *Dreaming, 11*(4), 195–202. doi:10.1023/A:1012240307661
6. Takeuchi, T., Miyasita, A., Inugami, M., & Yamamoto, Y. (2001). Intrinsic dreams are not produced without REM sleep mechanisms: evidence through elicitation of sleep onset REM periods. *Journal of Sleep Research, 10*(1), 43–52.
7. During REM dreams, a transmitter called acetylcholine, required for learning and memory in wakefulness, is at high levels, whereas serotonin, the feel-good messenger, and another transmitter, noradrenaline, which elevates mood but can trigger anxiety and controls concentration, are active in wakefulness but shut off during REM. Dopamine, a neurotransmitter that enables motor activity and governs responses to risks and rewards, is active during wakefulness. Dopamine release increases somewhat during REM. In contrast, during NREM sleep and dreams serotonin and noradrenaline are at about half the level they are while we are awake; acetylcholine is at very low levels but dopamine levels remain similar throughout the wake–sleep cycle. For more information, see pp. 67–70 in Hobson, J. A. (2002). *Dreaming: An Introduction to the Science of Sleep*. Oxford University Press, New York; and Gottesmann, C. (2002). The

neurochemistry of waking and sleeping mental activity: the disinhibition-dopamine hypothesis. *Psychiatry and Clinical Neurosciences*, 56(4), 345–354.

8. How are the mind and brain related? Philosophy Now. Available at: https://philosophynow.org/issues/65/How_Are_The_Mind_And_Brain_Related

9. Hobson, J. A. (2002). *Dreaming: An Introduction to the Science of Sleep*. Oxford University Press, New York, p. 33.

10. Nir, Y., & Tononi, G. (2010). Dreaming and the brain: from phenomenology to neurophysiology. *Trends in Cognitive Sciences*, 14(2), 88–100.

11. How dreams work. Available at: https://science.howstuffworks.com/life/inside-the-mind/human-brain/dream6.htm. Stages of sleep. Available at: https://www.ncbi.nlm.nih.gov/books/NBK10996/ and pp. 43–55 in Walker, M. (2017). *Why We Sleep: The New Science of Sleep and Dreams*. Penguin, London.

12. Yu, C. K. C. (2015). The vicissitudes of affective valence across the night: a high-density electroencephalographic study. *Dreaming*, 25(4), 274.

13. Nielsen, T. A. (2000). A review of mentation in REM and NREM sleep: 'covert' REM sleep as a possible reconciliation of two opposing models. *Behavioral and Brain Sciences*, 23(6), 851–866.

14. Monroe, L. J., Rechtschaffen, A., Foulkes, D., & Jensen, J. (1965). Discriminability of REM and NREM reports. *Journal of Personality and Social Psychology*, 2(3), 456–460.

15. Fosse, R., & Domhoff, G. W. (2007). Dreaming as non-executive orienting: a conceptual framework for consciousness during sleep. In D. Barrett & P. McNamara (Eds), *The New Science of Dreaming: Content, Recall, and Personality Characteristics* (Vol. 2, pp. 1–27). Praeger Press, Westport, CT.

16. Nielsen, T. A. (2000). A review of mentation in REM and NREM sleep: 'covert' REM sleep as a possible reconciliation of two opposing models. *Behavioral and Brain Sciences*, 23(6), 851–866.

17. Suzuki, H., Uchiyama, M., Tagaya, H., Ozaki, A., Kuriyama, K., Aritake, S., ... & Kuga, R. (2004). Dreaming during non-rapid eye movement sleep in the absence of prior rapid eye movement sleep. *Sleep*, 27(8), 1486–1490.

18. Siclari, F., Baird, B., Perogamvros, L., Bernardi, G., LaRocque, J. J., Riedner, B., ... & Tononi, G. (2017). The neural correlates of dreaming. *Nature Neuroscience*, 20(6), 872.

19. Siclari, F., Bernardi, G., Cataldi, J., & Tononi, G. (2018). Dreaming in NREM sleep: a high-density EEG study of slow waves and spindles. *Journal of Neuroscience*, 38, 9175–9185.

20. Offenkrantz, W., & Rechtschaffen, A. (1963). Clinical studies of sequential dreams: I. a patient in psychotherapy. *Archives of General Psychiatry*, 8(5), 497–508 and Kramer, M. (2011). REM sleep and dreaming: the nature of the relationship. In B. N. Mallick, S. R. Pandi-Perumal, R. W. McCarley, & A. R. Morrison (Eds), *Rapid Eye Movement Sleep. Regulation and Function* (pp. 40–48). Cambridge University Press, New York.

21. But see Nielsen, T. (2017). Microdream neurophenomenology. *Neuroscience of Consciousness*, 2017(1), nix001, https://doi.org/10.1093/nc/nix001 for a full consideration of what he terms 'microdreams' at wake/sleep transitions.

22. Nir, Y., & Tononi, G. (2010). Dreaming and the brain: from phenomenology to neurophysiology. *Trends in Cognitive Sciences*, 14(2), 88–100.

23. Ohayon, M. M. (2000). Prevalence of hallucinations and their pathological associations in the general population. *Psychiatry Research*, *97*(2–3), 153–164.

24. One study claims to have identified lucid dreams in NREM sleep, see Stumbrys, T., & Erlacher, D. (2012). Lucid dreaming during NREM sleep: two case reports. *International Journal of Dream Research*, *5*(2), 151–155.

25. Dream example (p. 223) from Barrett, D. (1992). Just how lucid are lucid dreams? *Dreaming*, *2*(4), 221–228. https://doi.org/10.1037/h0094362

26. What people choose to dream about: sex and flying. Available at: https://www.livescience.com/46755-flying-sex-lucid-dream-content.html

27. Saunders, D. T., Roe, C. A., Smith, G., & Clegg, H. (2016). Lucid dreaming incidence: a quality effects meta-analysis of 50 years of research. *Consciousness and Cognition*, *43*, 197–215.

28. Reed, H. (1977). Meditation and lucid dreaming: a statistical relationship. *Sundance Community Dream Journal*, *2*, 237–238; and Gackenbach, J., & LaBarge, S. (Eds) (2012). *Conscious Mind, Sleeping Brain: Perspectives on Lucid Dreaming*. Springer Science & Business Media, Plenum Press, New York and London.

29. Dresler, M., Wehrle, R., Spoormaker, V. I., Steiger, A., Holsboer, F., Czisch, M., & Hobson, J. A. (2015). Neural correlates of insight in dreaming and psychosis. *Sleep Medicine Reviews*, *20*, 92–99; Mota, N. B., Resende, A., Mota-Rolim, S. A., Copelli, M., & Ribeiro, S. (2016). Psychosis and the control of lucid dreaming. *Frontiers in Psychology*, *7*, 294; and Rak, M., Beitinger, P., Steiger, A., Schredl, M., & Dresler, M. (2015). Increased lucid dreaming frequency in narcolepsy. *Sleep*, *38*(5), 787–792.

30. Daydreaming example from Dorsch, F. (2015). Focused daydreaming and mind-wandering. *Review of Philosophy and Psychology*, *6*(4), 791–813. doi:10.1007/s13164-014-0221-4

31. Buckner, R. L., Andrews-Hanna, J. R., & Schacter, D. L. (2008). The brain's default network. *Annals of the New York Academy of Sciences*, *1124*(1), 1–38.

32. Buckner, R. L., Andrews-Hanna, J. R., & Schacter, D. L. (2008). The brain's default network. *Annals of the New York Academy of Sciences*, *1124*(1), 1–38.

33. Fox, K. C. R., Nijeboer, S., Solomonova, E., Domhoff, G. W., & Christoff, K. (2013). Dreaming as mind wandering: evidence from functional neuroimaging and first-person content reports. *Frontiers in Human Neuroscience*, *7*, 412. doi:10.3389/fnhum.2013.00412

34. Foulkes, D., & Fleisher, S. (1975). Mental activity in relaxed wakefulness. *Journal of Abnormal Psychology*, *84*(1), 66; and Foulkes, D., & Scott, E. (1973). An above-zero baseline for the incidence of momentarily hallucinatory mentation. *Sleep Research*, *2*, 108.

35. People spend half their waking hours daydreaming. Available at: https://www.bbc.co.uk/news/health-11741350

PART I
DREAM PATTERNS, DREAM BASICS, AND DREAM BACKSTORY

2

Dream to See Patterns

Introduction

Dreams are a puzzle. We don't know what to make of them. Familiar faces, identi-
fiable places, and remembered experiences appear but dreams mix them up. Why?
This book aims to convince you that dreams take people, places, and events out
of their waking life context to identify a complex pattern in your experience. But
dreams don't seem like complex pattern identifiers. They appear chaotic. To address this apparent paradox, we'll take a detour into pattern detection.

Discerning Patterns in the World

Your brain evolved to detect patterns.[1] My definition of pattern is: a discernible
form in the way something happens or is done, where this form can be visualized.
My theory is rooted in our pre-linguistic evolutionary past, when we would have
visualized patterns in human or animal behaviour in the world. For example, take
vomiting. In my experience I vomit when I'm on boats, but only when the sea is
rough. I also vomit if I eat shellfish, have a migraine, or travel in cars—but only if
I read. Occasionally, I vomit when I'm uneasy. I vomited the first time I met my
future (now past) in-laws. I have constructed this example while awake but if you
associate and visualize 'sea–rough–car–read–shellfish–migraine–in-laws' you can
see how the image is becoming bizarre and dream-like.

Across evolutionary time, it would have been important to detect patterns in
the way humans and animals behave as they move about to secure resources (food,
water, mating opportunities) in the world. Contemporarily, the term 'resources'
encompasses much more than this because we do more than meet our basic needs.

We humans share our visual pattern-recognition ability with animals. As we experience the world we *see* patterns: the pattern of features that make up a face; a pattern of food locations; and a pattern of gestures that communicates information,[2]
for example, sign language. Expert human skills depend on remarkable pattern
detection: playing chess, diagnosing illness, scientific discovery, military strategy,
and mathematical relationships. Some argue all brain functions depend on recognizing patterns in experiences.[3] I agree with this. We have dream experiences as
well as waking ones. If dreams have a function is this visual pattern detection too?

What Do Dreams Do? Sue Llewellyn, Oxford University Press (2020). © Oxford University Press.
DOI: 10.1093/oso/9780198818953.001.0001.

What is a visual pattern anyway? Perhaps you are thinking of those red checkered tablecloths, which used to feature in Italian restaurants. These are patterned by design and the visual checkered pattern is immediately obvious, requiring no detection skills. But simple detection skills are necessary to answer the question of whether all Italian restaurants have red checkered tablecloths. In other words, do red checkered tablecloths repeat over time and place in Italian restaurants? There used to be a cultural pattern (how things are done) that linked red checkered tablecloths and Italian restaurants—they went together in time and space. So back in the 1970–80s if you went to an Italian restaurant you expected a red checkered tablecloth.

In this book we are concerned with discernible patterns that happen in nature and can be visualized rather than cultural patterns about the way things are done. These natural patterns aren't designed but they do often repeat in space and time. Two eyes, a nose, and a mouth in the same spatial arrangement is the pattern we look for in a face. This pattern also repeats in time, so whenever we see two eyes placed symmetrically over a nose and mouth, we recognize a face. Faces also repeat in space. Many different creatures in many different places have faces. But not all faces look alike—an elephant's face is very different from a human one. So it makes sense to talk of discerning the pattern that makes up a face, whereas it doesn't make sense to speak of detecting the pattern of a red checkered tablecloth—the pattern is obvious.

Identifying Complex, Non-obvious Patterns in the World

On seeing a face, we know we are in the presence of another living being that moves about. The behaviour of living beings, as they interact with the world isn't obvious. It's a *complex, non-obvious* pattern that has to be detected. I propose dreams evolved to detect these complex, non-obvious patterns. By complex and non-obvious, I mean that the elements of the pattern are associated in a complicated way. Complexity also comes about because the elements of the pattern may not appear together in time. We recognize a face whenever the same elements (eyes, nose, and mouth) appear together at the same time. But not all patterns are like this. The elements of the pattern, which predict when I am likely to vomit don't all appear together in time. I'm never on a rough sea, reading a book while travelling in a car, eating shellfish at a restaurant, having a migraine at work, and meeting my future in-laws at their house, all at the same time. In this pattern, the vomiting happens at different times but also in different places. Across evolutionary time, one very significant pattern would have involved elements that happened at different times *but at the same place.* To take a contemporary example first.

Suppose there's another academic, called Len, and he's based at the same place as me, the university, but, like me, often works at home. Len is a bit of a pest, so I'm trying to avoid him. Without asking him, I'm trying to identify his 'being in the university' pattern through visual observation. I've seen him there if he has an important meeting or if he has to teach a class. Len also attends university graduation ceremonies. Len usually picks his kids up from school but I've observed him working late in his office when his partner, Liz, or her mother, Lorna, picks them up and drives them home. Len lives near the university. When his fridge is empty, I've seen him sometimes eating in the university café. Individually, these patterned elements repeat over time; for example, Len is repeatedly at the university when he is teaching, and he's a regular attendee at university graduations. However, the different patterned elements appear at different times; they don't usually all come together the same time. It's highly unlikely Len would be in the university for a meeting and to teach a class and because there is a graduation ceremony and because his partner or his mother-in-law is picking up the kids and because he's eating in the café. We don't always detect patterns to avoid people. If Len were attractive I could observe this same pattern and use it to be at the university at the same time as him.

In evolutionary terms, why would we need to detect a complex pattern that predicts 'a living creature being at a particular place'? Like animals, we can recall a pattern of food locations. So far so good—but across evolutionary time, it would have been much safer to visit dependable food and water sources at times when predators and competitors tended to be absent. Even better would have been to visit when there were no predators or competitors but potential mates were around. But how to know? Observation of their past patterns of behaviour in visiting places with desirable resources, like the waterhole, would have been the only way. For example, the general pattern of lion behaviour is to hunt at night. So usually it will be safer to visit the waterhole during the day. But lions do sometimes visit in the daytime—particularly in the dry season when they get very thirsty and when prey like zebra and wildebeest are around. So time of day, seasonality, thirstiness, and availability of prey are elements in the pattern.

Visiting at night, when the waterhole is surrounded by dense vegetation that affords ambush cover for predators and when prey animals are present, is very dangerous. Picturing a waterhole at night in the dry season surrounded by thick reed beds, with zebra and wildebeest should induce fear because it signals danger. If you were to picture a relatively, safe time to visit the waterhole you would visualize the daytime in the wet season with no zebra and wildebeest. Being able to imagine these scenes doesn't mean you have actually experienced them. You probably have not. For example, you may have glimpsed a lion hiding in thick reeds beds around the waterhole during the day in the dry season. Equally, you may have seen a lion drinking from the waterhole at night on a few occasions. Also you may have seen lions kill and eat zebra and wildebeest at the waterhole. Elements of lion-related experiences that happened at different times but *at the same place* are associated in the picture, in effect the pattern, because all are indications that predict the presence (or absence) of a lion at the waterhole.

But sometimes there would have been elements in the pattern that predicts 'lion at the waterhole' which happened *away from the waterhole*. For example, you saw elephants gathering near a clump of trees. When some lions appeared the elephants chased them away. This didn't happen at the waterhole. It happened at a different place—at the clump of trees. But from an 'away from the waterhole' experience you inferred that elephants may chase lions away from the waterhole too. Similarly, for the 'pest at the university' pattern, when Liz or Lorna pick the kids up from school, you inferred that Len is more likely to be at the university. But picking the kids up from school doesn't happen at the university, it happens at the school gate.

Probabilistic Patterns and Hybrids

Like the 'when I vomit' and 'pest at the university' patterns, 'the lion at the waterhole' pattern is only probabilistic—meaning that the pattern is made up of tendencies rather than certainties. I don't always vomit when I meet new people. Likewise Len often stays late at the university when his partner or her mother picks up the kids, but if he gets fed up during the day he may go home at 5pm anyway. Lions tend to visit the waterhole at night but they sometimes visit during the day. Their daytime visits tend to be in the dry season when they tend to be thirsty. We are dealing with probabilities or, in less technical language, tendencies. There are no dead certs when it comes to animal or human behaviour. Their behaviour isn't random but it's not deterministic, like day follows night.

When detecting complex patterns in past experiences, elements that have the same significance may be combined to make a hybrid. What do we mean by elements with the same significance? In the 'pest at the university' pattern, Len's partner, Liz, or her mother, Lorna, may pick up the kids. As far as the pattern is concerned his partner and mother-in-law are both patterned elements that have the same significance. So Liz and Lorna may be combined to make a hybrid Liz–Lorna person.

If we take the 'predator at the waterhole' pattern, hyenas will also attack humans and have been known to kill them. Like lions, they hunt at night, will kill prey at waterholes, and have yellow fur. Lions and hyenas also tend to be in the same places at the same time because they scavenge each other's food; incidentally, the popular notion that hyenas scavenge from lions but not the other way around is incorrect.[4] From the point of view of early humans avoiding predators, a hyena at a waterhole has the same significance as a lion. Imagining a 'liena'—a hybrid creature that merges a lion and a hyena—is an efficient way of combining elements of the pattern with the same significance into one.

Dreams Portray Complex Patterns in Your Experience

I propose we portray complex, non-obvious, probabilistic, divergent patterns in our experiences through the visual medium of dreams. In a nutshell, this is what dreams do. Dreams are complex patterns derived from our experiences. But these patterns have not usually been experienced. They associate elements from different experiences. So, we may say that dream construction doesn't only recognize patterns; it searches for and discovers patterns or even creates patterns. The liena is a patterned element I created through associating a lion and a hyena but a liena doesn't actually exist. The evolutionary imperative to obtain food and water and meet with mates while avoiding predators and competitors may have driven us to imagine the impossible in our dreams!

For example, returning to me working out when Len, the pest, will be at the university, if I dream the pattern that predicts this, it may go something like this:

Scene 1

I am at a university in a large room. I can see Len. He seems to be teaching a class but there are some of our colleagues sitting around, as if he is in a meeting. Suddenly Liz appears, she walks up to a very large open gate in the wall of the room. On the other side of the gate are two young children. Liz takes them away.

Scene 2

I can see Liz, or it may be her mother, Lorna. She is dressed like Liz but has the same hair as Lorna. She is sitting on the top of an empty, very small white car, but somehow Liz/Lorna is driving along. The car has lots of stickers on it—they look like fridge magnets. She drives past the university café. Through the café window I can see Len. He is dressed in a university gown and eating a sandwich.

These two scenes are formed by combining the individual elements of the pattern that predicts when Len will be at the university. This associative process mixes up people, places, and events because it extracts them from their real-life context to portray the 'Len, the pest, at the university' pattern. These combined patterned elements are then cast into a narrative.

A story structure seems to be the basic way that the brain organizes experience; we cast our experiences into narratives whether awake or dreaming.[5] This condensed dream narrative engenders bizarreness, even impossibilities: the wall of the university room has a gate (this gate represents the school gate from where Liz/Lorna picks up the kids); the fridge-car cannot take passengers, it can only be driven by sitting on top of it because it is so small, it is empty because the fridge has no food in it; Len is wearing a university gown (now only worn by UK academics for graduation ceremonies) while eating a sandwich in a café.

This narrative creates new people, objects, and events. A new person is produced through merging Liz and her mother Lorna—from the point of view of the pattern they have the same significance because they both sometimes pick the kids up from school. The new object is the small, white, empty fridge-car. When the fridge is empty, Len sometimes eats at the café in the university. Equally, when Liz/Lorna picks the kids up from school she drives them home and Len is more likely to be in the university. The fridge and the car may be merged into one object because they are associated and they share some characteristics: both are containers, one for food the other for people; both are metallic; white is a common colour for both; and now we have such large fridges and such small smart cars their sizes are not so dissimilar; and we humans decorate both our fridges, with magnets, and our cars, with personalized number plates and window stickers with messages such as 'Baby on Board'. A car and a fridge aren't obviously associated but, in several non-obvious ways, they are.

The last chapter distinguished rapid eye movement (REM) from non-rapid eye movement sleep (NREM) dreams. REM dreams are organized into narratives that are more associative and more bizarre than NREM dreams. I think complex pattern identification happens during REM sleep with the pattern portrayed in a REM dream.

What's the Difference Between the Complex Patterns We Detect in Wake and Those We See in Dreams?

Surely our brains when awake are smarter than our dreaming brains, so why can't we identify complex patterns while awake? Of course, as noted above, we can—think of playing chess or diagnosing illness—but the type of complex pattern we can detect in wake differs. I don't think you can say we are smarter in wake than in dreams or vice versa, just that our brains work differently. Consider the contrasts between the patterned associations we make in wake and those we see during REM dreaming (see Figure 2.1).

In wake we use sequentially directed logic to detect patterns and our thinking converges on an output. For example, if shown this ☺ we recognize 'It's a face', we make a definite judgement, even though the nose is missing. This definitive output reflects our thinking in wake; we may be wrong about what we see but we don't see two things at once. In REM dreams we tolerate ambiguity, which creates bizarreness. For example, in Scene 1 of the Len scenario/dream above, Len could be

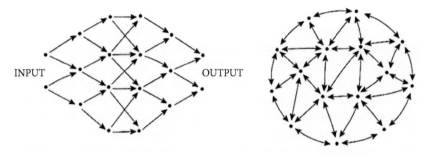

Figure 2.1 Contrasting associative patterns in wake (left) and REM dreaming (right).
Adapted with permission from: Hartmann, E. (2011) *The Nature and Functions of Dreaming*. Oxford University Press, Oxford, p. 70.

teaching or he could be at a meeting—somehow he is involved in both simultaneously. In Scene 2 I see a person who may be Liz but at the same time is also Lorna. In wake, our thinking is convergent on an output. In contrast, in REM dreams, we make divergent associations, our associational nets spread out.

During wake, our pattern detection is constrained by logic so if I saw a liena I would deduce I was hallucinating. Whereas, unconstrained by logic in dreams, I have no problem in seeing a visual pattern that looks a bit like a lion and a bit like a hyena. As discussed in the previous section, these differences are linked to the presence of hybrids and probabilistic associations in dreams.

Overall, the differing modes of perception in wake and dreaming result in better detection of patterns driven by logic, obvious associations, and sequencing during wake. Whereas, during dreaming, we excel at discerning divergent patterns underpinned by non-obvious associations. In the following chapters we will look more closely at the differences between wake and dreaming in terms of pattern identification and association, but, for the moment, we characterize dreams as identifying complex, divergent, non-obvious patterns.

You may buy this idea of dreams discerning complex, divergent, non-obvious patterns, but you may be thinking dreams are forgotten so how can they be used during our waking lives? Do dreams come from the unconscious? If the evolutionary purpose of dreams was to avoid predators and competitors while meeting mates, are dreams of any use now? The rest of the book addresses such questions.

Briefly...

In answer to the question: What is a dream? I propose: REM dreams portray complex, divergent, non-obvious patterns in past experiences but not patterns that have actually been experienced. If this sounds peculiar, well, dreams are strange—at least to our minds in wake. To create a pattern that hasn't been experienced you take associated elements of past experiences and put them together to make something new, as I did above in the 'pest at the university' example.

The evolutionary driver for discerning such patterns was, archetypically, to avoid meeting predators at places you wanted to go, like food sites and waterholes. To evade a predator at a waterhole you needed to work out what circumstances increased the probability of a predator at the waterhole visit and then associate them. Such circumstances include: night time, when there is dense vegetation to provide ambush cover around the waterhole, when the predator is thirsty, when it's hot, when elephants aren't there, and when prey animals are there. If you could avoid being eaten you stood a chance of reproducing. To meet a potential mate also required observation of their pattern of behaviour to work out when and where a safe encounter was likely.

Next

Chapter 3 looks more closely at *how* dreams associate elements of experiences to identify patterns.

Notes

1. Barkman, R. C. (2018). See the world through patterns. *Psychology Today*. Available at: https://www.psychologytoday.com/us/blog/singular-perspective/201801/see-the-world-through-patterns; Hale, J. (2018). Patterns: The need for order. Available at: https://psychcentral.com/lib/patterns-the-need-for-order/; and Basulto, D. (2013). Humans are the world's best pattern-recognition machines, but for how long? Available at: https://bigthink.com/endless-innovation/humans-are-the-worlds-best-pattern-recognition-machines-but-for-how-long

2. Mattson, M. P. (2014). Superior pattern processing is the essence of the evolved human brain. *Frontiers in Neuroscience, 8*, 265.

3. Fukushima, K., & Miyake, S. (1982). Neocognitron: a self-organizing neural network model for a mechanism of visual pattern recognition. In S. Amari & M. A. Arbib (Eds) *Competition and Cooperation in Neural Nets* (pp. 267–285). Springer, Berlin, Heidelberg, Germany; chapter 3 in Kurzweil, R. (2013). *How to Create a Mind: The Secret of Human Thought Revealed*. Penguin, London; Humans are the world's best pattern recognition machines, but for how long? Available at: https://bigthink.com/endless-innovation/humans-are-the-worlds-best-pattern-recognition-machines-but-for-how-long; and

Does the human brain work solely by pattern recognition? Available at: https://www.quora.com/Does-the-human-brain-work-solely-by-pattern-recognition

4. The predator chain Botswana wildlife guide. Available at: http://www.botswana.co.za/Botswana_Wildlife_Behaviour-travel/the-predator-chain.html

5. Pace-Schott, E. F. (2013). Dreaming as a story-telling instinct. *Frontiers in Psychology*, 4, 159.

3

Dream to Associate

Introduction

During sleep and dreaming, we aren't having experiences in the world. We aren't seeing or hearing anything from outside ourselves. So, without stimuli from the external world, our dreams must turn inwards to our memories.[1] If we reflect on dreams, we can often discern elements of our experiences, but dreams only very rarely portray actual experiences in their entirety. Magdalena Fosse and colleagues at Harvard Medical School found that memories of experiences were replayed in only 1–2% of dreams.[2] If you see one of your rapid eye movement (REM) dreams in your mind's eye I contend you are looking at the image of a complex pattern in your experience. This complex visual pattern merges elements of several experiences that are associated in non-obvious ways.

This may be the reason that REM dreams are often bizarre because they depict elements of experiences, which didn't belong together in time, associated in an image. Indeed, we use the word 'bizarre' to describe an incongruous person/object/place that has taken on multiple (apparently, inconsistent) elements.

To be able to identify a complex, non-obvious, divergent pattern, the mind/brain in REM sleep is more associative than the mind/brain during wake. More associative means: first, the mind/brain in REM sleep makes associations between more remotely connected things, i.e. the associations are non-obvious; second, the associations are made broadly rather than sequentially or logically; and, third, there are, simply, more associations.

This all sounds very abstract. To illustrate, we look at a dream in detail.

A dream to illustrate non-obvious associations between memories of experiences

'The white paper kite and the butterfly' is not one of my dreams. Some of these will feature later in the book. Although I'm passionately interested in dreams, I don't often remember them on waking. I tend only to recall dreams that provoke such anxiety they wake me up suddenly in the middle of the night. Consequently, my remembered dreams are usually fearful. I wanted my first illustrative dream in this book to be a pleasing one, so I have chosen one from my Swedish friend and colleague, A.

To start on this dream, we need two distinctions from psychology. The first is between an episodic memory, the memory of an experience or an episode (e.g. flying a

What Do Dreams Do? Sue Llewellyn, Oxford University Press (2020). © Oxford University Press.
DOI: 10.1093/oso/9780198818953.001.0001.

kite) and semantic memory, memory for knowledge (e.g. what a kite is). Dreams depict non-obvious associations between different episodic memories, although they also contain basic semantic knowledge. For example, if I dream of flying a kite, I must also know what a kite is. The second distinction is between recent and remote memories. Recent memories are from the immediate past. Freud called these 'day-residues'. Remote memories are from the more distant past. 'Distant' is rather ill-defined: we will use 'remote' for memories that are more than a week old when they appear in a dream.

'The White Paper Kite and the Butterfly'

A recalled the dream at home and wrote it down on the morning of Saturday, 30 April 2016. From Chapter 1, you will recall my definition of REM dreams: 'Vivid, bizarre, emotional, highly associative mental experiences which develop in a story-like manner during sleep and are embodied, but out of volitional control'. Against this definition I judge 'the white paper kite and the butterfly' to, probably, be a REM dream, although this can't be demonstrated because the dreamer wasn't awakened from REM sleep in a lab.

Dream Narrative

Scene 1 (normal perspective and zoomed in on the butterfly and kite)

We were two people, me (A) and my husband (T) outside a house but this house was rather in the distance. I held the line of a kite in my hand. It was not an ordinary kite which children play with, more of a square of white paper. The kite was flying very nicely high up in the air over some trees when it suddenly attracted a white butterfly, which had two rather big red dots, one on each of the top, front wings, symmetrically placed.

Scene 2

I was standing in front of some huge electric wires. I still had the kite with me so I had to watch out not to get the kite entangled in the wires. Suddenly, I found that I had released it and the kite flew up in the sky. I felt both surprised and satisfied.

This dream isn't particularly bizarre. The kite is a bit odd because it's 'more of a square of white paper'. Also why would a kite attract a butterfly? In the second scene, it's unusual to be 'satisfied' if a kite flies away because a kite is something to be held on to so it can be enjoyed again. But then this kite isn't a normal one for playing because it's 'more of a square of white paper'.

Were any non-obvious associations revealed when I asked A about whether her dream was based on her personal, episodic memories? A promising place to start would be the odd bits of the dream because I propose oddities are engendered through making non-obvious associations.

The episodic memories in Scene 1

So we start with the kite that is 'more of a square of white paper' and attracts a butterfly in Scene 1.

Recent episodic memory 1

On the evening before the dream A had been at a reception after a PhD award. She had been the academic supervisor of this PhD student. She wrote down episodic memory 1 as follows: 'During the reception I remembered overhearing CF (one of my close senior colleagues) talking to CG (another of my colleagues). CF told CG he was "like a butterfly", attracted to new academic ideas all the time—implying that CG flitted from one thing to another.'

But why was the butterfly attracted to the kite? In the dream A describes the kite as 'not an ordinary kite which children play with, more of a square of white paper'. Academics work with white paper, so academics are associated with paper. The white paper may visually represent one of the new academic ideas that attracts CG. This explains why the butterfly (CG has been told he is 'like a butterfly') was attracted to the white paper kite.

Why did the butterfly have large, red spots? Some butterflies do have red spots, but is there any other reason that is related to A's episodic memories? Apart from the 'like a butterfly' comment, A has another episodic memory in which CF is associated with butterflies.

Remote episodic memory 2

She wrote down this memory as follows: 'I remember I once made a mistake in a discussion with CF about butterflies. A group of us, from the university, were walking in the forest (but I am sure T, my husband, who is not an academic, was also with us) when we saw a white butterfly. CF told us this was a "kålfjäril" (cabbage butterfly). I interpreted this as "kolfjäril" (coal butterfly), remarking "Strange to call it a 'kolfjäril' as it is white". I was embarrassed at this mistake.' This embarrassment may be represented by one of the red spots on the butterfly because, in humans, embarrassment can cause blushing or red cheeks. It's worth pointing out here that embarrassment is a social emotion. Embarrassment occurs when people think that others will evaluate them more negatively because of what they have done or said.[3] If I make a mistake when alone, which no-one will find out about unless I tell them, embarrassment would not occur, rather I may be irritated with myself.

Remote episodic memory 3

A wrote down this kite memory, arguably the dominant memory in the dream, as follows: 'I got a nylon kite from T's mother and father as a birthday present. It was very expensive. I think T and I had all our three kids already but the thing is that T's parents knew I liked to play, not only with the kids. I have always been very childish (and very old at the same time). The first time T and I went out together with the kids to use it, I did not realize that the line was not attached at all to the handle. So as I let out more line and reached the end of it (it was a perfect day for kite-flying) the kite left and flew on its own and landed on the top of some trees. The kite was close to the railway with some electric wires. However, at the time, I was not really afraid the kite would get entangled in the wires—as I remember. But, I do remember I was very embarrassed I lost my present this way.' This embarrassment over a kite may be the other red spot on the butterfly. For A, embarrassment at mistakes is a non-obvious association with kites. The symmetrical placing of the two red spots on the butterfly may represent A's embarrassment, as blushing over mistakes (the incorrect butterfly identification and the kite loss) would result in red spots on each cheek of her face.

Remote episodic memory 4

A also related a fourth memory which seems to be associated with Scene 1: 'We got another kite (a silk butterfly type) bought in China for us by my elder brother. It was given to us some years after I had lost the one I got from my parents-in-law. We still have it. It has red parts on all four wings, but no red spots.'

This experience also involves kites, butterflies, presents and red marks. But what about Scene 2?

Scene 2

Given that, at the time, A was very embarrassed at the kite flying away, why was she 'surprised and satisfied' in Scene 2 of the dream? This may relate to one of A's current concerns, retained in her brain as a memory. Research demonstrates continuity between our concerns in waking life and those in our dreaming lives.[4] The things we care about in wake are remembered and appear as *memories of concerns* in our dreams, albeit that they are associated with the dream events. Some of the things A cares about in wake—kites, butterflies, presents, and embarrassment—have already appeared in her dream but she has another current concern.

Episodic memory/concern 5

She wrote down this concern as follows: 'The white paper kite flying away may relate to the issue that I have thought of leaving the academy so many times—but I am still working there. When I think of this I become sad as well. It's really mixed feelings. I knew I had come to the point where I felt I couldn't contribute any longer and I desperately needed a new environment which made use of what is me. But I couldn't leave because I was a supervisor on a PhD. When this suddenly finished [the recently awarded PhD] I was both surprised and satisfied because it meant I was released.'

The white paper kite that is released may also represent A herself.

In Scene 2 A is standing in front of some huge electric wires. Electric wires feature in episodic memory 3 because the released kite landed on top of some trees close to some electric railway lines. Some readers may have noticed that one feature of Scene 2 has not been linked to episodic memories/concerns: A's efforts 'not to get the kite entangled in the wires'. When I asked A about episodic memory sources for the dream, she wrote down eight but incorporating them all here would make for a very lengthy section so I have only looked at five.

Next we look at the non-obvious associations among memory elements in 'the butterfly and the white paper kite'.

Non-obvious associations among episodic memories in Scenes 1 and 2

I argue all four of the episodic memories (the relevant elements are outlined in the preceding paragraphs) are associated in Scene 1. In turn, this may indicate a clue about dream construction—in a dream only those elements of an episodic memory that are non-obviously associated with at least one other episodic memory will appear; everything else is omitted. In other words, the dream only embeds the memory elements that form part of the complex, non-obvious, divergent pattern.

For example, in episodic memory 1, A is at a reception with CF, CG, and others when she overhears the 'like a butterfly' remark. Obviously, at this reception, A would have encountered many people and had had several conversations; some of these would have been retained, at least in the short-term, as a 'whole' episodic memory of the reception that could be recalled during waking hours. I have put 'whole' in quotation marks to indicate that a memory never replays an experience in its entirety. Generally, we remember those aspects of an experience that are significant to us. But, in A's dream, there is no indication that she is at a reception; even CF and CG are omitted. Only the butterfly appears in the dream because it is associated with the 'butterfly kite' in episodic memory 4, with the kite in episodic memory 3 (because both butterflies and kites fly), and in episodic memory 2 it is associated with A's embarrassing mistake about butterflies.

Similarly, in episodic memory 3, A is with T (her husband) and her children flying an expensive kite when she lets out all of the string that isn't attached to the handle. She is embarrassed at losing the kite when it lands on the top of some trees. Only the kite, the trees, a house, and T appear in the dream. The abstract concept of embarrassment seems to be portrayed through red spots. The kite in episodic memory 3 is associated with the butterfly kite in episodic memory 4. The trees in episodic memory 3 are associated with the forest in episodic memory 2. T, in the kite-flying episodic memory 3, is also associated with episodic memory 2 because he was on the walk in the forest. Portraying embarrassment at the mistakes as red spots associates episodic memories 2, 3, and 4 because embarrassment at mistakes is an association between memories 2 and 3 and red marks characterize the butterfly kite in memory 4.

The dominant memory/concern in Scene 2 is clearly 5, but memories 1 and 3 also feature. The PhD reception marked the end of A's academic responsibilities, so she was released. The abstract concept of 'release' is associated with the kite flying off. Also the electric wires described in episodic memory 3 appear in Scene 2.

Dream scenes, particularly adjacent ones, show thematic continuity.[5] In A's dream, kite-flying demonstrates continuous thematic linkage, i.e. there are associations between scenes as well as within scenes.

Dreams Are Not True Memories; They Are Probabilistic Associations Between Memories

REM dreams don't depict what really happened. For example, in 'the butterfly and the white paper kite' dream, the white paper kite attracts a white butterfly. In reality, this never happened. This fictive dream event is engendered by associating the kite and butterfly (they both fly in the air), along with CG being a butterfly because he is always attracted to new academic ideas (the kite is a piece of white paper that represents a new idea), and also because A has a butterfly kite (the butterfly is attracted to the kite because in A's experience they came together in one object).

You will recall from the last chapter that dream associations are probabilistic, meaning they are tendencies rather than certainties. In her dream A makes two embarrassing mistakes, in front of others, over 'things that fly in the air'. The patterned association is probabilistic because it is by no means certain that A will again make a mistake over 'things that fly in the air'. Indeed, having had two such experiences may make her more circumspect about kites and butterflies. Similarly, having had two glimpses of a predator at different times at the waterhole doesn't mean that one will be encountered again, but caution would be called for.

This Contemporary Dream in an Evolutionary Context

In Chapter 2 I proposed an evolutionary driver for REM dreaming. Early humans would have obtained food and water from particular places that were also visited by predators, competitors, and potential mates. These other visitors created threats but also opportunities. Associating the relevant elements of living being-related experiences to identify any non-obvious patterns in their visits would have increased the chances of avoiding predators and competitors while meeting potential mates. Clearly the thought of meeting a predator at the waterhole would have been a terrifying but everyday concern in waking lives of early humans. Now such a concern doesn't feature on most peoples' horizons, but we still make regular visits to key places (both work and social) where there are other living beings whose presence creates threats and opportunities. These threats and opportunities feature as our concerns. A's everyday concerns are much less alarming than predators at the waterhole; nevertheless, they are concerns that contemporaries would readily relate to: embarrassment at losing an expensive gift given by significant others, making a mistake about butterflies in front of academic colleagues, and wondering whether to leave her job in academia.

Does my proposed evolutionary explanation for dreams, as complex patterns in experience, apply to a contemporary dream, like A's? To reiterate some of the evolutionary context: first, elements of experiences that happened at different times but at the same central place are extracted from their waking life context to form a complex pattern. Sometimes this complex pattern also includes elements of experiences that happened at different places but are related to the central place.

In A's dream the central place is an open space for kite-flying. But two of the memories (1 and 2) happened at different places: first, at the PhD reception; and, second, during a walk in the forest. Prima facie, the experiences of kite-flying, being at a PhD reception, and walking in the forest don't seem associated. The associations only appear when elements are extracted from the experiences. Confusion over butterflies during the walk in the forest is associated with losing the kite during kite-flying through both being embarrassing mistakes. The 'like a butterfly' remark at the PhD reception is associated with kite-flying through both kites and butterflies being 'things that fly in the air'.

The archetypical evolutionary context would have been avoiding a predator or a competitor at the waterhole, to increase the chances of survival. The emotional driver for such a dream would have been fear, although complex pattern identification would also apply to positive experiences for reproduction, like meeting mates at the waterhole. In this contemporary dream, A is trying to avoid mistakes rather than a predator, with embarrassment, rather than fear, as the emotional driver. Also the dream ends with a positive emotion because letting go of the kite becomes associated with release rather than loss.

This in-depth look at the 'the white paper kite and the butterfly' illustrates how the contemporary mind/brain in dreaming is still more associative than the mind/brain in wakefulness, just as it would have been in an evolutionary context. To reiterate, first, the dreaming mind/brain makes associations between more remotely connected things, i.e. the associations are non-obvious; second, the associations are made broadly rather than sequentially or logically; and, third, there are, simply, more associations.

Evidence on Associations in REM Sleep/Dreaming

As discussed in the preceding paragraphs, 'more associative' in REM dreaming means multiple, non-obvious, probabilistic associations are made broadly. Experimental evidence demonstrates this. In Chapter 1 I touched on the mind/brain issue. This is important, at this point, because in the following experiments on REM sleep I assume their results apply to the mind state in REM (i.e. REM dreaming) *and* the corresponding brain state (i.e. REM sleep).

Obviously you can't converse with people while they are dreaming, but if someone is awakened from REM sleep there is a 'carry-over' period when the mind/brain is in a more REM-like state, even though the person has woken up. Experiments that try to work out what dreaming does can use this carry-over period, when the mind is in a more REM dream-like state and the brain is also in a corresponding more REM dream-like state.

In 1999, Robert Stickgold, a psychiatrist at Harvard Medical School, and his colleagues used this carry-over period to show that, immediately after being awakened from REM sleep, people make more remote associations than they would if they had been fully awake.[6] For example, when prompted with the word 'table', participants in the carry-over REM state were more likely to respond with, for example, 'altar', whereas, with a fully awake brain, 'table' would probably elicit, for example, 'chair'. Table–chair is a more obvious association because they co-occur (go together) in space. Tables are associated with altars because a simple altar is made in the shape of a table, but this association is non-obvious.

In 2009, Denise Cai, a psychologist at the University of California, and colleagues gave a test, the Remote Associates Test (RAT), to people in which three words are associated with another word but the associated word was non-obvious.[7] For example, what word is associated with 'falling', 'actor', and 'dust'? People who had REM sleep during a daytime nap were better able (than the group who stayed awake) to come up with the word that was associated with all three words—in this instance, 'star'. Denise Cai and colleagues applied their test in the morning and the afternoon (before and after the nap for the group who napped). Because the group who had REM sleep had improved results on the RAT they concluded that something happens to the mind/brain during REM sleep/dreaming that enhances the ability to make non-obvious or remote associations. During wake, the mind/brain tends to approach this task in a sequential or logical way: thinking of a word associated with falling then seeing if that word is also associated with actor and so on. But success on the RAT test requires a broad and encompassing search to identify the associated word.

In 2015 Murray Barsky, a sleep researcher at Harvard Medical School, and colleagues did a further study on non-obvious associations. They asked their participants to predict one of two probabilities: 'sun' or 'rain' based on multiple associations between 'sun' or 'rain' and eight other things.[8] A probabilistic association is more difficult to spot because either it only becomes apparent after multiple observations or multiple conditions are required for the association to emerge, i.e. the task is complex. On the weather prediction task, Barsky and colleagues compared the performance of participants who had a nap, with REM sleep, with those who stayed awake. The research showed improvement on the weather prediction task depends upon REM sleep; there is no performance enhancement over the same period of time awake.

The above three experiments were all with human participants. Experiments that restrict REM sleep have been done with rats. One such study showed that restricting REM sleep impaired performance on a complex, associative spatial task.[9]

To sum up on this section, there is experimental evidence indicating that REM sleep/dreaming makes multiple, non-obvious, probabilistic associations across a broad domain.

Associations During Wake and NREM Sleep/Dreaming

Basic psychology teaches that associative learning, through pattern identification, occurs in three main ways: first, associations among things that are alike in some way; second, associations among things that happen together either in time or space or both, i.e. co-occurrences; and, third, associations between things that occur in sequence or, more strongly, when one thing causes another.

I propose during REM sleep/dreaming: likenesses are non-obvious; things are associated that occur at different times and, sometimes, different places; and, although there are narrative sequences and one thing appears to cause another, these sequences and causations sometimes violate the expectations we have formed in wake.

Making associations during wake

Dreaming defies our expectations because during wake we identify and learn different patterns and make more obvious associations. For example, I have three sisters; for me they are alike. The input 'sister' is instantly associated with the output *my* sisters: R, D, and M. They constitute an obvious sister pattern. During wake we encounter co-occurrence patterns when things repeat across time and space. For example, on my desk just now I can see a computer, a coffee mug, a scanner, my iPhone, papers, pens, and books. These items are a co-occurrence pattern for a desk. Sequential patterns are important in wake. We learn when one thing always or usually follows another. For example, day always follows night. In contrast, rain usually, but not always, follows black clouds. Sometimes, the first thing not only precedes but can cause the second. For example, a heart attack causes pain or a poisonous berry causes vomiting.

Making associations during NREM

Are associative patterns also generated in NREM sleep/dreaming? You will recall from Chapter 1 that there are different types of NREM sleep/dreaming. At this point we consider deep slow-wave sleep (SWS), where very few dreams occur. In the section on 'This Contemporary Dream in an Evolutionary Context', we noted we still make regular visits to key places as part of journeys or to gather food. Take, for example, railway stations or supermarket visits. It is fairly unusual for people to retain episodic memories of such mundane events. Of course, if I had met my partner at a railway station I would remember that episode, but, without any such emotionally significant encounters, such memories quickly fade.

What we do retain, though, is what scientists call a knowledge 'schema', 'script', or pattern for such visits. Penny Lewis, a psychologist at Cardiff University, UK, argues these patterns form during SWS.[10] (SWS is depicted by the jagged line on the arrow in Figure 3.1.) During SWS I replay, for example, memories of visits to

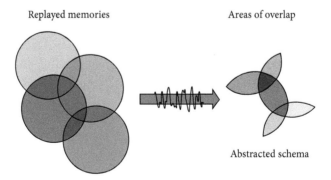

Replayed memories   Areas of overlap

Abstracted schema

Figure 3.1 Abstracting knowledge elements from experiences during slow-wave sleep.
Adapted with permission from Lewis, P. A. (2013). *The Secret World of Sleep*. Palgrave Macmillan, London. p. 109.

railway stations—four such visits are depicted by the bubbles on the left. These visits have idiosyncratic elements (on one visit I missed my train, on another I laddered my tights, on yet another I saw a colleague from the university) but all four visits also have common elements. These elements are overlaps: I know that I can buy a ticket from a person at ticket office; or I can buy one from a ticket machine; I know that trains leave from numbered platforms; and if I have luggage there is a lift. These facts about railway stations help me prepare for a visit. They are *common elements extracted from many visits*. These commonalities would have had clear evolutionary significance, conferring knowledge of what to expect at daily visits to dependable food sites and the waterhole.

These emotionally neutral, commonalities or *co-occurrences* extracted during SWS constitute knowledge. The associations made to identify the overlaps are simple, neutral binary ones of the 'what–where' type. For example, station–ticket office, station–ticket machine, station–numbered platforms, and station–lift, or waterhole–vegetation, waterhole–pebbles, and waterhole–insects. We can contrast them with the complex, emotionally significant, probabilistic associations we make between elements of episodes during REM sleep. However, both are patterns extracted from experiences and both are formed through making associations between memory elements across time.

You will recall from Chapter 1 that most SWS happens in the first half of the night, with most REM in the second half of the night. It seems likely these two sleep stages serve complementary functions, and that the sequencing of sleep stages, with SWS coming before REM, is important.[11] We know from the above discussion that SWS can extract or abstract knowledge elements from experiences, but the abstracted pattern is one of commonalities, associations between things that are always and so, obviously, associated (see Figure 3.1). Whereas, during REM, we make non-obvious, probabilistic associations between elements of experiences.

So, during SWS, we can extract elements of different memories. Also, during SWS, we can spot obvious associations to identify patterns made up of common elements. But we need REM to make non-obvious, probabilistic associations to identify complex patterns. Next we briefly consider how these patterns are represented in the brain.

Associative Memory in Brain Networks

All memories are fundamentally associative.[12] Chapter 1 explained that brain cells, or neurons, communicate with each other across the tiny gaps, or synapses, between them. This communication is chemical through neurotransmission across the synapse as the first cell releases a chemical, or neurotransmitter, that the second takes up. The more neurons communicate with other neurons across synapses, the more the linkages between them are strengthened. These strengthened linkages are the physiological basis for association and, hence, for creating memories.

Memories exist in brain networks. The basic structure of a memory network is one of 'nodes' or 'junctions' connected by 'pathways'.[13] Figure 3.2, in the approximate shape of the brain (side view), is a much simplified illustration of this.

An episodic memory is represented along a pathway in a brain network.[14] There is much that could be said about how events are represented in the brain but our focus here is on association; we will avoid a long digression on 'representation'. This pathway represents the elements (or smaller events) that occur as part of the larger episode or experience. For example, the first time I ate blackberries with my friend J on a walk during wakefulness could be said to have six elements. The episode went something like this:

Element 1: As a child of about 12, I was walking along a path in the country with my friend J.

Element 2: We noticed some black shapes in the hedge.

Element 3: We moved closer.

Element 4: We saw they were blackberries.

Element 5: We picked some.

Element 6: We ate the berries while we walked along, chatting about our favourite books.

Each of these elements is associated with the following one, making up a sequential, associative pattern. In the brain, we can think of these six elements as represented, in turn, along a linear pathway. The episode is sequential, moves forward in time, and is represented along a brain network pathway. The more these

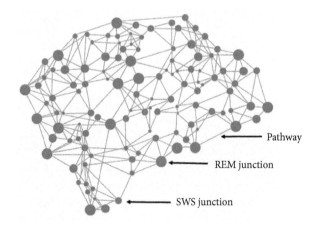

Figure 3.2 Schematic, simplified representation of brain networks.

particular memory elements are strengthened in the brain through the linkages created by neurotransmission, the stronger the whole memory becomes as the individual elements are repeatedly associated.

But we have noted that a network consists of pathways *and junctions*. The function of pathways in memory networks is better understood than that of junctions, but one well-recognized feature is that memory networks share constituent elements.[15] One way of sharing elements is at junctions.

We have seen two examples of this sharing of elements to identify patterns. The first, complex pattern is identified during REM sleep/dreaming where non-obvious associations are made between elements of different experiences that happened at different times. The second, simpler pattern is identified during deep SWS, where more obvious associations are made, again between elements of different experiences at different times, but the pattern is one of commonalities.

Another way of thinking about these patterns is that they *integrate* different episodic memories because, in the brain, different pathways meet and overlap at junctions. In Figure 3.2 the REM dreaming patterns are represented by larger junctions because associations are being made more broadly, whereas the smaller junctions would represent the commonality patterns identified in SWS.

The patterns identified in SWS are knowledge or semantic patterns. In the railway station example given earlier, SWS extracts knowledge of commonalities in experience, of what to expect at a railway station (i.e. a ticket office, ticket machines, platforms, and a lift), whereas REM dreams associate elements of experiences to identify a complex, non-obvious, probabilistic pattern. This pattern isn't one of commonalities but of different elements of episodes, i.e. REM patterns are still episodic in nature. As along a pathway, the more neurons communicate with each other at junctions, the stronger the pattern becomes.

In the brain, semantic or knowledge memories are held at a higher level than episodic ones; the highest level is abstract or conceptual knowledge.[16] Memory networks are interconnected at all levels (as shown in Figure 3.2) but episodic networks, shown with larger junctions, are lower in the hierarchy than semantic or knowledge networks, shown with smaller junctions.

We conclude this chapter by exploring the image-based nature of REM dreaming.

The Image-based Nature of REM Dreaming

REM sleep is generated in very ancient brain mechanisms[17] when both animals and humans may have thought in images. Image-based thought may be conserved (i.e. retained) in REM dreams. Sometimes, in REM dreams, people speak but, more commonly, the content is purely visual. Reflecting its ancient origins, REM sleep is found not only in humans but also in mammals and birds, it has also, recently, been found in lizards,[18] and, even cuttlefish,[19] albeit in a different form from that in mammals. We can't ask animals if they dream but it seems very likely.[20] The current scientific consensus is that animals think, in ways similar to humans.[21] Animals have only rudimentary language skills, and their thinking is probably in images; early humans, too, before they acquired language,[22] would have thought in images.[23]

Antonio Damasio, a Portuguese-American neuroscientist at the University of Southern California, believes we still think, mostly, in images. In his book, *Descartes' Error* (pp. 106–108), he writes 'It is often said that thought is made up of much more than just images, that it is made also of words and non-image abstract symbols ... [but] ... Images are probably the main content of our thoughts, regardless of ... [where] ... they are generated and regardless of whether they are about a thing or a process involving things.'[24] The philosopher Stephen Asma at Columbia College, Chicago, argues image-based thinking is making a comeback—in the sense that scientists are now questioning the assumption that human thought is based on words and symbols.[25] Antonio Damasio argues that for a word to be known it must become an image, however fleetingly.[26]

Lawrence Barsalou, a psychologist at Emory University, Atlanta, proposes that a visual experience—like seeing a specific chair—gives rise to an image of a generic chair (or chair symbol).[27] Barsalou argues that this image is then retained at an unconscious level in the brain,[28] underpinning memory (e.g. what is a chair is like), thought (e.g. I think this chair would be more comfortable with a cushion), and action (e.g. I can stand on a chair to reach this high cupboard). Also he proposes images can be dynamic; they can portray events as well as objects. So once images are combined in a sequence they become like a film or movie.

In the earlier 'blackberry' example, once an early human had discovered blackberries s/he most probably formed a dynamic image of themselves seeing blackberries on hedges and reaching out to pluck and eat them. This image would have been retained in memory to trigger the blackberry-hedge-eat association whenever s/he walked along in a place where blackberries were possible. Now words, rather than images, may underpin our thinking during wake but, in any case, image-based thought persists in REM dreaming.

As argued earlier, image-based thought in REM dreams portrays non-obvious associations. The experiment conducted by Robert Stickgold and colleagues showed that the mind/brain forges non-obvious associations in the 'carry-over' period after REM sleep. The visual sense is the only one that readily conveys non-obvious associations[29] because apparently dissimilar things can be merged in a single image. The associative power of dreams can, perhaps, be seen most clearly in dream characters. About half of dream characters appear with unusual combinations of features.[30]

The liena was mentioned in Chapter 2. The mind/brain's ability to create visual associations in dreaming may have produced the mash-ups that often feature in art

Figure 3.3 The liena.

and myths, like centaurs, mermaids, satyrs, griffins, sphinxes, and winged horses like Pegasus. These fantastic creatures take some elements from one living creature and combine them with elements from a different creature. This results in a new creature that, in mythologies, sometimes, has superior powers. Figure 3.3 portrays the liena, an imaginary creature that associates the features of a lion and a hyena.

The image-based ability to associate may be the reason that REM dreams are still so vividly visual.

Briefly...

During REM sleep, dreaming depicts non-obvious associations between elements of experiences that identify complex, probabilistic patterns. These patterns haven't been experienced. The associative patterns we make during wake are between things that are more obviously alike, co-occur in time/space, or are sequential in nature. During SWS we extract commonalities from different experiences to generate patterns. Our memories are based on association and are represented in networks, specifically in pathways and junctions, in the brain. Pathways represent episodic memories that are integrated at junctions. These junctions can be either patterns from REM or SWS sleep. REM sleep is of very ancient origin, from a time when both animals and humans thought in images. We retain this image-based thought in REM dreams probably because it facilitates non-obvious associations.

Next

The next chapter focuses on the dangers faced by early humans as they visited places with food and water. REM dreams may have been retained at an unconscious level to ensure the fast responses to dangers that enhanced the survival chances of early humans.

Notes

1. Stickgold, R. (2002). EMDR: a putative neurobiological mechanism of action. *Journal of Clinical Psychology, 58*(1), 61–75.
2. Fosse, M. J., Fosse, R., Hobson, J. A., & Stickgold, R. J. (2003). Dreaming and episodic memory: a functional dissociation? *Journal of Cognitive Neuroscience, 15*(1), 1–9.
3. Lamia, M. C. (2011). Embarrassment. Available at: https://www.psychologytoday.com/blog/intense-emotions-and-strong-feelings/201112/embarrassment
4. Domhoff, G. W. (1996). *Finding Meaning in Dreams: A Quantitative Approach*, Plenum Press, New York; Hartmann, E. (1998). *Dreams and Nightmares: The Origin and Meaning of Dreams*. Perseus, New York; and Schredl, M. (2006). Factors affecting the continuity between waking and dreaming: emotional intensity and emotional tone of the waking-life event. *Sleep and Hypnosis, 8*, 1–5.
5. Seligman, M., & Yellen, A. (1987). What is a dream? *Behaviour Research and Therapy, 25*, 1–24; and Stickgold, R., Rittenhouse, C. D., & Hobson, J. A. (1994). Dream splicing: a new technique for assessing thematic coherence in subjective reports of mental activity. *Consciousness and Cognition: An International Journal, 3*(1), 114–128.
6. Stickgold, R., Scott, L., Rittenhouse, C., & Hobson, J. A. (1999). Sleep-induced changes in associative memory. *Journal of Cognitive Neuroscience, 11*(2), 182–193.
7. Cai, D. J., Mednick, S. A., Harrison, E. M., Kanady, J. C., & Mednick, S. C. (2009). REM, not incubation, improves creativity by priming associative networks. *Proceedings of the National Academy of Sciences, 106*(25), 10130–10134.
8. Barsky, M. M., Tucker, M. A., & Stickgold, R. (2015). REM sleep enhancement of probabilistic classification learning is sensitive to subsequent interference. *Neurobiology of Learning and Memory, 122*, 63–68.
9. Bjorness, T. E., Riley, B. T., Tysor, M. K., & Poe, G. R. (2005). REM restriction persistently alters strategy used to solve a spatial task. *Learning & Memory, 12*(3), 352–359.
10. Durrant, S. J., Taylor, C., Cairney, S., & Lewis, P. A. (2011). Sleep-dependent consolidation of statistical learning. *Neuropsychologia, 49*(5), 1322–1331; and Lewis, P. A., & Durrant, S. J. (2011). Overlapping memory replay during sleep builds cognitive schemata. *Trends in Cognitive Sciences, 15*(8), 343–351.
11. Giuditta, A., Ambrosini, M. V., Montagnese, P., Mandile, P., Cotugno, M., Zucconi, G. G., & Vescia, S. (1995). The sequential hypothesis of the function of sleep. *Behavioural Brain Research, 69*(1–2), 157–166.
12. See p. 2 in Fuster, J. M. (1999). *Memory in the Cerebral Cortex: An Empirical Approach to Neural Networks in the Human and Nonhuman Primate*. MIT Press, Cambridge, MA.

13. See p. 85 in Fuster, J. M. (1999). *Memory in the Cerebral Cortex: An Empirical Approach to Neural Networks in the Human and Nonhuman Primate*. MIT Press, Cambridge, MA.

14. Buzsáki, G. (2005). Theta rhythm of navigation: link between path integration and landmark navigation, episodic and semantic memory. *Hippocampus*, *15*(7), 827–840.

15. See p. 97 in Fuster, J. M. (1999). *Memory in the Cerebral Cortex: An Empirical Approach to Neural Networks in the Human and Nonhuman Primate*. MIT Press, Cambridge, MA.

16. Fuster, J. M. (1999). *Memory in the Cerebral Cortex: An Empirical Approach to Neural Networks in the Human and Nonhuman Primate*. MIT Press, Cambridge, MA.

17. Shein-Idelson, M., Ondracek, J. M., Liaw, H. P., Reiter, S., & Laurent, G. (2016). Slow waves, sharp waves, ripples, and REM in sleeping dragons. *Science*, *352*(6285), 590–595.

18. Shein-Idelson, M., Ondracek, J. M., Liaw, H. P., Reiter, S., & Laurent, G. (2016). Slow waves, sharp waves, ripples, and REM in sleeping dragons. *Science*, *352*(6285), 590–595.

19. Daley, J. (2019). Cuttlefish are dazzling but do they dream? *Scientific American*. Available at:https://www.scientificamerican.com/article/cuttlefish-are-dazzling-but-do-they-dream/

20. Langley, L. (2015). Do animals dream? *National Geographic*. Available at: http://news.nationalgeographic.com/2015/09/150905-animals-sleep-science-dreaming-cats-brains/

21. England, R. (2012). Animals think like humans, scientists declare. Available at: https://www.positive.news/2012/environment/8831/animals-humans-scientists-declare/

22. For those interested in when and how humans acquired language, see FAQ: How did language begin? Available at: https://www.linguisticsociety.org/resource/faq-how-did-language-begin

23. Baumeister, R. F., & Masicampo, E. J. (2010). Conscious thought is for facilitating social and cultural interactions: how mental simulations serve the animal–culture interface. *Psychological Review*, *117*(3), 945.

24. See p. 107 in Damasio, A. R. (2006). *Descartes' Error*. Random House, London.

25. See pp. 112–117 in Asma, S. T. (2017). *The Evolution of Imagination*. University of Chicago Press, Chicago, IL.

26. See p. 106 in Damasio, A. R. (2006). *Descartes' Error*. Random House, London.

27. Barsalou, L. W. (1999). Perceptions of perceptual symbols. *Behavioral and Brain Sciences*, *22*(4), 637–660.

28. Retention of unconscious mental images does not imply that 'pictures' reside in the brain any more than 'words' do. Rather brain cells represent images. This book cannot cover the complex debates about how images and words are represented in brain cells.

29. Paivio, A. (1990). *Mental Representations: A Dual Coding Approach*. Oxford University Press, Oxford.

30. Revonsuo, A., & Tarkko, K. (2002). Binding in dreams—the bizarreness of dream images and the unity of consciousness. *Journal of Consciousness Studies*, *9*(7), 3–24.

4

Dream to Survive

Introduction

Theodosius Dobzhansky (1900–1975), a Ukrainian-American population geneticist, wrote an essay entitled 'Nothing in biology makes sense except in the light of evolution'.[1] To see the evolutionary driver for dreaming, we need to take a, necessarily somewhat speculative, excursion into the lives of early humans to capture the backstory of dreams.

Hunter-gatherers or Gatherer-hunters?

Early humans[2] were hunter-gatherers of food. Farming didn't develop until about 10,000 years ago. Our pre-agricultural period, when we had to find rather than grow our food, occupied about 99% of human history.[3] 'Human history' is a contested term. So is 'early human'. When did we become human? When did human history begin? I'm dating human history as beginning, roughly, 2.5 million years ago. When bones from early forms of the genus *Homo* were found, along with early stone tools, it was decided that tool-making defined being human and these bones and tools dated back 2.5 million years.[4] Hence my choice of 2.5 million years of early human history. Our species *Homo sapiens* evolved about 250,000 years ago but, before this, early humans gathered food, pair-bonded, spoke a proto-language, tamed fire, and used it to cook the food they had gathered.[5] This all happened during the Palaeolithic era (Old Stone Age). The date at which human history began may be contested but that our early ancestors gathered food is not.

The idea of our ancient ancestors being hunters first and gatherers second is appealing to some, conjuring up images of the noble savage in a state of nature.[6] But hunting is dangerous and precarious. Surprisingly, even tigers are successful only 5–10% of the time, although kill rates, for specific prey, are reckoned to be higher.[7] We can't know how effective our early ancestors were but modern day human hunters of moose have a success rate of less than 25% on hunts that take 2–4 days[8]. More energy may have been expended in the hunting than became available to the hunter through the amount that could be eaten. In any case, until the advent of weapons such as spears, about 500,000 years ago, early humans would not have been able to kill large animals.[9]

An alternative, rather repellent but more realistic, hypothesis on the meat-eating habits of our ancestors is that we were scavengers, taking meat, fat, organs, and bones (for bone marrow) from prey killed by other animals.[10] For example,

What Do Dreams Do? Sue Llewellyn, Oxford University Press (2020). © Oxford University Press.
DOI: 10.1093/oso/9780198818953.001.0001.

leopards actually store meat high in trees, where it's safe from lions and hyenas, but early humans could certainly have climbed up to reach.[11] We were more gatherer-scavenger-hunters than hunter-gatherers, spending much more time gathering nuts, fruit, roots, insects, bird or reptile eggs, and wild plants, scavenging from dead prey and capturing fish or small animals than hunting big game.[12] During the Palaeolithic era, when we used simple stone tools, we ate 1.65–1.9 kg (3.6–4.2 lb) per day of fruit and vegetables.[13]Clear evidence of considerable gathering and certainly way exceeding our current intake, despite exhortations from health experts.

A nomadic or semi-nomadic way of life has been linked to early humans as hunter-gatherers, but this too may be misleading. Few animals are nomads; most stay within a fairly confined 'home range'.[14] Early humans lived much like animals—nothing special in their way of life distinguished them from baboons, chimpanzees, and elephants.[15] Their home range was much larger than that of animals[16] and may have varied enormously in size, but early humans would not, normally, have strayed outside of known turf. Only natural disasters, violent conflicts, pressure of numbers, or the decision of a charismatic leader would have impelled wider exploration.[17]

A home range has many advantages for food gathering *and* hunting. Once early humans had invented spears, their hunting technique was, probably, to choose a known clump of trees, wait in their branches until herds of wildebeest, antelope, or gazelle passed underneath, and then spear an animal at point blank range.[18] This strategy did not depend on a nomadic way of life, it required local knowledge of when the prey herd passed the particular clump of trees. Food gathering in a home range is much quicker and more efficient, as are actions to avoid predators because of familiarity with escape routes to shelters and the way back to the home base.[19]

Several issues weigh against the presumption of a nomadic way of life for early humans. First, a physiological issue: our kidneys are not very efficient; we need water each day to get rid of waste products, without frequent access to water supplies we would have died.[20] Second, water availability would have been a preoccupation for early humans because, most probably, they had limited means of carrying liquids.[21] A third factor is the extended period of dependency for human offspring: foraging adults would have had to return to the home base each day to feed and care for young children. A nomadic way of life would have exposed young children to many hazards. Clearly, if food supplies across the whole home range became exhausted, then the family or group would have had to search for another home range, but it's unlikely they would have been nomads out of choice—the preference would have been to find new food sites within the home range. How is food and water distributed in the home range?

Our Patchwork Planet and Moving About in the Home Range

We live on a patchwork planet—most natural resources, including food and water, are patchy, clumped or clustered; they aren't evenly or randomly distributed.[22] We need to move to get what we need. Indeed, the evolutionary driver for the whole of human brain development was not to think or feel but to move about.[23] Animals that don't move about don't have brains. They don't need them. For example, carnivorous sea sponges don't have brains and don't move about, they trap prey that comes floating their way.

In contrast to sea sponges, within any home range, animals that move about regularly return to those places with resources (i.e. food, water, shelter, mates) while, if possible, avoiding those where they have encountered aggression. Consequently, the home range has core locations of intense use such as dependable food sites and natural shelters from predators. Animals undertake regular, sometimes daily, tours of such places followed by a return to the home base.[24] To consume and gather food, early humans would have made tours too using regular routes or pathways to known places, some of these served as visual aids to navigation, some were actual destinations to consume food or water, shelter, or meet potential mates.

Unless they covered a very large area, tours would have ended with a return to the home base. Figure 4.1 is a much simplified, schematic version of such a tour, where only one food site (C), the blackberry bush, is shown. On this tour the early human visited the blackberry bush (C), a shelter (D), and the waterhole/pond (E) in that order; the clump of trees, from which hunting sometimes took place, (B) and big tree (F) were used as visual aids only.

Our brains construct representations of the world. These representations evolved, through natural selection, to enable early humans to move about to find food, water, and mates, to stay alive and reproduce. Once you know that the brain represents its environment, it's not surprising to find that the brain is made up of a

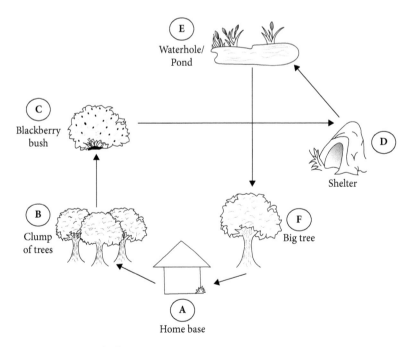

Figure 4.1 A tour in the home range.

network of pathways and junctions (as described in Chapter 3) because, over a period of 2.5 million years (less the 10,000 years when farming began), early humans walked along pathways and spent time at junctions to survive. The structure of our brains is not independent of our experiences.

Pathways in Brain Networks

You will recall from Chapter 3 that memories for experiences are called *episodic* memories—remembering episodes. For early humans, a very frequent episode would have been walking along a familiar pathway to reach a destination in the home range. György Buzsáki, a neuroscientist at Rutgers, the State University of New Jersey in America, is interested in the relationship between memory for pathways and places, 'spatial memory', and memory for experiences.[25] It's not difficult to see how spatial memory for a pathway co-evolved with an episodic memory for the experiences that happened as the early human walked along. An experience such as walking along a pathway and stopping to pick blackberries off a bush, followed by going to a shelter, then walking to a waterhole/pond to consume water is a memory for a pathway or route but also a memory for an experience or episode that unfolds over time as various things (blackberries, sheltering, and drinking) happen in order. György Buzsáki points out that, in the brain, learning and remembering things that happen sequentially during an experience is equivalent to remembering sequential places along a pathway. Also in both you are moving forward, in one direction, in time.

Junctions in Brain Networks

Junctions were frequently visited places for both early humans and animals. On the tours of early humans, what type of places would have been *landmark* (i.e. significant) junctions? The human body is 60% water. In the absence of physical exercise humans can survive 3–5 days without water, but early humans took lots of exercise, so we can surmise that most of their tours would have included a visit to a waterhole (a pool, pond, or lake), making this a landmark junction. Water is vital for humans *and* mammals. This makes waterholes often crowded places, relative to the surrounding area. More than this, waterholes are 'landscapes of fear'[26] because both prey and predators congregate there. Chapter 2 raised the example of lions, they are 'sit and wait' predators at waterholes, ambushing their prey through hiding in the vegetative cover that surrounds them.[27]

On tours within the home range, if there was only one waterhole available, our dependence on water meant early humans couldn't avoid visiting for long, out of fear of lions. You will recall from Chapter 2, the behaviour of humans and animals is not determined, nor is it random, it's probabilistic, meaning humans and animals tend to act in certain ways but they can always surprise us.

Any *complex probabilistic pattern* in lion behaviour that indicated when they would be present at the waterhole would have enhanced the survival of early humans. To identify the pattern, early humans would have to extract elements through observing lions during different experiences. For example, one element would be lions tend to visit waterholes at night.[28] Another element is that they, generally, sleep during the day but, in dry seasons, they can get so thirsty they go to the waterhole in the midday sun. Yet another is lions hunt not far from waterholes throughout the seasons but, during the dry season, lions are more likely to be near waterholes due to prey abundance.[29] Making associations between these elements would have created 'lion–waterhole–night' and 'lion–waterhole–dry season–day–prey' probabilistic patterns.

To remember patterns, they must, somehow, be represented in the brain. We noted earlier that memories are represented in brain networks, composed of pathways and junctions. Pathways represent *single* episodes of experience that move forward in time. But to remember the 'lion–waterhole–visit–night' and 'lion–waterhole–dry season–visit–day–prey' patterns requires a different type of memory. To remember these patterns, early humans would have had to identify lion-related elements across *many different* past experiences at a waterhole. How might such a memory have evolved?

On any tour within the home range, say there are six alternative pathways to the waterhole, making this an *omnidirectional* landmark junction, as shown in Figure 4.2.

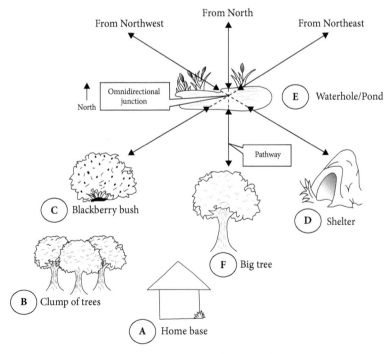

Figure 4.2 The six paths to the waterhole/omnidirectional junction.

Junctions are places where paths meet and have *crossed* multiple times. Supposing an early human has already visited the waterhole 20 times and, on each visit, has taken one of the six different approach/exit pathways. We can think of the landmark area as composed of crisscrossing paths that are layered on top of one another, intersecting at the landmark, assuming, for simplicity, that the pool, pond, or lake was sufficiently shallow to walk through.

We noted above that episodic memories evolved from spatial memories of moving forward along a pathway. Experiences that happened at the landmark can be thought of as elements of a whole pathway which represents an episodic memory. Looking at Figure 4.3(below), suppose that the home base is (A) and, on this particular day, the waterhole is the third place visited on a tour. Having left the blackberry bush (C) the early human stops at the waterhole (D) to drink and then continues straight on in a north-easterly direction until reaching point (X). Clearly, experience is continuous. Nevertheless, we remember experience in discrete episodes, usually to highlight events of some significance to us. If the episodic memory is counted as starting at (C) and ending at (X), then only the middle part of the memory is the experience at the waterhole (D). This experience at the waterhole can be thought of as an element of the episode that began at (C) and ended at (X). See Figure 4.3.

If this visit is the 20th, then there are 19 past sets of experiences at the waterhole. These 19 previous sets of experiences are a series of crisscrossing paths/events that happened at the same place. Waterhole experiences would not always be the

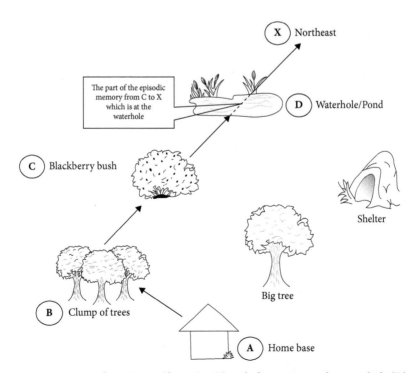

Figure 4.3 An episodic memory (from C to X) including a visit to the waterhole (D).

middle part of a whole episodic memory. If the early human arrived and left by the same or a different pathway, events at the waterhole could be said to constitute the end of one pathway and/or the beginning of another. We said earlier that pathways in brain networks evolved into representing single episodic memories in the brain. What did the landmark junctions, which are formed by crisscrossing parts of episodic memories, evolve into?

I argue these junctions evolved into representing the associative patterns between the elements of past episodes that happened at landmarks, like the waterhole.[30] In Figure 4.4 we consider waterhole visits over 20 consecutive days where

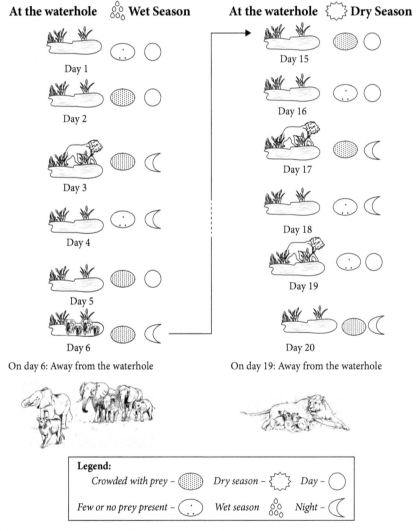

Figure 4.4 Identifying the lion at the waterhole pattern.

the wet season ends and the dry season begins sometime between days 7–14; for simplicity these intermediate days are omitted.

To reiterate, an early human would identifying any *complex probabilistic pattern* in lion behaviour that indicated when they would be present at the waterhole. To identify the pattern, early humans would have to extract elements through observing lions during many different experiences. For example, lions are more likely to visit the waterhole at night when prey are abundant; these conditions are associated with the presence of a lion on Day 3 and Day 17. But we need to remember that these associations, i.e. night-crowded with prey at the waterhole-lion, are only probabilistic. On Day 20 it is night and the waterhole is crowded with prey so it is potentially dangerous but no lion is there. Equally, lions get so thirsty in the dry season that they sometimes visit during the day, especially when the waterhole is crowded with prey—these conditions are met on Day 15 but no lion is there. Obviously the knowledge of the pattern is continually constructed over many visits; over just 20, only part of the pattern is evident.

Sometimes, as discussed previously, the dangers of a lion at the waterhole may be linked to an event that happens *away* from the waterhole. For example, elephants enjoy eating tree bark.[31] In natural conditions they only sleep 2 hours, mainly at night.[32] On Day 6 during the day and away from the waterhole an early human sees elephants chase away a lion who had been resting under a tree,[33] (see the bottom left of Figure 4.4). On the following night on Day 6 the early human sees elephants at the waterhole, given that they had seen elephants chasing a lion away from the tree they deduced that the presence of elephants at the waterhole offers some degree of safety—even though it is night and the waterhole is crowded with prey. On this occasion it seems the presence of elephants means no lion is present. Equally, during the dry season, lions can get so thirsty that they visit during the day, particularly at midday when the sun is high in the sky. On Day 19 the early human sees a female lion suckling cubs away from the waterhole (see bottom right of Figure 4.4)—she gets so thirsty that she visits the waterhole during the day even though there are few prey present.

What has all of this got to do with dreams?

Dream to Survive! A Dream is a Landmark Junction

You will recall from Chapter 3 that rapid eye movement (REM) sleep is of very ancient evolutionary origin. Brain activity during REM sleep indicates evolutionarily early behaviours such as foraging, eating, and dealing with fear and anxiety,[34] suggesting that REM sleep and dreaming served an evolutionary imperative. Foraging involves visiting places. John O'Keefe and Jonathan Dostrovsky at University College London found a type of brain cell that fires when an animal visits a particular place, they called these place cells[35]. The place cells that fire when animals visit dependable food sites fire again during sleep, indicating that animals may dream about their goals—the places they wish to go.[36] I think humans dreamt about the places they visited too; the evolutionary imperative was to identify complex, associative patterns in the behaviour of predators, competitors, and potential mates at landmark places, such as dependable food sites and waterholes.

Dream associations are non-obvious. I argue that, across evolutionary time, landmark junctions in the world were represented as junctions in brain networks, through portraying non-obvious associations between those elements of different episodic memories that happened at the landmark junction in the world—along with elements of some episodic memories that happened away from the landmark but were relevant to the behaviour of other living beings at the landmark. I argue that a dream scene, which identifies a complex, pattern through associating elements of past experiences, is represented at an omnidirectional junction in brain networks.[37] Archetypically, this pattern was predator behaviour. We dreamed to survive!

At this point, some readers may object. Few dreams are remembered. Even when we recall dreams on waking we usually rapidly forget them. This forgetting leads many people to think dreams have little, if any, impact on their lives. But there's a difference between forgetting, in the sense of 'do not remember during wakefulness', and retention. Dream associations may have evolved to be retained at an unconscious level.

Chapter 1 points out that dreams, while being dreamt, are conscious experiences. But, the initial process of dream construction from elements of different episodic memories may be unconscious.[38] Introspection indicates this because we don't consciously search our memory banks for elements of experiences that are non-obviously associated. Dream scenes appear—already formed and out of our control—unless we are having a lucid dream. After being both constructed and consciously dreamt, I think dreams 'go to' the unconscious. The retained, unconscious dream pattern can to be accessed unconsciously by the conscious mind/brain in wakefulness.

This may sound unlikely but we are actually quite familiar with previously conscious patterns being retained unconsciously. Take driving a car. When we first learn to drive a car we're very conscious of the sequential pattern involved. Switch on the engine, depress the clutch, go into first gear, release the clutch until the engine engages, then press the accelerator and move forward. But once this pattern is well learnt it becomes unconscious. If you start to think consciously about what to do, starting the car becomes clumsy and slow. The reason why dream patterns become unconscious may be very similar to this car-starting scenario. We retain memories of actions, like starting a car, unconsciously in 'how to do' memories, formally called 'procedural' memories. We know REM sleep benefits procedural memory.[39] This gives some support to the idea that REM dreams are retained unconsciously, in a similar way to procedural memories.

Dreams in Dangerous Situations

Identifying a complex pattern created through associating elements extracted from many past experiences would have enhanced the survival of early humans. Anticipating likely events at a landmark junction, such as a waterhole, would have enabled early humans to take advantage of possible rewards, obviously water but also meeting potential mates, while avoiding risky encounters. To reiterate the example of lions, they tend to visit waterholes at night.[40] Lions, generally, sleep during the day but in dry seasons they can get so thirsty they will go to the waterhole to drink in the midday sun. Lions hunt near waterholes throughout the seasons but, during the dry season, lions are more likely to be there due to prey abundance.[41] Identifying these patterns 'lion–waterhole–visit–night' and 'lion–waterhole–dry season–visit–day' and portraying them in unconscious images would have enabled early humans to respond immediately to danger and increased their survival chances.

Given that lions tend to visit waterholes at night, if an early human had identified this association, to avoid them s/he would have come during the day. On any tour, the approach to a landmark, such as a waterhole, is the most dangerous time; vigilance on approach is greater than either drinking at or departing from the landmark.[42] If, on approach to a waterhole during the day, an early human saw a flash of yellow in the vegetation surrounding the waterhole, what is the chance this is a lion waiting to ambush? It may just be a yellow butterfly. If it's the dry season the chances of a lion ambush are higher than if it's the rainy season. A glimpse of a life-threatening predator requires an immediate flight, fight, or freeze response. For an early human 'fight' with a lion doesn't seem a good strategy; contemporarily 'freeze' is the advice usually given for mountain lions, but new research disputes this; based on an analysis of the different strategies of survivors, flight was the best response.[43]

Whatever the response to a predator, the identification of danger and the response to danger must be fast to be effective. Unconscious processes and responses are much faster than consciously deliberated ones. We know fear-related visual stimuli can be processed unconsciously in the brain.[44] Evolutionary adaptation to predator threats would have driven unconscious processing because it's quick. Another significant reason for unconscious retention of dream images is that, in the evolutionary context of predator threat, it would have been vital to maintain visual perception to track the movements of the predator; a conscious dream image would have interfered with visual perception.[45] Fast unconscious processing, through mental images, would have been foremost in evolutionary terms.[46]

We know that forming an unconscious mental image that predicts and projects what we are about to do is essential for bodily movement.[47] Unconscious processing, through retained dream images, may portray memories of action appropriate to the circumstances. Unconscious mental images also enable unconscious bodily responses that reflect the situation. If sensory input indicated, for example, a predator, the probabilistic pattern can be integrated with the appropriate action in an unconscious image that facilitates a rapid response.

For example, Figure 4.5 illustrates a daytime tour, during the dry season. An early human has progressed to the shelter (D) and spent time there. Then, while on approach to the waterhole/pond (E), s/he sees a flash of yellow in the surrounding vegetation. This flash of yellow triggers an unconscious mental image, retained from a dream, portraying 'lion–waterhole–dry season–visit–day', which immediately leads to a retreat from the waterhole back to the shelter, hopefully before the lion has seen its potential prey.

Chapter 2 mentioned the possibility of two or more apparently dissimilar things being merged in a single dream image when they have the same meaning and significance for the dreamer. We talked about the liena. Both lions and hyenas can attack humans. Also both occupy the same territories in Africa.[48] So if the early human sees a flash of yellow in the vegetation surrounding a waterhole this could be the fur of a lion or a hyena. A dream may associate these two animals in a fused image—to be mobilized, unconsciously, whenever a flash of yellow is seen.

It is worth recognizing that 95% of brain activity is fast and unconscious.[49] Previously, we noted that all mind states have corresponding brain states because

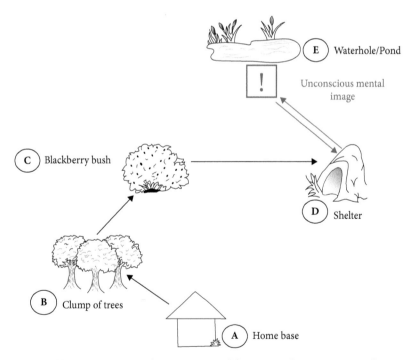

Figure 4.5 Unconscious mental image, retained from a rapid eye movement dream, causes retreat.

the brain generates the mind. By definition, unconscious brain activity doesn't reach the mind. A mind state can't be more than a brain state but a brain state is more than a mind state because of unconscious brain activity. The unconscious processing of retained dreams is an aspect of the 95% of fast, unconscious brain activity that happens during consciousness in wake. This illustrates how our conscious mind/brain and our unconscious mind/brain work together. How do the conscious and the unconscious relate to pathways and junctions in our brain networks?

Unconscious Landmarks and Conscious Pathways

To start on this question, we need a more nuanced understanding of consciousness. As noted earlier, 95% of brain activity is unconscious. While unconscious we can engage in parallel processing of different streams of information but, sometimes, information becomes conscious, resulting in a subjective experience that we can report.[50] Why does this happen? We don't really know the answer. As noted earlier, unconscious processing is fast and efficient, in many ways superior to conscious processing. The philosopher Thomas Metzinger, at the University of Mainz, Germany, thinks of conscious thoughts using the analogy of dolphins who briefly leap from the unconscious ocean only to rapidly return to their natural habitat. He says '"our conscious thoughts" are really like dolphins in our mind, jumping briefly out of the ocean of our unconscious for a short period before they submerge themselves once again'.[51] Consciousness makes us suffer—if we had no subjective experiences we would have no torments and no sense of our own mortality.

But consciousness also allows us to reflect; to think ahead on possible different courses of action. It may have evolved whenever there were no immediate dangers requiring rapid action. The pathways, between landmark junctions, afforded interludes between threats. Walking along in a particular direction towards a goal also engenders 'always follows' thinking. What we call step-by-step logic may have arisen as early humans walked step-by-step along pathways. Experiences along the pathways on a daily tour would have been more predictable than those at junctions. Regularly occurring, successive visual landmarks along a pathway (passing trees and bushes, crossing streams) made for serial, sequential, more stereotyped associative knowledge. Conscious reflection may have arisen in these walks between landmarks, enabling deliberation about future possibilities.[52] For example, to plan the precise route to take on any particular day, given past experiences, current food availability, and the weather conditions.

If consciousness evolved in this way, as we walked step-by-step along pathways that held no immediate dangers, it explains why consciousness is serial thinking—as opposed to the 'massive parallelism'[53] of the unconscious brain as it juggles different information from disparate sources. But consciousness comes in different forms.

Gerald Edelman (1929–2014) was an American biologist who became a professor of neurobiology. He made a distinction between primary and 'higher order' or secondary consciousness.[54] Primary consciousness equates to an awareness of things in the world, through forming mental images of them in the present. Animals, like humans, have primary consciousness. Secondary consciousness imparts abilities to recreate the past and imagine the future, along with knowing about having these capabilities. During wake you know you can rerun past events and think about how you might act differently in the future, faced with the same events. Given this, you must conceive of yourself as a self—as an agent in the world. During your waking hours you know you are conscious. You're also aware of an alternative consciousness—that of dreaming.

During dreaming you lose secondary consciousness, you don't reflect on the past, and can't imagine the future. You're always in the present. You don't know you're dreaming because you can't reflect on your state of mind/brain. During normal (non-lucid) dreaming your mind/brain runs on primary consciousness. The unconscious retention of dreams, as images, reflects how, across evolutionary time, dreams were used in dangerous situations during waking hours. There's more than dreams in your unconscious, however. Earlier, I used the example of starting a car becoming an unconscious process. Starting a car is faster and smoother when it becomes an unconscious procedural memory. Escaping from dangers requires fast, efficient responses too—this was imperative at landmark junctions whenever predators or competitors were around.

In contrast, on the pathways between junctions, the danger of predation, while still present, would have been less. Thus secondary, conscious thought in wake and primary conscious thinking in REM dreaming would have become patterned in different ways. Secondary conscious thought emerged to support the logical, ordered, step-by-step, more predictable associations experienced along a trajectory that went forward in time. In contrast, dreams are constructed from parallel, non-obvious associations that identify patterns inherent in the behaviour of other living creatures at a particular place but at different times.

But, in conscious form, both dreaming and waking thought give rise to seriality. When we dream consciously the dream scenes follow each other in a serial way. Also both types can give rise to unconscious retention—the logical, step-by-step associative pattern to start a car and the non-obvious, associative behavioural patterns of other living creatures.

One implication of identifying the behavioural patterns of living creatures is that *new* associations can be identified in REM sleep and retained for later use. In contrast, during wake, we have already identified the associations that give rise to schema or scripts in slow-wave sleep (SWS). Consequently, the associations, or commonalities, like station–ticket–platform–train that form a schema in SWS aren't new, we have already noticed them in wake, but REM associations seem to be new. There is research supporting this hypothesis of us learning new associations and their unconscious retention during REM.

Research on REM Sleep and Unconscious Associations

In 2012, Anat Arzi and colleagues at the Weizmann Institute of Science in Israel investigated how associations, formed in REM sleep, are retained at an unconscious level and then impact on their participants' behaviour when they were awake.[55] This study drew on the brain's ability to process some sensory input during sleep. We are interested in visual associations but it would be impossible for researchers to present pictures to sleeping subjects and ask them to associate the images. Anat Arzi and colleagues played a tone to their sleeping participants followed by an odour.[56] Perhaps surprisingly, we react in the same way to odours during sleep as we do in waking hours. We sniff deeply in response to a pleasant smell but only shallowly when exposed to an unpleasant one. Over the course of the night many tones, followed by smells, were presented, with the same pairs repeated for reinforcement. While still asleep, the participants associated the tone with the odour so that, when only the tones were heard, they sniffed deeply or shallowly—as if the odours had been present as well.

When the participants heard only the tones on the next day, although they did not remember hearing them during the night, their sniffing behaviour showed the same pattern: deep sniffs for pleasant smells and shallow sniffs for unpleasant ones. The associations formed between tones and sniffs during REM sleep remained unconscious, but on the following day they provoked deep sniffing, which prolonged the participants' exposure to pleasant aromas, or shallow sniffing, which limited their exposure to unpleasant smells. This shows that associations formed during REM sleep are retained unconsciously and, at this unconscious level, can influence behaviour during waking hours.

The above study only investigated paired associations. Juliana Yordanova and colleagues at the Institute of Neurobiology, Sofia, Bulgaria looked at more complex associations.[57] During waking hours, they gave their participants the task of finger-tapping a sequence of numbers that has a hidden regularity or pattern. This task is analogous to the identification of a non-obvious pattern in past experiences. About half of the participants seemed to unconsciously identify the hidden or nonobvious pattern because their response times were faster and their finger-tapping speeded up. Then the researchers divided their participants into two groups. Both groups slept for 3 hours but one group didn't have much REM sleep. About half of the participants in the group without much REM sleep became consciously aware of the pattern and could say what the pattern was after sleep. In contrast, very few participants in the group who had REM sleep became consciously aware of the pattern—the pattern was stabilized in its unconscious brain form. I suspect most people's reaction to this experiment will be that it is better to have conscious knowledge of the pattern than not. But this ignores the issue that acting on unconscious knowledge is faster—thinking takes time. In dangerous situations at landmark junctions, there was no time to think—you must act. Unconscious retention of patterns after REM sleep enables this fast action.

Although I argue dreams function unconsciously, the dreams we consciously remember are certainly worthy of attention. So far we've considered a single dream, the case study method as applied to dreams, but there is research on the *general* characteristics of dreams. Does this research support the evolutionary context for dreams outlined here?

General Dream Characteristics

The dreamer is, almost always, in their own dreams.[58] We experience both dreams and wake from the first-person, 'I' perspective. During REM dreams the action always happens somewhere, a single dream scene is located at a place.[59] Dreams aren't like abstract art, for example, which is placeless. Clearly landmark junctions were significant places. Earlier we discussed how, sometimes, events at the landmark junction were associated with events occurring away from the landmark. This may explain why we dream of events that happened at different places at the same place.

In a study undertaken by Susan Malcolm-Smith and colleagues at the University of Cape Town, 73% of dreams portrayed approach behaviours.[60] We noted earlier that approach to the landmark place was the most dangerous time. Dreams prioritize significant events which have a high value for survival.[61] Seventy-nine per cent of REM dreams involve movement of the lower extremities, as would be required for activity at landmarks such as food sites or waterholes. Content analyses on dream reports derive typical themes that may reflect evolutionary landmark origins; for example, the themes of 'being chased or pursued', 'falling', and 'a person now alive as dead' occurred in 92.2%, 87.1%, and 75.0% of one student sample and 94.6%, 76.8%, and 69.6% of another.[62] On the other hand, many activities central to our contemporary lives are absent. For example, we almost never dream about reading, writing, or calculating.[63] Equally, we don't dream about watching the TV. These activities didn't feature at landmark junctions.

Dreamers don't engage in periodic, mundane, habitual behaviours. For example, we rarely wash, dress, or groom ourselves during dreams. Early humans would have been unlikely to engage in these behaviours at landmark junctions—at least if predation was a possibility. But there's another reason why these activities don't tend to feature in REM dreams. Chapter 3 argued we extract the common elements of different experiences during SWS to give us a schema or script for what to expect at frequently visited places like a railway station (buying tickets, using ticket machines, and finding platforms) or a restaurant (securing a table, perusing the menu, and calling a waiter over). Another way of thinking about common elements is that they are habitual. If habitual, they almost always happen. We don't dream about reading, writing, calculating, or watching the TV, nor do we dream about washing, dressing, or grooming ourselves. We don't dream about these activities because they are habitual (e.g. after getting up, you wash in the shower, then you get dressed, then comb your hair) and so are well remembered through our 'always follows' type of thinking during wake.

We noted previously that landmark places, such as waterholes, would be 'social', interactive places because they attract mates, competitors, and predators. Dream reports include more social interactions than reports of activity during wake, and REM dreams portray more aggressive interactions than non-rapid eye movement (NREM) dreams—the difference was threefold.[64] REM dreams are emotionally charged, particularly with elation, fear, and anxiety.[65] Elation may reflect securing rewards (food, water, or mates) at a landmark place in situations of considerable risk. Fear and anxiety would have followed from the danger of predators and aggressive encounters with competitors at landmarks.

Dreams are consistently and continuously visual; we sometimes hear sounds but these are sporadic rather than constant.[66] Our other senses, touch, smell, and taste, are generally absent. In one study on non-visual senses, from 635 REM dream reports, 76% had some sound, 1% had taste, 1% had touch, and <1% smell.[67] In another on 3,372 reports, not distinguishing between REM and NREM dreams, 53% had some sound, 1% had smell, <1% had taste, and 0% had touch.[68] In *The World as Will and Idea* Arthur Schopenhauer (1788–1860), the German philosopher, wrote: 'Life and dreams are leaves of one and the same book'. Yet, as these dream report studies show, our experiences in waking life and dreams are different in that dreams, generally, lack touch, taste, and smell. These sense deficiencies may reflect the archetypical dream that portrayed a pattern of predator behaviour. Predators are best observed through sight and sound at a safe distance. If early humans had got close enough to touch, taste, and smell a predator, they would have been eaten!

These general dream characteristics give support to the idea that dreams, originally, had a survival function in that they portrayed visual associations between elements of past events, archetypically, involving predators, competitors, and potential mates at a landmark junction. During the 2.5 million years (less the 10,000 years when farming began) when early humans gathered, scavenged, and hunted for food these general dream characteristics would have been appropriate and may be conserved in contemporary dreams.

On the other hand, the brain represents its environment. Our current environment is very unlike that faced by our early ancestors. So we would expect that dreams have evolved to better reflect the contemporary environment. For example, A's dream reflects some general dream characteristics: she is in her dream, the two dream scenes are both located at places, her husband (or mate) is present in the first scene, the dream involves motor activity (flying the kite), and is emotionally charged because it relates to her concerns, albeit these are clearly contemporary.

Briefly...

The key argument in this chapter is: in REM dreams, non-obvious associations between elements of different episodic memories originally happened at (or were related to) a landmark place, most usually a food site or a waterhole. These associations were made to identify a pattern between elements of past events at the landmark place. Archetypically, this pattern was predator, competitor, or potential mate behaviour. The associative pattern between, say, predator-relevant elements of past events would have been retained in an unconscious image. On approach to the landmark place during waking hours, any momentary sight or sound that may be indicative of a predator would trigger the unconscious image which portrayed the pattern. This would have given early humans an indication of the present risk based on past experiences at the landmark. We dreamed to survive!

Contemporarily, most of us still do make regular tours to 'landmark' places from our home base. For example, a tour may consist of a car trip to the railway station, a train to the city where we work, a walk from the station to work, followed by spending time at work, then possibly a trip to a supermarket to devote time to gathering food, followed by the return trip back to the home base. The most significant landmark on this particular contemporary tour is the workplace. We only encounter predators there in a metaphorical sense! We come across competitors at work. There are also opportunities to meet mates. The other landmark place is, naturally, the home, where were interact with our most significant others—our partners and families.

The brain evolved to represent the environment. Clearly, contemporarily, our environment is much less dangerous than that inhabited by early humans. We do not need to remember associative patterns in the past behaviour of fearsome predators. As human beings evolved into the people we are today, home, social and work interactions became much more significant. Rather than foraging, getting along with significant others and, for some people, getting ahead in social groups and at work became paramount. Our most personally significant memories are likely to involve other people in social, work, or intimate one-to-one situations. Identifying associative patterns between our experiences and retaining them in unconscious images will cause us to make fast, unconscious assessments of the people we meet and the situations we find ourselves in and, sometimes, to react to these people and situations quickly and unconsciously.

Next

The next chapter will focus on how making non-obvious associations between our experiences helps us remember them. We will also compare REM dream images with the associative images that memory champions use to win competitions. One of their associative image techniques is the Method of Loci, where the items to be remembered are placed at locations along a familiar route. Readers will anticipate a connection between this Method of Loci and the food-gathering tours that our early human ancestors made. But we will also consider what happens when the daily tour is no longer viable—when changes become necessary because waterholes have dried up or food sites are depleted. These modifications may have given rise to the flexible memory systems we have today.

Notes

1. Dobzhansky, T. (1973). Nothing in biology makes sense except in the light of evolution. *The American Biology Teacher, 35*(3), 125–129.
2. I use the term 'early humans' rather than the scientific terms 'hominid' or 'hominine' because these terms are linked to differing classification systems. For my purposes in this chapter, all that really matters is that up until 10,000 years ago we were gatherer-scavenger-hunters or foragers.
3. Chapter 7 in Leakey, R. E., & Lewin, R. (1979). *People of the Lake: Mankind and its Beginnings*. Avon Books, New York; and Hill, K. R., Walker, R. S., Božičević, M., Eder, J., Headland, T., Hewlett, B., ... & Wood, B. (2011). Co-residence patterns in hunter-gatherer societies show unique human social structure. *Science, 331*(6022), 1286–1289. Available at: http://science.sciencemag.org/content/331/6022/1286.full
4. Chapter 4 in Christian, D., Brown, C., & Benjamin, C. (2014). *Big history: Between Nothing and Everything*. McGraw Hill, New York.
5. Chapter 4 in Christian, D., Brown, C., & Benjamin, C. (2014). *Big History: Between Nothing and Everything*. McGraw Hill, New York.
6. Rousseau, J. J. (1968). *The Social Contract (1762)*. Rousseau developed the concept of a 'state of nature' as a time and place when human beings lived uncorrupted by social systems but, although often attributed to him, he did not speak of people in a state of nature being noble savages.
7. Hunting success rates: how predators compare. *Discover Wildlife*. Available at: http://www.discoverwildlife.com/animals/hunting-success-rates-how-predators-compare
8. Willson, M. (2014). On the trails: hunting success. Available at: http://juneauempire.com/outdoors/2014-11-14/trails-hunting-success
9. Hunter-gatherers. Available at: https://www.history.com/topics/pre-history/hunter-gatherers
10. Lewin, R. (1984). Man the scavenger; hominids of 2 million years ago ate meat: but were they hunters or scavengers? *Science, 224*, 861–863.

11. Bunney, S. (1989). Science: meat from the trees made early hunters redundant. Available at: https://www.newscientist.com/article/mg12316813-200-science-meat-from-the-trees-made-early-hunters-redundant/

12. Harari Y. (2014). *Sapiens: a Brief History of Humankind*. Harvill Secker, London, see pp. 11–12 and What kinds of food did early man eat? Available at: https://www.reference.com/history/kinds-food-did-early-man-eat-602b1e319637ed44

13. Cristian, R. (2018). The return to simplicity: a guide to the paleo diet thu, 09.13.2018. Available at: https://sodelicious.recipes/healthy-eating/guide-paleo-diet/

14. Powell, R. A. (2000). Animal home ranges and territories and home range estimators. *Research Techniques in Animal Ecology: Controversies and Consequences*, *1*, 476.

15. Harari, Y. (2014). *Sapiens: A Brief History of Humankind*.Harvill Secker, London, see p. 4.

16. Home range size. Available at: https://carta.anthropogeny.org/moca/topics/home-range-size

17. Harari, Y. (2014). *Sapiens: A Brief History of Humankind*. Harvill Secker, London, see p. 53.

18. McKie, R. (2012). Humans hunted for meat 2 million years ago. *The Observer*. Available at: https://www.theguardian.com/science/2012/sep/23/human-hunting-evolution-2million-years

19. Stamps, J. (1995). Motor learning and the value of familiar space. *The American Naturalist*, *146*(1), 41–58.

20. See p. 286 in Horrobin, D. F. (2001). *The Madness of Adam and Eve: How Schizophrenia Shaped Humanity*. Bantam Press, London.

21. See p. 93 in Leakey, R. E., & Lewin, R. (1979). *People of the Lake: Mankind and its Beginnings*. Avon Books, New York.

22. Macdonald, D. W., & Johnson, D. D. P. (2015). Patchwork planet: the resource dispersion hypothesis, society, and the ecology of life. *Journal of Zoology*, *295*(2), 75–107.

23. The real reason for brains. Available at: https://www.ted.com/talks/daniel_wolpert_the_real_reason_for_brains

24. Undertaking these regular tours to gather food has been demonstrated in animals as different as bees, Janzen, D. (1971). Euglossine bees as long-distance pollinators of tropical plants. *Science*, *171*(3967), 203–205, and baboons, Noser, R., & Byrne, R. W. (2007). Travel routes and planning of visits to out-of-sight resources in wild chacma baboons. *Animal Behaviour*, *73*(2), 257–266.

25. Buzsáki, G. (2005). Theta rhythm of navigation: link between path integration and landmark navigation, episodic and semantic memory. *Hippocampus*, *15*(7), 827–840.

26. Willems, E. P., & R. A. Hill (2009). Predator-specific landscapes of fear and resource distribution: effects on spatial range use. *Ecology*, *90*(2), 546–555.

27. Hopcraft, J. G. C., Sinclair, A. R. E., & Packer, C. (2005). Planning for success: Serengeti lions seek prey accessibility rather than abundance. *Journal of Animal Ecology*, *74*(3), 559–566.

28. Valeix, M., Fritz, H., Loveridge, A. J., Davidson, Z., Hunt, J. E., Murindagomo, F., & Macdonald, D. W. (2009). Does the risk of encountering lions influence African herbivore behaviour at waterholes? *Behavioral Ecology and Sociobiology*, *63*(10), 1483–1494.

29. Kittle, A. M., Bukombe, J. K., Sinclair, A. R., Mduma, S. A., & Fryxell, J. M. (2016). Landscape-level movement patterns by lions in western Serengeti: comparing the influence of inter-specific competitors, habitat attributes and prey availability. *Movement Ecology*, *4*(1), 17 Available at: https://movementecologyjournal.biomedcentral.com/articles/10.1186/s40462-016-0082-9

30. Llewellyn, S., & Hobson, J. A. (2015). Not only … but also: REM sleep creates and NREM Stage 2 instantiates landmark junctions in cortical memory networks. *Neurobiology of Learning and Memory*, *122*, 69–87.

31. Elephants: diet and eating habits. Available at: https://seaworld.org/animal-info/animal-infobooks/elephants/diet-and-eating-habits

32. Briggs, H. (2017). Mysteries of elephant sleep revealed. Available at: https://www.bbc.co.uk/news/science-environment-39126993

33. Elephants scare off a pride of lions. Available at: https://www.youtube.com/watch?v=YJLC1mLp_Rs

34. Horne, J. (2013). Why REM sleep? Clues beyond the laboratory in a more challenging world. *Biological Psychology*, *92*(2), 152–168.

35. O'Keefe, J., & Dostrovsky, J. (1971). The hippocampus as a spatial map: Preliminary evidence from unit activity in the freely-moving rat. *Brain Research, 34,* 171–175. https://doi.org/10.1016/0006-8993(71)90358-1

36. Wilson, C. (2015). Rats dream about the places they wish to go. *New Scientist.* Available at: https://www.newscientist.com/article/dn27788-rats-dream-about-the-places-they-wish-to-go/

37. Llewellyn, S., & Hobson, J. A. (2015). Not only … but also: REM sleep creates and NREM Stage 2 instantiates landmark junctions in cortical memory networks. *Neurobiology of Learning and Memory*, *122*, 69–87.

38. Barcaro, U., Paradisi, P., & Sebastiani, L. (2019). (2019). A hypothesis about parallelism vs. seriality in dreams. *Frontiers in Psychology.* doi:10.2299.10.3389/fpsyg.2019.02299.

39. Smith, C. (2001). Sleep states and memory processes in humans: procedural versus declarative memory systems. *Sleep Medicine Reviews, 5*(6), 491–506; and Plihal, W., & Born, J. (1997). Effects of early and late nocturnal sleep on declarative and procedural memory. *Journal of Cognitive Neuroscience, 9*(4), 534–547.

40. Valeix, M., Fritz, H., Loveridge, A. J., Davidson, Z., Hunt, J. E., … & Macdonald, D. W. (2009). Does the risk of encountering lions influence African herbivore behaviour at waterholes? *Behavioral Ecology and Sociobiology*, *63*(10), 1483–1494.

41. Kittle, A. M., Bukombe, J. K., Sinclair, A. R., Mduma, S. A., & Fryxell, J. M. (2016). Landscape-level movement patterns by lions in western Serengeti: comparing the influence of inter-specific competitors, habitat attributes and prey availability. *Movement Ecology*, *4*(1), 17. Available at: https://movementecologyjournal.biomedcentral.com/articles/10.1186/s40462-016-0082-9

42. Valeix, M., Fritz, H., Loveridge, A. J., Davidson, Z., Hunt, J. E., Murindagomo, F., & Macdonald, D. W. (2009). Does the risk of encountering lions influence African herbivore behaviour at waterholes? *Behavioral Ecology and Sociobiology*, *63*(10), 1483–1494; and Périquet, S., Valeix, M., Loveridge, A. J., Madzikanda, H., Macdonald, D. W., & Fritz, H. (2010). Individual vigilance of African herbivores while drinking: the role of immediate predation risk and context. *Animal Behaviour*, *79*(3), 665–671.

43. Subramamian, S. (2009). Should you run or freeze when you see a mountain lion? Available at: https://www.scientificamerican.com/article/should-you-run-or-freeze-when-you-see-a-mountain-lion/

44. Öhman, A., Carlsson, K., Lundqvist, D., & Ingvar, M. (2007). On the unconscious subcortical origin of human fear. *Physiology & Behavior*, *92*(1), 180–185.

45. Llewellyn, S. (2016). Dream to predict? REM dreaming as prospective coding. *Frontier in Psychology*, *6*, 1961. doi:10.3389/fpsyg.2015.

46. Paivio, A. (2014). *Mind and its Evolution: A Dual Coding Theoretical Approach*. Psychology Press, Hove.

47. Cuthbert, B. N., Vrana, S. R., & Bradley, M. M. (1991). Imagery: function and physiology. In J. R. Jennings, P. K. Ackles, & M. G. H. Coles (Eds) *Advances in Psychophysiology* (pp. 1–42). Jessica Kingsley Publishers, London.

48. See Relationship between lions & hyenas. Available at: http://animals.mom.me/relationship-between-lions-hyenas-3692.html

49. 95% of brain activity is beyond our conscious awareness. Available at: http://www.simplifyinginterfaces.com/2008/08/01/95-percent-of-brain-activity-is-beyond-our-conscious-awareness/

50. Dehaene, S., & Changeux, J. P. (2011). Experimental and theoretical approaches to conscious processing. *Neuron*, *70*(2), 200–227.

51. Metzinger, T. Are you sleepwalking now? Available at: https://aeon.co/essays/are-you-sleepwalking-now-what-we-know-about-mind-wandering

52. See p. 62 in Tucker, D. M. (2007). Mind from Body: Experience from Neural Structure. Oxford University Press, New York.

53. Baars, B. J., Franklin, S., & Ramsøy, T. Z. (2013). Global workspace dynamics: cortical 'binding and propagation' enables conscious contents. *Frontiers in Psychology*, *4*, 200.

54. See p. 9 in Edelman, G. M. (2004). *Wider Than the Sky: A Revolutionary View of Consciousness*. Penguin, New York.

55. Arzi, A., Shedlesky, L., Ben-Shaul, M., Nasser, K., Oksenberg, A., Hairston, I. S., & Sobel, N. (2012). Humans can learn new information during sleep. *Nature Neuroscience*, *15*(10), 1460–1465.

56. Arzi, A., Shedlesky, L., Ben-Shaul, M., Nasser, K., Oksenberg, A., Hairston, I. S., & Sobel, N. (2012). Humans can learn new information during sleep. *Nature Neuroscience*, *15*(10), 1460–1465.

57. Yordanova, J., Kolev, V., Verleger, R., Bataghva, Z., Born, J., & Wagner, U. (2008). Shifting from implicit to explicit knowledge: different roles of early-and late-night sleep. *Learning & Memory*, *15*(7), 508–515.

58. Snyder, F. (1970). The phenomenology of dreaming. In L. Madow and L. D. Snow (Eds) *The Psychodynamic Implications of the Physiological Studies on Dreams* (pp. 124–151). Charles C. Thomas, Springfield, IL.

59. For example, see Llewellyn, S. (2011). If waking and dreaming consciousness became de-differentiated, would schizophrenia result? *Consciousness and Cognition*, *20*(4), 1059–1083; and Llewellyn, S. (2016). Crossing the invisible line: de-differentiation of wake, sleep and dreaming may engender both creative insight and psychopathology. *Consciousness and Cognition*, *46*, 127–147.

60. Malcolm-Smith, S., Koopowitz, S., Pantelis, E., & Solms, M. (2012). Approach/avoidance in dreams. *Consciousness and Cognition, 21*(1), 408–412.

61. Perogamvros, L., Dang-Vu, T. T., Desseilles, M., & Schwartz, S. (2013). Sleep and dreaming are for important matters. *Frontiers in Psychology, 4.*

62. Yu, C. K.-C. (2008). Typical dreams experienced by Chinese people. *Dreaming, 18*(1), 1; and Yu, C. K.-C. (2011). The constancy of typical dreams. *Asia Pacific Journal of Counselling and Psychotherapy, 2*(1), 51–70.

63. Hartmann, E. (2000). We do not dream of the 3 Rs: implications for the nature of dreaming mentation. *Dreaming, 10,* 103–111.

64. McNamara, P., McLaren, D., Smith, D., Brown, A., & Stickgold, R. (2005). A 'Jekyll and Hyde' within aggressive versus friendly interactions in REM and non-REM dreams. *Psychological Science, 16*(2), 130–136.

65. Smith, M. R., Antrobus, J. S., Gordon, E., Tucker, M. A., Hirota, Y., . . . & Emery, R. N. (2004). Motivation and affect in REM sleep and the mentation reporting process. *Consciousness and Cognition, 13*(3), 501–511; and Hobson, J. A. (2002). *Dreaming: An Introduction to the Science of Sleep.* Oxford University Press, New York,

66. Schredl, M. (2010). Characteristics and contents of dreams. *International Review of Neurobiology, 92,* 135–154.

67. Snyder, F. (1970). The phenomenology of dreaming. In: L. Madow & L. D. Snow (Eds) *The Psychodynamic Implications of the Physiological Studies on Dreams* (pp. 124–151). Charles C. Thomas, Springfield, IL.

68. Zadra, A. L., Nielsen, T. A., & Donderi, D. C. (1997). The prevalence of auditory, olfactory, gustatory and pain experiences in 3372 home dreams. *Sleep Research, 26,* 181.

5

Dream to Remember

Introduction

Chapter 4 proposed that early humans dreamt about the places they visited as they moved about in the home range. Their dreams created complex, associative images composed of, archetypically, patterned elements from predator-related past events at those places. These dream images were visuospatial, i.e. they demonstrated visual perception of the relationships among people, objects, and places. This chapter emphasizes how visuospatial, associative dream images work mnemonically, i.e. how they work in memory retention.

So far, we've taken memory retention for granted, in the sense of not thinking about *how* we remember experiences. 'Taking memory for granted' echoes our everyday mindset. We are apt to think of remembering as the effortless result of experiencing. But this common-sense view may be mistaken. Does dreaming of experiences improve remembering?

Research on visuospatial tasks, similar to the tours undertaken by early humans, shows it does. Dreaming of navigating a virtual (online) maze followed by a rapid return to the exit improves memory for the task, both after a nap[1] and after overnight sleep.[2] The nap study showed a 10-fold greater performance improvement for those who dreamt about navigating the maze over those who did not. As is usual, the dreams did not replicate the maze navigation. Rather, element(s) of the recent experience of navigating the maze were associated with elements of previous maze-associated experiences. These associations between the new maze task and previous experiences enhance memory for navigating the maze because the previous maze-associated experiences are already present in memory networks.

The focus on memory in this chapter shouldn't be thought of as a different function for dreaming. The mnemonic power of dreaming is an integral aspect of associating different memory elements to produce an image. To be remembered, an experience (or some new knowledge) has to be integrated with memories of what has already been experienced or is already known. In other words, the experience or knowledge has to 'find a place' in brain networks composed of pathways and junctions. To be integrated it has to be associated in some way to become part of a pattern. We aren't inclined to think of complex associative patterns as key to remembering, but they are. Chapter 3 explained that memory is fundamentally associative.[3] To be associated the experience or knowledge has to be meaningful. The more personally meaningful, the easier to associate and integrate.

What Do Dreams Do? Sue Llewellyn, Oxford University Press (2020). © Oxford University Press.
DOI: 10.1093/oso/9780198818953.001.0001.

I can't remember the names of my Chinese students, for example, Xiaojing, because I don't have any associations to them. Associations convey meaning. Meaningful association is fundamental to remembering. Chinese names don't mean anything to me so it's hard to remember them. In other words, I struggle to get Chinese names into my brain networks. On the other hand, suppose I meet a person called William. I have lots of meaningful associations to 'William': it was my father's name, the name of my favourite uncle, it's my eldest son's second name, and the name of my partner's son. So it's relatively easy for me to remember the name of a new person called William.

This chapter looks first at techniques that people employ to help them remember during wake. These special mnemonic techniques build associations with things people want to remember and portray the associations in images. These images are similar to those created during rapid eye movement (REM) dreams. I argue we can go some way to understanding how dream images work mnemonically through looking at these memory techniques. We then move on to thinking about how, when early humans adapted their daily tours to incorporate new landmark places, these modifications may have given rise to the flexible memory systems that, generally, serve us so well today.

Overall, in this chapter I maintain we dream to remember. We concentrate again on episodic pathways and landmark junctions. First, we look at the techniques memory champions employ to engender bizarre, mnemonic images and compare these to REM dream images.

The Ancient Art of Memory (AAOM)

Mnemonic techniques are not new. They've been around since Classical Antiquity. Right up to the Early Middle Ages, the educated social elite used mnemonic techniques to enable them to remember information for presentation before live audiences, at events such as lectures, disputations or sermons. Pre-modern minds recognized the power of emotion for memory. They knew the more bizarre, dramatic, disgusting, absurd, or obscene the associations portrayed in their private mental images, the more persistent the memory and the easier the process of recall.

Modern psychology distinguishes between three memory processes: first, 'encoding'; second, 'storage' or 'consolidation'; and, third, 'retrieval'. Pre-modern scholars used different labels, 'composition', 'retention', and 'recollection', for, broadly speaking, the same processes. Encoding during waking hours integrates experiences (or knowledge) into memory networks. For example, I can encode the name of a person called William because I already know people with that name. Encoding is 'elaborate' or 'deep' when associations are consciously formed between the new experiences (or knowledge) and experiences (or knowledge) already firmly established in memory networks. This process of integrating new experiences with older, more remote ones intensifies and expands memory networks through making new associations or connections. Personally meaningful associations are the most mnemonic. Pre-modern scholars called the process of encoding 'composition' because they composed a striking, mental image to incorporate all of the to-be-remembered material. Like REM dream images, the images created by pre-modern scholars could be taken in at a single glance—being simple and sparse but, also, organized and in 'real time'.

I use the pre-modern AAOM concept of 'retention' rather than 'storage' or 'consolidation' because memories change over time. The historians Mary Carruthers and Jan Ziolkowski critique the modern storage idea,[4] ' "storage" … .is a curious intellectual model, for it suggests that our memories are essentially passive impressions of experiences … that can be taken out whole and unchanged'. Associations between memories clearly impact on how they are remembered. For example, memories of a usually painful experience, like divorce, may, at first, be closely associated with other distressing life events but, over time, become associated with more positive experiences as, say, perceptions that the divorce was inevitable and 'for the best' grow. In this way, the emotional tenor of memories can change. At the same time, some aspects of the experience become more pronounced, while others fade into the background. Nevertheless, despite changes in memories over time, it still makes sense to speak of remembering the factual details of an experience, such as a divorce, and for those to be more or less accurate.

Memories may be retained but retrieval or recollection can fail. I use the pre-modern AAOM term 'recollection' in preference to retrieval. It's a common experience to know something, often a person's name, is 'in' memory networks but can't be accessed when required. Then the name pops up later, seemingly, 'of its own accord'. Recollection is an unconscious process, it cannot be consciously willed, but the way that memories are encoded affects whether they can be successfully retained and recollected. The more elaborate the encoding, the easier the retrieval because there are more associations that act as triggers to aid recall. Recollection implies that some elements of the memory may be recovered more easily or at different times from others. Also elements of the memory may be retained at different locations in the brain so they have to be 'collected' from different places in memory networks.

The next sections look at three AAOM encoding techniques that you can use in wake to improve your memory. These techniques improve memory because they conform to your brain's memory network structure.

AAOM Technique 1: The Method of Loci (MoL)

To understand how the MoL works, we return to the tour in the home range. I argue this underlies the efficacy of the MoL. Chapter 4 proposed that early humans undertook regular, even daily, tours. I noted that farming developed only 10,000 years ago. For all of our pre-farming history, our most pressing and important tasks were to move about, to navigate to gather food and consume water at dependable, yet risky, landmark sites, followed by a speedy return to the safety offered by the home base. You will recall the brain models (or represents) its environment. Consequently, the brain structures that underlie memory are networks composed of pathways and landmark junctions, reflecting almost 2.5 million years of tours to visit known food and water sites. The MoL takes to-be-remembered material and makes it conform to a 'pathways and landmarks' structure.[5] Consequently, we would expect better retention in the brain.[6]

For example, a simple case is to remember a shopping list without taking the list out with you. If the to-be-remembered items are coffee, firelighters, sugar, adhesive tape, and butter, I imagine depositing them in places along a familiar route and visualize them in these locations. Then, when out shopping, I mentally revisit all the places along the route to remember the items I wish to purchase. In terms of the tours made by early humans, the items to be remembered are being placed at the landmark junctions, which would have been very memorable locations because of their highly emotional risk/reward associations.

For me, a very familiar tour is my route to work. I visualize the coffee in the first landmark (the porch) as I leave the house, then I see the firelighters at the second landmark (the bus stop), then I visualize the sugar on the third landmark (the seat of the bus beside the one I am sitting on). Next I see the adhesive tape at the fourth landmark (the bus stop outside the university) and, finally, visualize the butter in the fifth landmark (the lift after I enter the university building). So the tour goes like this:

The porch + coffee → The bus stop + firelighters → The bus + sugar → The bus stop at the university + adhesive tape → The lift + butter.

Along this route, one place triggers the next through 'always follows', sequential association, so, for example, the porch triggers the bus stop as they are both landmark places where I spend time (to lock the door and wait for the bus, respectively) on my familiar journey to work.

You will recall from the last chapter that remembering these ordered, step-by-step associations (experienced along a habitual, and therefore, highly familiar, journey that goes forward in time) is well supported by our logical, sequential thought during wakefulness. This sequential thought conforms to the pathway structures in our brain networks.

AAOM Technique 2: Binary Associations and the MoL

Conforming to the brain network structure of pathways and landmark junctions will help retention in the brain. But, currently, the placing of the items at landmarks is arbitrary. So it's not that easy to remember their locations. How do I remember the firelighters are at the bus stop rather than in the porch? I stand a much better chance of remembering the item locations if I build in associations with my previous memories of events at the places. For example, to take just two of the places, sometimes as I approach the bus stop, one of my neighbours is already there. We chat. I can easily visualize him holding firelighters at the bus stop because he's something of a pyrotechnist. The spectacular bonfires in his garden threaten life and limb. A very different association with previous memories already in my brain networks is: the lift at work recently broke down so I can visualize the lift mechanism being greased with butter.

As well as being personal, these two associations 'neighbour with firelighters–bus stop' and 'greasing with butter–the lift' are mnemonic because they're bizarre. We remember unusual events much more easily than we remember ordinary ones—unless the ordinary ones are habitual and frequently rehearsed such as if I always took sugar into work. In the last chapter we discussed non-obvious associations. Greasing with butter–lift is a non-obvious association, so is neighbour with firelighters–bus stop. But the associations are still only binary, what–where associations.

When we remember 'what', the 'where' is the context for the 'what' memory. Suppose I go to a huge bonfire, this may trigger memories of other spectacular ones, but where did they happen? The 'where' is the context for the 'whats'—in this case, bonfires. One past context is: in my pyrotechnist neighbour's garden.

On the early tours our ancestors undertook, remembering 'what–where' would have been crucial. The 'whats' were 'resources' or 'what to do to get resources'. The 'wheres' were the landmarks. Blackberries (what) are found on bushes (where). Hunting with spears (what) takes place from a clump of trees (where). We can certainly form these what–where, contextual associations during wakefulness but sleep strengthens and stabilizes them. Non-rapid eye movement (NREM) sleep is important for this.[7] We encountered a special instance of this in Chapter 3, the commonalities extracted during slow-wave sleep (SWS), the 'whats' that are always found at a particular place. For example, you expect to find tickets and platforms at a railway station.

If you learn word pairs during wakefulness (e.g. brick–fur, wall–cat, or clock–tree) these are also strengthened and stabilized during NREM sleep.[8] Word pairs aren't always what–where associations but they are simple, binary ones. We can even learn new word pairs during SWS without any previous learning in wakefulness.[9] These learning and strengthening processes may give rise to the more thought-like NREM dreams we have during the first half of the night.

But are there AAOM techniques that come closer to the hyperassociative state of mind/brain we experience during REM dreaming? I think memory champions try to mimic this kind of state.

AAOM Technique 3: Multiple Associations and the MoL

Memory champions who compete in the World Memory Championships, USA Memory Championship, and UK Open Memory Championship have to do much more than remember simple, binary associations. How do they do it? They aren't born with fantastic memories, they use the memory techniques outlined here[10] to retain, recollect, and recite such things as the order of a shuffled deck of playing cards, 50 lines of poetry, or a page of 1,000 random digits. For these memory feats, they have to be much more ambitious and creative than putting a single item in a location, associated with a single memory—like firelighters held by my neighbour at the bus stop. Several items need to be combined into a single, striking image and then visualized in an associated place.

In 2006 a journalist and science writer, Joshua Foer, won the USA Memory Championship after only 1 year's preparation in mnemonic techniques. Then he wrote a book about it: *Moonwalking with Einstein*. At the US Championships competitors have 5 minutes to memorize a shuffled deck of 52 playing cards. Here's how Foer did it.[11] First, he picked up some tips on what makes for a good mnemonic image. We've already said bizarreness is good. So is putting yourself, your friends or relatives, and famous people in your image, anything to do with sex, death, food, or drink is memorable—as are images that arouse strong emotions, like fear, elation, and disgust, or portray dramatic personal or public events. Foer immersed himself in this mnemonic world, to create 52 subject/action/object images to portray a deck of cards. These images aren't static. They're dynamic, portraying actions and events. Such movement is also mnemonic. Foer's image for the king of hearts was Michael Jackson moonwalking with a white glove. The king of clubs was John Goodman eating a hamburger. The king of diamonds: Bill Clinton smoking a cigar.

I'm not Joshua Foer so I don't know why he made these particular associations but I can guess. Take the king of hearts: Michael Jackson was the self-styled *King* of Pop. He died suddenly, seemingly of a *heart* attack. The heart symbolizes *emotion*. Jackson engendered huge displays of emotion when on stage performing his trademark *moonwalk* dance. At its premier he wore his emblematic rhinestone-studded *white glove on his left hand*. So closely associated was this glove with Jackson that it sold, after Jackson's death, for US$420,000. Most people think the heart is on the left side of the body (actually it's central but tips to the left). The moon looks white from the earth. Many more possible associations between the king of hearts and Michael Jackson exist. These associations are much more complex than my neighbour holding firelighters at the bus stop. They are closer to the complex nexus of associations that characterizes A's dream. Consequently, they render the connection between the king of hearts and Michael Jackson much more memorable. Associations can be thought of as 'hooks'[12] that secure the king of hearts to the image of Michael Jackson. The more hooks, the stronger the connection.

Once all the cards have been connected to a memorable image, the mnemonist has to assign the images to landmark places. To remember the deck of cards in order would require 52 places. Most mnemonists combine three images into one. This reduces the number of locations to 17 (52 divided by 3) with one card left over. So if the order of the cards-to-be-remembered begins with the king of hearts, followed by the king of clubs, and then the king of diamonds, to combine the cards in a single dynamic image you take the person from the first card-image (Michael Jackson moonwalking with a white glove), the action from the second (John Goodman eating a hamburger), and the object from the third (Bill Clinton smoking a cigar). This ordered combination to portray three cards (king of hearts, king of clubs, and king of diamonds) in a single image would be Michael Jackson eating a cigar—this would be the image Joshua Foer located in his first place on his familiar route with 17 landmarks.

Using AAOM Techniques in Everyday Life

Memory champions use these multiple associations to remember a page of 1,000 random digits, but, in everyday life, you are unlikely to want to do this. However, you often do need to remember semantic material, i.e. knowledge, for exams or simply to remember people's names at a party. AAOM techniques depend upon six principles: one, visualization, two, bizarre association, three, organization, four, narration, five, embodiment, and six, location. All of these principles are mnemonic, i.e. they make to-be-remembered material more memorable.[13] So you can use AAOM principles to improve your memory.

An example illustrates. I am using knowledge, rather than my own episodic memories, so readers stand a chance of guessing its source. However, as in the examples of remembering lists, cards, or digits, some of the associations are personally relevant because this enhances the mnemonic effect. As noted earlier, when discussing memory champions, remembering semantic material is much easier if it is associated with information already in memory networks, whether this is semantic or episodic. As mentioned earlier, this process of associating to-be-remembered things with material already in memory networks is termed elaborative encoding.

An Illustrative AAOM Example: The Man With a Spear

Scene 1

I am walking along beside a canal. On the canal there are long, curved, narrow boats. Suddenly a man wearing leggings and a padded jacket with a high white collar appears. He is holding a spear. He shakes my hand.

Scene 2

The man with a spear stands aside and gestures with a flourish as if to show me two people. By the canal, an old man dressed in black with long white hair and a small, red cap on the back of his head gives money to a wealthy-looking man, who looks to be trading from one of the boats.

Scene 3

I am in a courtroom. A woman with a sieve is using it to try to catch some rainwater coming from a hole in the roof. She isn't able to retain the water in the sieve but she stops the old man, dressed in black, from cutting the wealthy-looking man with a knife. Then the old man takes off his hat.

Scene 4

I am in a room, it seems like a hotel. The old man, dressed in black, locks some money away in the safe then he quickly turns away from me and leaves the room.

To remember this material I visualize and organize it in four, separate images (Principles One and Three). The four scenes have a story-like progression (Principle Four). All of the scenes happen in places (Principle Six). I am embodied in the scenes and so are all the other characters (Principle Five). The scenes feature bizarre associations (Principle Two); for example, it would be odd for someone in a courtroom to be trying to catch rainwater in a sieve, which is in any case, impossible, wherever it is undertaken.

As is clear this mnemonic composition in four image scenes has a dream-like quality. Impossible events occur. Although an image-based narrative, there are strange discontinuities between the scenes: I am by a canal then a courtroom, then in a hotel. No-one—including me—comments on the odd events, which are seemingly accepted as normal.

Yet 'the man with a spear' is not a dream. I composed it, using mnemonic techniques, during my waking hours. I imagined I was a high school student who is beginning to learn about Shakespeare—he is visualized as the man with the spear who shakes my hand. When he shows me the two people, these are characters from one of his plays: *The Merchant of Venice*. The old man dressed in black is Shylock, the moneylender. He is generally portrayed dressed in long black robes with flowing white hair, wearing the traditional Jewish skullcap or yarmulke. In the Elizabethan era all Jews had to wear a red hat when outdoors. The man to whom he lends money is Antonio, the merchant for whom the play is named. Antonio appears to be a rich. He makes money from international trading, which is why he is in a boat. The location for the play is Venice, hence the boats are long, narrow, curved gondolas. When Shylock loans the money to Antonio he asks for a pound of Antonio's flesh if the debt is not repaid. When Antonio borrows the money from Shylock he is already in debt. Shylock asks for his money back. Antonio cannot repay him and the case ends up in court. Portia is depicted with a sieve that fails to catch rainwater because one of the greatest speeches in Shakespeare begins: 'The quality of mercy is not strain'd, It droppeth as the gentle rain from heaven. Upon the place beneath.' Her eloquence persuades Shylock to be merciful and not to take his pound of flesh from Antonio but, in turn, Shylock is forced to convert to Christianity so he takes off his hat. The final scene depicts the name 'Shylock' through the locking action and the way he turns quickly away from me and departs—as a shy person might.

If I were a high school student, these scenes depict key aspects of new to-be-remembered material about *The Merchant of Venice*; they also associate with some of my remote episodic memories—so they integrate this new material with personally relevant past experiences, which makes the new material much easier to remember. I love Venice, I love to arrive by the water boat, but I have some sad memories too. The one time I went in a gondola was with a colleague who died, suddenly, soon afterwards. My first husband was Jewish so I have many associations with Jewish history and culture. As a pedestrian, I was seriously injured by a car. The driver was charged by the police so I have experienced the adversarial nature of a courtroom. When looking on the internet I was surprised to find two hotels named Shylock. I don't usually put my money in the room safe but recently, staying with a friend in a hotel, she locked my money in her safe.

To further enhance the mnemonic effect of these scenes I could locate them at the first four places on my familiar route into work. If these scenes were dream scenes, they are related thematically to *The Merchant of Venice*.

So both memory champions and ordinary mnemonists try to access a state of mind close to REM dreaming during wakefulness. There are similarities but what are the differences?

AAOM Techniques and REM Dreaming

The AAOM creates memorable, associative images, then in the MoL these images are, mentally, placed at landmarks along a familiar route. In my simple shopping list, the images were of single items at landmark places. The memory champions associate three things in an image, which they locate at a landmark place. I associated four things (Venice–gondolas–canals–Shakespeare) in my first scene of *The Merchant of Venice* mnemonic above. But REM dreaming is much more associative—think of A's dream. She identified eight associated memory elements to a place for kite-flying, but I only used five to limit the length of the discussion.

On the daily tour, landmark junctions were the most rewarding but also the most dangerous places because they attracted predators and competitors. Chapter 4 emphasized the origin of REM dreams in associative pattern identification, which, archetypally, enabled us to gain rewards while avoiding dangers. Visiting landmark junctions would have been very emotionally arousing because they augured food, water, and opportunities to meet potential mates but also harboured predation threats that could mean death. Highly emotional events are also very memorable. We all remember the dramas in our lives much better than the routine events. This evolutionary context for landmark junctions may explain the mnemonic power of the MoL. When items are mentally placed at landmark junctions along a familiar route they become associated with places that, in an evolutionary sense, were highly memorable. These AAOM associations with highly memorable places along a familiar route make the items themselves much easier to remember.

But this raises two significant differences between the AAOM and REM dreaming: first, during REM dreaming, we aren't remembering items of knowledge, we are remembering elements of episodic memories; and, second, different REM dream scenes don't seem to follow a familiar route, whereas the MoL depends on using a familiar route. Next I discuss the first difference. The second is more complex: it will take me longer to explain.

First, during REM dreaming we associate or encode elements of episodic memories. For example, in A's dream we discussed the associations between elements of five episodic memories/concerns: first, overhearing an academic colleague tell another colleague he is 'like a butterfly' because he is constantly attracted to new ideas—here the PhD reception is the episode and the 'like a butterfly' remark is the element; second, A's embarrassing mistake over a butterfly when out on a walk with colleagues in the forest—here the walk is the episode and the mistake over butterflies the element; third, the kite present from A's relatives that was mistakenly released during kite-flying—here the kite-flying is the episode and the mistaken release the element; fourth, a butterfly kite present—here the present-giving is the episode and the butterfly kite the element; and, fifth, a memory/concern about leaving academia that, after the PhD completion, engendered a feeling of release—here the memory/concern over leaving academia is an ongoing episode and the feeling of release is the element. These episodic memories/concerns are represented along pathways that meet at a landmark junction/REM dream that portrays the associations between them, see Figure 5.1. The associations are: butterfly–mistake–embarrassment; butterfly–kite–present–embarrassing loss; butterfly–kite–academia–freedom or release.

The nexus of associations is made up of five elements from five different episodic memories. For ease of representation in Figure 5.1, these elements all appear to be 'at the end of' the five episodic pathways. Actually, as explained in the last chapter, the elements that appear in the dream could be from the beginning, middle, or end of a pathway.

Second, why don't REM dream scenes follow a familiar route like the MoL? This issue relates to the dynamism of our environment. The nature of our experience in our environment isn't fixed. We are continually having new experiences.

In A's dream, the 'like a butterfly remark' was a new, recent memory of a new, recent experience that associated an academic colleague with butterflies because he

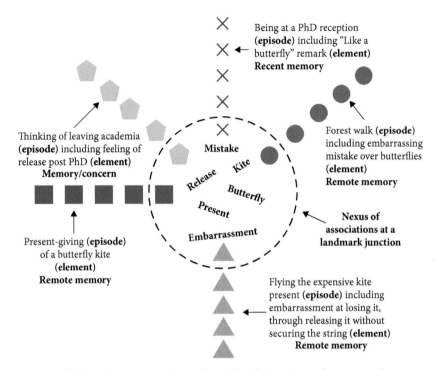

Being at a PhD reception (**episode**) including "Like a butterfly" remark (**element**) **Recent memory**

Forest walk (**episode**) including embarrassing mistake over butterflies (**element**) **Remote memory**

Thinking of leaving academia (**episode**) including feeling of release post PhD (**element**) **Memory/concern**

Mistake

Release   Kite

Butterfly

Present

Embarrassment

Nexus of associations at a landmark junction

Present-giving (**episode**) of a butterfly kite (**element**) **Remote memory**

Flying the expensive kite present (**episode**) including embarrassment at losing it, through releasing it without securing the string (**element**) **Remote memory**

Figure 5.1 Schematic representation of a landmark junction and its nexus of associations, formed from elements of different episodic memories that are associated at the junction.

was said to behave like one. In Freudian terminology the remark is a 'day-residue'. She overheard this comment at a PhD reception on the evening prior to the dream. This recent memory, when integrated with the other four, associated, remote memories/concerns, would have updated the associative pattern represented at the landmark junction. This recent association may have been added to the four previous associations at an existing junction (see Figure 5.1).

You will recall from Chapter 1 that, during REM sleep, memory elements are extracted, reorganized, and then integrated. So, more radically, the recent 'like a butterfly' remark/element may have caused brain network reorganization to integrate or 'tie' the five memories together through creating a *completely new* landmark junction. In other words, the four remote memories/concerns were already incorporated in brain memory networks but may not have been associated with each other before the 'like a butterfly' remark triggered this new complex, associative pattern.

Across evolutionary time, after environmental circumstances changed, brain network reorganization of episodic memories, with the instantiation of a *new* landmark junction, may have occurred. Clearly, any new landmark junctions would have changed the familiar route.

New Junctions, After Route Modification

Chapter 4 explored the dynamism of the environment inhabited by early humans. If a food site became exhausted or a waterhole dried up, our early ancestors would, most probably, have searched for alternatives within the home range rather than taken off to find a new one. For example, on a daily tour the previously visited waterhole/pond (E) has dried up (see Figure 5.2) but the early human has discovered another waterhole/pond (B1) at some distance from the clump of trees (B). Consequently, the daily tour (shown schematically and simply in Figure 5.2) has been modified to include (B1) but exclude (E), the dried-up waterhole/pond.

However, the position of the dried-up waterhole/pond at (E) is still known and retained—as a landmark—although the site is no longer visited on the tour. Also the routes previously used between: first, the clump of trees (B) and the blackberry bush (C); second, the (now dried-up) waterhole/pond (E) and the shelter(D); and, third, the waterhole/pond (E) and the big tree (F) would also be retained as they would be useful for flexible navigation to, for example, escape from predators or merely seek refuge in the shelter. Consequently the brain network changes to incorporate the new landmark in a modified tour but retains the landmarks and pathways from the original tour (see Figure 5.3).

Briefly, as the environment changed, early humans were compelled to seek out new places with resources but knowledge of the locations of the old ones was

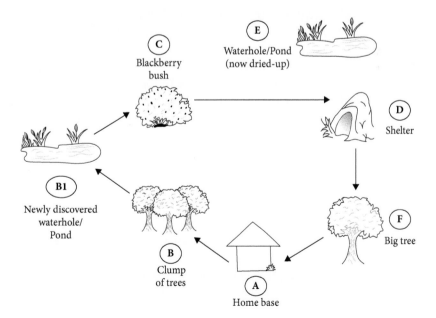

Figure 5.2 A modified tour in the home range.

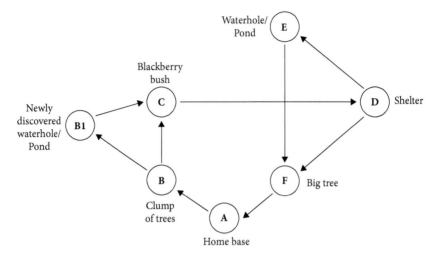

Figure 5.3 Modified brain network, which instantiates a new junction B1 and retains previous routes.

retained. Consequently, their brain networks, representing the external world, became complex with many landmark junctions and pathways—whether currently used or not.

Using Landmark Junctions to Remember: The Cerebral Cortex and Hippocampus

To reiterate from Chapter 3, networks in the brain evolved to represent the spatial networks (pathways and landmark junctions) used by early humans in the world. A rather surprising consequence of this is that navigating in real and mental space is fundamentally the same.[14] You can get lost in both.[15] To avoid getting lost when moving about in the world you use landmarks because they signal where you are in world space. When we want to find memories in brain networks we use landmark junctions to do so, although we aren't conscious of this. In other words, werely on the landmark junctions in brain networks to avoid getting lost in our minds when we remember past experiences.

Memory networks are widespread throughout the brain so recollecting a specific episodic memory will not be easy. Landmark junctions signal 'where you are' in the mental space of brain networks. In doing so, they assist in memory recollection. The network pathways that represent memories of specific past experiences overlap at a landmark junction that 'ties' elements of several episodic memories together through associating them. If this landmark junction can be located in brain networks, then the episodic memory/pathway becomes much easier to recollect.

Memory networks form in an area called the cerebral cortex—this is the most familiar part of the brain. Most people would readily recognize it *as* the brain with its wrinkly surface and wobbly consistency. If the two halves of the cerebral cortex were opened out and flattened, the brain resembles a walnut. Diagram 2 in Chapter 2 gives a simplified, schematic view of one half of the cerebral cortex, with its memory networks. But there is another brain structure that is essential to both spatial and episodic memory: the hippocampus. This organ, which is named after the Greek for 'seahorse' because of its shape, is located under the cerebral cortex, roughly in the centre of the brain.

The cortex and hippocampus interact during episodic memory recollection. An influential interaction theory is that the hippocampus acts as an 'index' for locations in the cortex.[16] The index in a book provides the several locations (i.e. pages) where related content can be found. If the index metaphor applies to brain networks, a hippocampal index would enable access to one or more landmark junctions at which several episodic memory pathways meet.

To reiterate, a landmark junction is a nexus of associations among elements of episodic memories (see Figure 5.1). The hippocampus is thought to be a 'store' for *associations among* memories rather than the memories themselves.[17] The hippocampus also associates elements of episodic memories[18] and is more active in REM dreaming than during wake. During REM dreaming the hippocampus has enhanced access to recent and remote memories.[19] But how does a landmark junction get retained in the hippocampus as an index?

Chapter 2 discussed how non-obvious associations between episodic memories are made during REM sleep. These associations form a landmark junction. The hippocampus receives inputs from the cortex during REM sleep (when the memory flow is from the cortex to the hippocampus) and then feeds them back during NREM (when the flow is from the hippocampus to cortex)[20]. This suggests that the hippocampus is responsible for associating elements of different episodic memories during REM sleep, giving rise to a dream.

During the period of NREM sleep that follows REM sleep this nexus of associations may be relayed back to the cortex to constitute a landmark junction, but also retained in the hippocampus as an index. As mentioned in Chapter 1, events called sleep spindles occur periodically during NREM sleep; these may represent the transfer of representations from the hippocampus to the cortex, followed by their integration into cortical networks.[21] At the same time as sleep spindles occur in the cortex, bursts of activity called sharp wave/ripples take place in the hippocampus.[22] These ripples may signal the retention of a landmark junction as an index in the hippocampus.

NREM Dreams Later in the Night

Sharp wave/ripples can support new associations between elements of recently acquired and remote memories,[23] such associations occur during REM dreams. You will recall from Chapter 1 that the late night/early morning NREM dreams, which occur in the second half of the night, are more like REM dreams: they are less thought-like and more hallucinatory. These late night/early morning NREM dreams may arise when landmark junctions, formed in REM sleep and giving rise to REM dreams, are instantiated in the cortex during NREM sleep.

You will also recall from Chapter 1 that one explanation for NREM dreams is that they are actually dreams remembered from previous REM periods. The creation of new landmark junctions in NREM sleep may trigger repeats of the REM dreams that formed the junctions. But these NREM dreams wouldn't exactly replicate the previous REM dreams because the brain/mind state is different in NREM. This process would explain why NREM dreams become more like REM dreams later in the night.

Indexing in the Hippocampus

The use of an index-type process during recollection is supported by evidence of unconscious hippocampal activity several seconds before memories come to mind.[24] How would this indexing process work in actual memory recall?

Suppose A sees a butterfly when out walking, and this memory trigger leads her to remember that she overheard one person saying to another that he was 'like a butterfly' at the PhD reception. If the hippocampus has an index of landmark junction associations, the butterfly association can be used by the hippocampus to locate all the landmark junctions in A's brain networks that relate to her personal episodic memories of butterflies. In Figure 5.1, this episodic memory of the 'like a butterfly' remark is represented by a green cross. At this landmark junction there are two other 'butterfly' associated memories: the mistake over butterflies on a walk in the forest (represented by a red circle) and the butterfly kite that was given as a present (represented by a blue square), but neither of these relate to the PhD reception, so the correct memory can be recovered from this junction.

Although the associations at this junction are with butterflies, the memories themselves are quite distinct—they are non-obviously associated. To be able to adequately recollect an episodic memory, its location in memory networks should be such that it isn't easily confused with memories of other similar experiences. For example, if there were a landmark junction that associated memories of all the PhD receptions A had attended, recollection of the unique event, when A went to a PhD reception where a 'like a butterfly' remark was made, would be much more difficult.

This attribute of landmark junctions in episodic brain networks may have derived from spatial networks in the world. Back in evolutionary time it would have been important to have distinct, segregated pathways that early humans could easily recognize if fleeing from a landmark with a predator in pursuit. In consequence, as episodic memories evolved from spatial pathways, the episodic memories at landmark junctions would also be distinct but associated in non-obvious ways.

Flexible Memories and the Hippocampus

I argued, in the previous section, that if A saw a butterfly while she was out walking, she may recollect the 'like a butterfly' remark. For this to happen, a butterfly index in the hippocampus would have triggered a search for all landmark junctions with associations with butterflies. So far we only considered one landmark junction with butterfly associations but many more are likely.

For example, suppose A had been to a lecture on the 'butterfly effect'. First used by the meteorologist Edward Lorenz: he remarked the flap of a butterfly's wings in Brazil could cause a tornado in Texas.[25] This chaos theory metaphor captures how diminutive events can, ultimately, have considerable, far-reaching consequences. Suppose, that CF, the colleague who made the 'like a butterfly remark', was also at the butterfly effect lecture. A and CF meet up to chat after the lecture. Consequently, the next time A sees a butterfly, this may trigger the memory of the butterfly effect lecture rather than the 'like a butterfly' remark at the PhD reception. Alternatively, A may recollect the 'like a butterfly' episodic memory but this could also trigger the other 'butterfly effect' memory.

This means there is no certain memory output for any specific brain input (e.g. seeing a butterfly). In other words, human memory is flexible. But, of course, flexible doesn't mean random because seeing a butterfly would only trigger the activation of butterfly-associated landmark junctions. Although these butterfly associations may then lead to kite associations and so on.

The hippocampus is essential for this flexible use of memory.[26] In turn, flexible memory relies on the associational role of the hippocampus where many different but associated experiences can be 'recollected' from landmark junctions.

We can trace flexible memory back to modifying the daily tour in the home range.

Flexible Memories and the Modified Tour

As explained earlier, early humans would have modified their daily tours after, for example, waterholes dried up or food sites became depleted. Flexible navigation implies that the brain representation of the daily tour could incorporate both new pathways and new landmark junctions. For example the modified tour in Figure 5.3 has a new pathway from (B) the clump of trees to (B1) the newly discovered waterhole/pond, and another new pathway from (B1) to (C) the blackberry bush.

In addition, animals can imagine travelling along a pathway never actually experienced, to, for example, make a short cut.[27] For example, when first taking the modified tour, the early human has not travelled from the clump of trees at (B) to the shelter at (D) but can visualize doing so (see Figure 5.4).

Knowledge of this short cut to the shelter could be life-saving, if, say, predators threatened when hunting at the clump of trees. As episodic memories developed from pathways in spatial networks, the ability to picture travelling along a pathway never actually taken may have given rise to imagining a future experience that has not yet occurred (or a fantasy experience that could never happen) from within a network of memories of experiences that have occurred.[28]

So the human mind/brain can undertake flexible spatial navigation, through imagining new routes and forging new paths. But what about the complex associative patterns at landmark junctions? Were they used flexibly too?

Any associative patterns among the experiences at, for example, one waterhole would also have been relevant to any newly discovered ones. All waterholes attract predators, competitors, and mates. The best guess on their patterns of behaviour at a new waterhole is how they behaved at the previously experienced one. For example, the associative patterns of visits to one waterhole 'lion–waterhole–visit–night' and

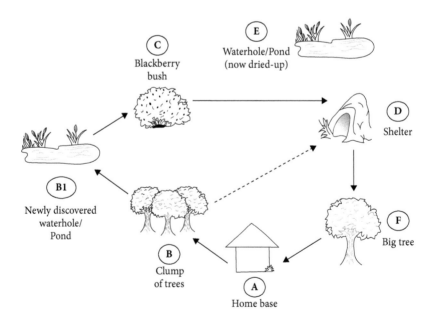

Figure 5.4 A modified tour in the home range showing an imagined pathway (dashed line).

'lion–waterhole–dry season–visit–day' would, at least potentially, be applicable to all waterholes.

Hence, any associative pattern would not have been tied to a particular waterhole. In consequence, REM dream images may have evolved to portray an associative pattern among, for example, lion-related experiences at all waterholes rather than just one particular waterhole. In other words, if the waterhole usually visited on the daily tour dried up but another one was found, then the complex, associative image of, for example, elements of lion-related experiences at the first waterhole would be transferred to the new one. This is the simplest evolutionary forerunner of the flexible use of landmarks—memories of any complex patterns in experiences at one waterhole could be transferred to another. Memories of patterns weren't tied to one particular place. They could be used flexibly at another.

But a similar context can mean that memories can be useful not just at a different place of the same type but at a different type of place. All waterholes are dangerous places. Lions are 'sit and wait' predators in the surrounding vegetation. But lions have also been known to use cover away from waterholes to surprise prey.[29] So, for example, bushes are also dangerous places because they too provide cover for lions. Whether they are lurking in the vegetation around waterholes or hiding in bushes, lions only usually hunt at night so 'lion–visit–night' is an associative pattern that holds for both waterholes and bushes because they both provide cover, wherever they are located in space. But the 'lion–dry season–visit–day' is not as likely to apply to bushes because they don't provide water; this associative pattern probably only applies to waterholes.

Higher-order Associations

The common feature of the waterhole surrounded by vegetation and the spreading blackberry bush is that they provide cover. The concept of 'cover' is a more abstract notion than vegetation around a waterhole or a spreading blackberry bush—these are both concrete things. Specifically, the association 'lion–visit–cover–night' has become detached from the specific locations of waterholes and bushes through their common attribute of cover. 'Lion–visit–cover–night' is a 'higher-order' association than either 'lion–waterhole–visit–night' or 'lion–bush–visit–night'. Sighting a lion in the cover of a waterhole or a bush is an episodic memory. The associations among episodic memories held by the hippocampus are organized hierarchically with 'higher-order' associations being above spatial associations in the hierarchy.[30] 'Lion–visit–cover–night' is a higher-order association that is not linked to a specific location but applies to any place that offers cover to lions (see Figure 5.5).

You may recall that I embarked on this lengthy discussion of flexible memory, the hippocampus, indexing, and higher-order associations to explain why different

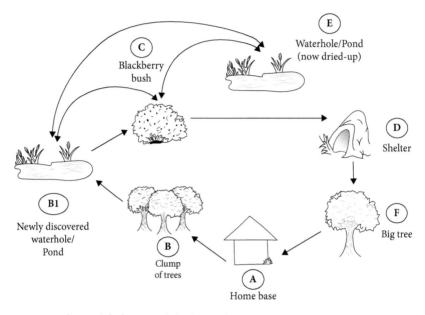

Figure 5.5 The modified tour with higher-order associations.

REM dream scenes don't follow a familiar route. We conclude this discussion by identifying what links different REM dream scenes, given that they aren't usually linked through following a familiar route as is the MoL.

What Links Different REM Dream Scenes?

As described earlier, in the MoL, the locations for the images are along a familiar route—akin to the tours made by early humans. If dream scenes were, originally, formed through identifying any associative pattern in, archetypically, predator, competitor, or mate-related events at landmark junctions on a daily tour, we would expect consecutive dream scenes to be located along a familiar route.

Looking at the only dream illustration we have so far: in Scene 1 A is outside a house; in Scene 2 she is in front of some huge electric wires. These two locations could be landmarks on a familiar pathway but we don't have enough recorded dream scenes to find out. In my dream in Chapter 12 the locations do follow in sequence and the dreamer returns, albeit in an unusual manner, to the first location. But studies of many dream reports offer little evidence of dream scenes being located along a familiar route. Dream *themes*, however, continue across the night and can be seen, most easily, in adjacent dream scenes.[31]

Studies of REM dreams across the night identify two types of thematic connection: first, a progressive-sequential one where a problem-related theme repeats in different forms, eventually finding some resolution; and, second, a traumatic, re-petitive one where a problem-related theme is experienced and repeats in different forms but little or no progress is made.[32] In A's dream, the kite theme repeats across Scenes 1 and 2. The problem of embarrassment at the loss of the kite does seem resolved in Scene 2 when A experiences surprise and satisfaction, rather than em-barrassment, when the kite flies off.

The above section discusses how higher-order associations evolved between places that did not follow each other sequentially on the daily tour but that were connected through a common context or theme. For example, the newly discovered waterhole/pond, the blackberry bush, and the now dried-up waterhole/pond in Figure 5.5 do not follow each other sequentially on the daily tour but they are connected, thematically or contextually, through the higher-order concept of 'cover'. The evolution of higher-order associations may explain why dream scenes do not now follow each other along a familiar route. Rather, dream scenes are connected thematically. However, the evo-lutionary roots of these higher-order associations still lie with spatial memory and the daily tour, which explains why the MoL is so effective mnemonically.

Across evolutionary time, as the daily tour ceased to dominate human existence, theme-based higher-order associations between dream scenes would have begun to take increasing precedence over spatial ones. However, dream events still, al-most always, happen at a place. As these theme-based or contextual links between dream scenes (and between landmark junctions/hippocampal indices) began to dominate spatial ones, our memories became much more flexible, which makes us much more creative—for more on this, see Chapter 10. But is flexible memory entirely beneficial?

Is There a Downside to Flexible Memory?

Sometimes, yes. Association can create false memories[33] through misattribution. Contemporarily, this can be unfortunate; for example, when witnesses to a criminal act mistake the perpetrator for another similar person whom they saw in a different place or at a different time but in the same context.[34] As we have seen, at landmark junctions in our memory networks we associate events/people/objects across time, i.e. time is ignored. Also the pattern identified through associating events/people/objects can be transferred from one place to another when the context or theme is the same or similar. It's not hard to see how this can lead to misattribution.

Briefly...

This chapter shows how identifying associations among recent and past (or remote) experiences is mnemonic, i.e. it helps us remember by connecting new experiences to past ones that are already held in brain networks. This associative process is called elaborative encoding. Like memory champions, we can elaboratively encode memories in wake but I propose we excel at this skill during REM dreams. Connecting new and past experiences through association can also identify a pattern in events—the last chapter focused on this. It's worth emphasizing again that I'm not proposing a completely *new* function for REM dreams in this chapter: *pattern identification* and *elaborative encoding* are two different ways of looking at the same process. Also we looked at how landmark junctions, created in REM dream scenes through associating elements of different episodic memories, aid recollection, which is necessary for conscious remembering. An episodic memory may be retained in the brain but if you don't know where to 'find it' you can't recollect and consciously relive it.

REM dreaming is comparable with the AAOM elaborative encoding techniques that are practised by memory champions but can be used by anyone which wants to improve their memory. There are clear similarities between the AAOM and REM dreaming. Both rely more on visualization than the other senses, both engender often bizarre and counterfactual (in the sense of, 'did not actually happen') images, and both sets of images are organized. By 'organized' I mean the images conform to normal spatial arrangements and are populated by people/animals/objects in normal relationships with one another. Famous people or people we know well are particularly memorable—both feature in REM dreams and the AAOM. Both progress in a story-like manner, both provoke strong emotions, both feature embodied action (although in REM dreams the action almost always starts from the active, embodied self, whereas the AAOM tends to rely more on other people), and in both the scenes are located—the events always happen somewhere.

These similarities suggest that REM dreams are elaborative encoding devices. But there are differences between REM dreams and the AAOM. The latter are more complex, both in terms of the memories they embed and the associations they create between these memories. Also, as argued in the last chapter, REM dream associations are probably constructed unconsciously before they are consciously portrayed in REM dreams and then retained unconsciously. In contrast, the AAOM images appear to be created consciously during waking hours and can be retrieved into consciousness. On the other hand the associations that underlie the AAOM images may be unconscious. For example, Joshua Foer may not have been conscious of all the associations that underpinned his depiction of Michael Jackson as the king of hearts.

The MoL locates images created through associative AAOM techniques at landmark junctions along a familiar route, echoing the daily tour in the home range. The chapter argues that REM dream scenes don't usually follow each other along a familiar route; rather, they are linked thematically. The chapter demonstrates how thematic, contextual links would have developed as 'higher-order' associations between locations on the daily tour. Through evolutionary time, as the daily tour became less important, thematic or contextual, rather than spatial, associations, may have taken precedence as the connections between REM dream scenes. This development made our memory systems much more flexible.

This chapter introduced two brain structures intimately involved in memory: the cerebral cortex and the hippocampus. The cerebral cortex is formed by folded grey matter and makes up the outer surface of the brain. It is the site of long-term memories, maintained through networks: omnidirectional landmark junctions and unidirectional, in the sense of moving forward, pathways. The hippocampus is a seahorse-shaped structure below the cerebral cortex, near the centre of the brain. Moving about in space and episodic memory both depend on the hippocampus; its involvement in both these functions is another pointer that memory for experiences evolved from spatial memory.

Next

The next chapter looks at the role of emotions in REM dreams. For early humans a close encounter with a predator would have been very emotional and memorable. We think of emotions as feelings but they are also drivers for actions. Positive emotions generate approach behaviours, whereas negative emotions trigger avoidance. The next chapter explores the connections between the emotionality of REM dreams, memory, and reactivity.

Notes

1. Wamsley, E. J., Tucker, M. A., Payne, J. D., Benavides, J. A., & Stickgold, R. (2010). Dreaming of a learning task is associated with enhanced sleep-dependent memory consolidation. *Current Biology*, *20*, 850–855. https://doi.org/10.1016/j.cub.2010.03.027
2. Wamsley, E. J., & Stickgold, R. (2019). Dreaming of a learning task is associated with enhanced memory consolidation: replication in an overnight sleep study. *Journal of Sleep Research*, 28, e12749. https://doi.org/10.1111/jsr.12749
3. See p. 2 in Fuster, J. M. (1999). *Memory in the Cerebral Cortex: An Empirical Approach to Neural Networks in the Human and Nonhuman Primate*. MIT Press, Cambridge, MA.
4. See p. 1 in Carruthers, M., & J. M. Ziolkowski (2002). General introduction. In M. Carruthers and J. M. Ziolkowski (Eds) *The Medieval Craft of Memory* (pp. 1–31). The University of Pennsylvania Press, Philadelphia, PA.
5. Method of loci. Available at: https://en.wikipedia.org/wiki/Method_of_loci
6. The conventional wisdom on the MoL is its origins lie in the story of Simonides of Ceos (c.556 BC–468 BC) remembering the positions of seated guests who died and were buried under rumble after a banqueting hall collapsed. I think the power of the MoL arises from much earlier events—the tours made by early humans to gather good and consume water from landmark places and their representation in our brain networks.

7. Cox, R., Van Bronkhorst, M. L., Bayda, M., Gomillion, H., Cho, E., Parr, M. E., ... & Stickgold, R. (2018). Sleep selectively stabilizes contextual aspects of negative memories. *Scientific Reports, 8*(1), 17861.

8. Stickgold, R. (2006). Neuroscience: a memory boost while you sleep. *Nature, 444*(7119), 559.

9. Züst, M. A., Ruch, S., Wiest, R., & Henke, K. (2019). Implicit vocabulary learning during sleep is bound to slow-wave peaks. *Current Biology, 29*(4), 541–553.

10. Maguire, E. A., Valentine, E. R., Wilding, J. M., & Kapur, N. (2003). Routes to remembering: the brains behind superior memory. *Nature Neuroscience, 6*(1), 90–95.

11. See p. 166 in Foer, J. (2011). *Moonwalking with Einstein: The Art and Science of Remembering Everything*. Penguin, London.

12. See p. 99 in Foer, J. (2011). *Moonwalking with Einstein: The Art and Science of Remembering Everything*. Penguin, London.

13. Llewellyn, S. (2013). Such stuff as dreams are made on? Elaborative encoding, the ancient art of memory, and the hippocampus. *Behavioral and Brain Sciences, 36*, 589–659.

14. Buzsáki, G., & Moser, E. I. (2013). Memory, navigation and theta rhythm in the hippocampal-entorhinal system. *Nature Neuroscience, 16*(2), 130–138.

15. See p. 2 in Bond, M. (2020). *Wayfinding: The Art and Science of How We Find and Lose Our Way*. Picador: New York.

16. Hirsh, R. (1974). The hippocampus and contextual retrieval of information from memory: a theory. *Behavioral Biology, 12*(4), 421–444; Teyler, T. J., & DiScenna, P. (1986). The hippocampal memory indexing theory. *Behavioral Neuroscience, 100*(2), 147; and Teyler, T. J., & Rudy, J. W. (2007). The hippocampal indexing theory and episodic memory: updating the index. *Hippocampus, 17*(12), 1158–1169.

17. Johnson, M. K., & Chalfonte, B. L. (1994). Binding complex memories: the role of reactivation and the hippocampus. *Memory Systems, 1994*, 311–350; Eichenbaum, H. (2000). A cortical–hippocampal system for declarative memory. *Nature Reviews Neuroscience, 1*(1), 41–50; and Eichenbaum, H., & Cohen, N. J. (2001). *From Conditioning to Conscious Recollection: Memory Systems of the Brain*. Oxford University Press, Oxford.

18. Henke, K., Buck, A., Weber, B., & Wieser, H. G. (1997). Human hippocampus establishes associations in memory. *Hippocampus, 7*(3), 249–256.

19. Desseilles, M., Dang-Vu, T. T., Sterpenich, V., & Schwartz, S. (2011a) Cognitive and emotional processes during dreaming: a neuroimaging view. *Consciousness and Cognition, 20*(4):998–1008.

20. Buzsáki, G. (1996). The hippocampo-neocortical dialogue. *Cerebral Cortex, 6*(2), 81–92.

21. Buzsáki, G. (1996). The hippocampo-neocortical dialogue. *Cerebral Cortex, 6*(2), 81–92; Buzsáki, G. (2006). *Rhythms of the Brain*. Oxford University Press, Oxford; and Tamminen, J., Payne, J. D., Stickgold, R., Wamsley, E. J., & Gaskell, M. G. (2010). Sleep spindle activity is associated with the integration of new memories and existing knowledge. *Journal of Neuroscience, 30*(43), 14356–14360.

22. Siapas, A. G., & Wilson, M. A. (1998). Coordinated interactions between hippocampal ripples and cortical spindles during slow-wave sleep. *Neuron, 21*(5), 1123–1128; and Clemens, Z., Mölle, M., Erőss, L., Jakus, R., Rásonyi, G., Halász, P., & Born, J. (2011).

Fine-tuned coupling between human parahippocampal ripples and sleep spindles. *European Journal of Neuroscience, 33*(3), 511–520.

23. Buzsáki G. (2019). *The brain from inside out.* Oxford University Press, USA.

24. Gelbard-Sagiv, H., Mukamel, R., Harel, M., Malach, R., & Fried, I. (2008). Internally generated reactivation of single neurons in human hippocampus during free recall. *Science, 322*(5898), 96–101; and Burke, J. F., Sharan, A. D., Sperling, M. R., Ramayya, A. G., Evans, J. J., Healey, M. K., ... & Kahana, M. J. (2014). Theta and high-frequency activity mark spontaneous recall of episodic memories. *Journal of Neuroscience, 34*(34), 11355–11365.

25. When the butterfly effect took flight. Available at: https://www.technologyreview.com/s/422809/when-the-butterfly-effect-took-flight/

26. Chen, N. J., & Eichenbaum, H. (1993). *Memory, Amnesia, and the Hippocampal System.* MIT Press, Cambridge, MA.

27. Tolman, E. C., Ritchie, B. F., & Kalish, D. (1946). Studies in spatial learning. I. Orientation and the short-cut. *Journal of Experimental Psychology, 36*, 13–24.

28. Byrne, P., Becker, S., & Burgess, N. (2007). Remembering the past and imagining the future: a neural model of spatial memory and imagery. *Psychological Review, 114*(2), 340.

29. Kenny, J. (2017) How do lions hunt? Available at: https://owlcation.com/stem/Lions-Hunting-Behaviour

30. McKenzie, S., Frank, A. J., Kinsky, N. R., Porter, B., Rivière, P. D., & Eichenbaum, H. (2014). Hippocampal representation of related and opposing memories develop within distinct, hierarchically organized neural schemas. *Neuron, 83*(1), 202–215.

31. Nielsen, T. (2013). The method of loci (MoL) and memory consolidation: dreaming is not MoL-like. *Behavioral and Brain Sciences, 36*(06), 624–625; McNamara, P. (2014). Why some of your dreams have sequels. *Psychology Today.* Available at: https://www.psychologytoday.com/blog/dream-catcher/201412/why-some-your-dreams-have-sequels; and also Llewellyn, S. (2013). Such stuff as dreams are made on? Elaborative encoding, the ancient art of memory, and the hippocampus. *Behavioral and Brain Sciences, 36*(06), 589–607, which reviews several studies on thematic continuity across dream scenes.

32. Kramer, M. (2011). REM sleep and dreaming: the nature of the relationship. In B. N. Mallick, S. R. Pandi-Perumal, R. W. McCarley, & A. R. Morrison (Eds) *Rapid Eye Movement Sleep. Regulation and Function* (pp. 40–48). Cambridge University Press, New York.

33. Neuroscientists create false memories in the brain. Available at http://news.mit.edu/2013/neuroscientists-plant-false-memories-in-the-brain-0725

34. For several examples of witness misattribution, see pp. 88–98 in Schacter, D. L. (2003). *How the Mind Forgets and Remembers: The Seven Sins of Memory.* Souvenir Press, London.

PART II
DREAM EMOTIONS, MEANINGS, AND UNCONSCIOUS IMPACT

6

Dream to Emote

Introduction

To 'emote' means to express emotion, to make emotions very clear, to convey intense emotionality. Rapid eye movement (REM) dreams are emotional. The emotional areas of the brain are up to 30% more active during REM sleep as compared to wakefulness,[1] so this is when we emote the most! Unless you happen to be an actor, when your job is to emote for an audience.

REM dreams generally express and convey primary or basic emotions such as fear, anxiety, elation, happiness, anger, and disgust rather than the, evolutionarily later, socially derived, emotions such as pride, shame, and embarrassment.[2] If the evolutionary context for REM dreams is discerning a pattern in the past behaviour of predators, competitors, and mates at high-risk but high-reward landmark junctions, the prevalence of unambiguous primary emotions such as fear and elation isn't surprising. For example, patterned associations are made between events that cause fear or ones that generate joy. As discussed in Chapter 5, the evolutionary context for this was the transfer of patterns between similar places (e.g. from one waterhole to another) or similar types of places (from a waterhole surrounded by vegetation to a large bush because they both provided cover for predators). When present in a dream such patterns would cause fear. In a contemporary context, the powerful emotions aroused by one situation may be transferred to another associated situation during a dream. As REM dreams evolved, after our gatherer-scavenger-hunter days were over, the emotion itself may drive the dream to associate the patterned behaviour of living creatures at one place to similar places or similar types of place.

Your dreams are probably more revealing of your inner emotional and psychic state than your reports of your emotions during wake, because, during dreaming, the emotional areas of your brain (i.e. the limbic system) are 'revved up' and the brain region (i.e. the prefrontal cortex) that inhibits your emotional expression during wake is 'switched off'.[3]

Debate continues over the overall emotional tone of dreams. When independent judges assess dream emotions, they find dream life to be mostly negative. In the first large-scale study in 1966, only 20% of dreams were judged as positive.[4] Similarly, a representative sample found 54% of dreams to be negative, 26% positive, and 20% neutral.[5] Another study reported negative emotions in 68% of dreams.[6] More recently, studies have used self-assessments of dream emotions, resulting in positive

What Do Dreams Do? Sue Llewellyn, Oxford University Press (2020). © Oxford University Press.
DOI: 10.1093/oso/9780198818953.001.0001.

emotions being reported as often[7] or even more frequently than negative ones.[8] A comparison between independent judging and self-assessment concludes that negative dream emotions can be identified more reliably than positive ones.[9]

This chapter focuses on negative emotions in dreams not because I've concluded dreams are more often negative than positive in tone, but because there are interesting findings on negative emotion that, I think, relate to the evolutionary origins of dreams. First, if people are deprived of sleep, particularly REM sleep, they retain more negative than positive memories. On the other hand, after REM sleep, negative emotional experiences have less power to disturb and cause distress. At first these two sets of findings seem rather at odds. How can this apparent inconsistency be resolved?

To illustrate, I introduce a second REM dream, 'quicksand', one of my own dreams. Its driving emotions are fear and anxiety. If people are asked to produce reports of dreams and reports of events in their waking lives the presence of fear is more common in dreams than in the waking reports.[10] The same is true for the incidence of threat.[11] As mentioned in Chapter 4, dream reports include more social interactions than waking ones, specifically, aggressive encounters happen three times more often in REM dreams than non-rapid eye movement (NREM) dreams.[12] The dreamer is involved in around 80% of the aggressive interactions in dreams and is more often the victim of aggression than the attacker.[13] Given these findings, it isn't surprising that many REM dreams are characterized by fear, anxiety, vulnerability, and helplessness.[14] Questionnaires identify being chased or pursued as the most prevalent dream theme; two others, falling and sexual interactions, are also common.[15] These three events would be expected at populous landmark junctions, frequented by predators, competitors, and potential mates. As should be clear by now, this chapter, like the others, isn't presenting another distinct function for dreaming—rather we just take a somewhat different perspective on how close on 2.5 million years of the daily tour impacted on our brains and minds.

We, perhaps especially the English, think of emotions as internal feelings to be managed or even ignored. But this is somewhat misguided. Emotions enable animals and humans to meet the demands of their environment.[16] For example, back in evolutionary time, a flash of yellow in the vegetation around a waterhole (an important stimulus in the environment that could signal a lion) triggers a fear of predation. An evolutionary perspective on emotions is: first, they motivate animals and humans to act; and, second, our basic emotionally based action sets or dispositions are to approach or to avoid/withdraw.[17] As Matt Walker, a neuroscientist and sleep/dream researcher at the University of California, points out 'Emotions make us do things, as the name suggests (remove the first letter from the word)'.[18] Across evolutionary time, approach behaviours followed from feeling this is good, this is what I want, or this is right for me. Feeling this is bad, will harm me, or is wrong for me triggered avoidance or withdrawal. Emotions motivate action through anticipating an experience. We feel elated or happy when looking forward to rewards. This elation triggers approach. Fear or disgust triggers avoidance or withdrawal. We begin by looking at negative emotions in REM dreams.

REM Dreams and Negative Emotions

As noted earlier, actors emote for a living. In his darkest tragedy, Shakespeare has Macbeth say:

Life's but a walking shadow, a poor player,
That struts and frets his hour upon the stage
And then is heard no more.

Light casts shadows. The line that precedes the famous 'Life's but a walking shadow' is 'Out, out brief candle!' We all have negative experiences in life. Do we carry them, like candles, into our dreams? Do dreams then cast an unconscious shadow over our waking lives?

In our dreams we, generally, act in the first person, i.e. 'I am walking along', but, especially in lucid dreams, we can also take something of a dispassionate, more disconnected, third-person perspective on events, i.e. 'I see myself walking along'. Dreaming neurochemistry, specifically the reduction in noradrenaline (see footnote 7 in Chapter 1) reduces the stress associated with experiencing negative events.[19] This can also induce some emotional distance between the dream self and the dreaming events resulting in the more detached third-person perspective. Sometimes this distance is evident in the dream content.

In one of my dreams I was travelling around Edinburgh hanging on to the top of a double decker bus. If I were to do this in waking hours I would be terrified, but, in the dream, it seems quite normal and I'm quite composed. Consequently, the dream self can have a certain role-playing, theatrical-like character.[20] The Shakespearean words 'struts and frets upon the stage' may suggest we emote on the stage of dreams to try to dispel the shadow they can cast over our lives. Do we succeed? The evidence from neuroscience seems to point in two different directions.

On the one hand, our negative experiences seem to be compounded in dreams. As discussed above, threats, aggressors, being chased, and falling are all more frequent occurrences in dreams than in our waking lives. If we are sleep deprived we retain negative memories in preference to positive ones.[21] Many negative memories provoke fear. Memory for fearful experiences is improved after sleep;

the improvement is linked to the time spent in REM sleep.[22] Freud familiarized us with the idea of repressing traumatic, negative experiences and their reappearance in dreams. Recent research supports this Freudian idea: REM sleep improves the recall of unwanted memories, defined as ones that are consciously repressed during waking hours.[23] All of this points to REM dreams and sleep expressing and improving the recollection of negative and fearful memories.

On the other hand, REM sleep and dreams may have a cathartic function for negative experiences, as suggested by Freud.[24] Rosalind Cartwright, a psychologist, founded the Sleep Disorder Service and Research Center at Rush University in the United States. She undertook research into the dreams of depressed people who had experienced devastating divorces or relationship break ups. She found only people who dreamt of these traumatic events involving their ex-partner got relief from their depression.[25] Also, people who experience fear in their dreams showed less emotional arousal to fear-inducing stimuli during wakefulness.[26] When people identify waking life experiences in their dreams, they rate the dreamt version as less emotionally intense than the original experience.[27] After REM sleep, when people remember negative experiences or re-experience similar negative events, their fearful, emotional reactivity is reduced.[28] Relatedly, REM sleep deprivation increases emotional reactivity to threatening visual stimuli.[29] So far the research discussed in this paragraph is concerned with depression and the basic, primary emotion of fear. What about socially derived emotions like embarrassment? A recent study (unfortunately this research did not focus specifically on REM sleep) caused embarrassment by exposing participants four times to their out-of-tune singing after a karaoke session; time awake did not reduce their embarrassment but time asleep did.[30]

How could dreaming improve the recollection of negative experiences but reduce the distress they cause? In Chapter 3 'the butterfly and the white paper kite' dream had two embarrassing elements: first, the mistake over butterflies in front of work colleagues; and second, letting go of, and so losing, an expensive kite, bought as a present. We know from the last chapter that association is the bedrock of memory. These memories of embarrassment at a mistake and a loss are strengthened, through association, in the dream. But in the dream, A isn't embarrassed. Instead she speaks of releasing (rather than losing) the kite, feeling surprised and satisfied. The emotions of surprise and satisfaction seem to relate to the PhD completion. Once the PhD completion is associated in the dream with the mistake and the lost kite, embarrassment is superseded by surprise and satisfaction, and A is released from her responsibility to remain at her current university. She can choose to go elsewhere. Associating and integrating recent positive experiences with older negative ones during dreams may partly account for a reduction in reactivity.

As used here, 'reactivity' is a different concept from 'response'. Earlier, when emotions driving responses were discussed, these responses were actions—basically either to approach or avoid. Reactivity can be physiological or psychological. It can refer either to the bodily changes (think of 'it makes my skin crawl' for a negative experience) that accompany experiences or psychological assessments of the emotional intensity that goes along with negative (or positive) experiences. This emotional intensity has two different dimensions. The first is the nature of the emotion experienced: happy or sad, disgusted or delighted. The second is the level of arousal: on a continuum from calm to agitated.

Naturally, negative and positive experiences elicit both reactivity and responses. It's not difficult to see that excessive fearful reactivity may inhibit a fast, appropriate response that could threaten survival in a dangerous situation. On the other hand, when seeing a flash of yellow for a second time on approach to the waterhole, a calm, fearless reaction to the threat would not provoke a fast, appropriate response either. Therefore, if REM sleep and dreaming reduces (but does not extinguish) subsequent reactivity during waking hours, this would enhance evolutionary fitness, particularly for responses to danger.

Chapter 5 introduced two brain structures: the cortex and the hippocampus. These structures interact to encode, retain, and recollect memories. This chapter describes another related structure: the amygdala—a small, almond-shaped structure situated next to the 'tail' end of the seahorse-shaped hippocampus. The amygdala controls our reactivity to emotional experiences, particularly how we react to threatening and dangerous events,[31] archetypically, potential death by predation. It also works with the hippocampus to engender emotional memories, particularly fearful ones.[32] The amygdala and hippocampus are more active during REM sleep.[33] Specifically, a brain circuit involving the amygdala, the hippocampus, and a part of the cortex (medial, prefrontal) controls emotional processing and fear memory and is most active during REM sleep.[34] The amygdala makes us afraid of risks that we can't control: it's the reason people are more afraid of flying (we can't influence what's happening in the flight deck) than driving (I'm in control of the car) despite the statistic that, in the US for example, 48 people per year die in air transport accidents compared with over 30,000 in car accidents.[35] Death by predation is extremely unlikely for me but my amygdala still works as if it's an everyday possibility.

Chapter 5 also mentioned research on REM dreams across the night and identified two types: first, a progressive-sequential type that, eventually, resolves the dreamer's concern or problem; and, second, a traumatic, repetitive type where the concern/problem is not resolved.[36] In terms of REM sleep reducing reactivity, in the first type, reactivity may decrease after one night's sleep, but the second, severe type may require multiple periods of REM sleep, even extending over several nights, to reduce reactivity[37]; over only one night of REM sleep, reactivity may be preserved.[38]

To illustrate both types of REM dream, I use one of my own dreams. Scene 2 of this dream associates several experiences, including some negative ones, and may reduce my reactivity to them. On the other hand, after the traumatic nature of Scene 3, I wake up terrified. The dream expresses negative experiences and the associations between them. Making these associations should improve my memory for the experiences. Considering this dream will aid further understanding of how REM sleep and dreams could improve recollection for the memory content of negative experiences while diminishing their emotional charge and reducing reactivity in wakefulness through identifying a pattern in past experience.

Quicksand—a Dream Illustration of a Pattern

The dream occurred in November 2003 and has been reported elsewhere.[39] An abbreviated version, which focuses on the dream emotions, is given here.

Scene 1

I am walking along a quiet suburban road of neat houses with open front gardens approaching a huge bridge over a river. Something is a bit wrong. I start to feel uneasy. The last house down by the bridge at the end of the road seems to be still under construction. I wonder: will anyone buy it? It's probably going to be too noisy. Buying this house may be a mistake. As I approach this last house I notice how odd it looks—its shape appears rounded but is not clearly delineated. Then I see that something is covering the house. But I can't work out what this covering is—maybe it's a vast piece of cloth. Then I perceive the colour—it's yellow, I see the house is covered in sand. I feel afraid.

Scene 2

Suddenly the scene ahead has changed—now I am approaching a beach rather than a river. The view ahead is very enticing. The tide is in. The sun is sparkling on the water. There are lots of happy children playing on the beach but no adults. Suddenly a bad thing happens. A 'grown up' appears in the foreground and throws a child out across the sand. The child (now a small white bundle, a baby?) lands on his/her ear and rapidly disappears. Then another child/baby is thrown. I realize that this child/baby too may be swallowed up by the sand.

The dream ends as I wake up, terrified.

The episodic memory sources in Scenes 1 and 2

Recent episodic memory 1
The evening before the dream my eldest son, J, phoned me about a house he and his girlfriend, G, had seen and were thinking of buying. The house is on the edge of an old housing estate but adjacent to a 'good' part of town. The house is now empty. The previous occupant, an elderly lady, died in it. I fear this house may be 'unlucky' but don't voice this concern. I don't want to appear irrational. But I still hope they won't buy the house.

Remote episodic memory 2
Second, the dominant remote memory: in 2002 I had a working holiday driving around upstate New York with my then-partner N and his sister. N is interested in bridges and loves to photograph them. One day we pull up next to an interesting sight—a massive new bridge is under construction immediately next to an elegant, graceful, but collapsing, old bridge. Both stretch out over a wide, fast flowing river.

N is keen to take photos but access isn't easy. The bridge is on the edge of a small housing estate. We find the road in this estate closest to the bridge, get out of the car, and walk along the road to the house closest to the bridge. Here there is good place to take photos right under where the massive new concrete bridge is being built. N and his sister are happily shooting away. Suddenly in this place I start to get a 'bad' feeling; the new bridge from right up close looks like a 'dead' bridge to me—cold, hard, concrete, looming overhead. And the spot where we are standing is lonely—a kind of no man's land. I want to move on and escape this sudden irrational fear.

Remote episodic memory 3

The most remote memory: as a small child my mother warned me against wandering off across beaches. She said children can die if they stray. Quicksand can suddenly swallow them up. In my childish imagination I saw this 'quick' sand as very fine, soft and sparkly, attractive but so fine that children (especially small ones) could quickly slip through and be engulfed. I loved being by the sea and playing on the beach; that something as delightful as a bright, sandy seashore should harbour a dreadful quicksand 'death trap' seemed unbelievable, but my mother said it was true.

Memory/concern 4

At the time of the dream my second son, T, had a long-standing and worrying problem with his hearing. As a result he found it impossible to tolerate being in noisy surroundings. In Scene 1 the house is under construction and would have been noisy. In actuality, in the US holiday it was the bridge not the house that was under construction. The new bridge was being constructed from concrete. Sand is a component of concrete. When I stood below the new bridge I experienced the irrational fear that I described above. For my second son, T, the UK/US house would be a bad buy as construction work would render it too noisy.

The episodic memory sources in Scene 2

Recent episodic memory 2

On evening before the dream the BBC TV news reported Michael Jackson had been arrested on charges of child molestation (http://news.bbc.co.uk/1/hi/entertainment/3222806.stm). The item carried a clip from the previous year (2002) when Jackson was seen dangling his baby son Blanket from a third-floor hotel balcony. The baby's head and torso were covered by a small blanket. The fans on the ground below the balcony feared Jackson may drop the baby (http://news.bbc.co.uk/1/hi/entertainment/2494249.stm).

Remote memory 5

I had a fourth son, Sam, who died suddenly and unexpectedly as a baby—a 'cot death' in our family house. After his death I read research on overheating increasing the risk for cot death. Did I cover Sam with too many blankets on the night he died? Michael Jackson's baby, Blanket, was covered with a blanket in the dangerous dangling incident. Scene 2 may associate my childish quicksand engulfment fear when crossing a beach with Michael Jackson seemingly on the point of dropping a baby to the ground. Associating 'crossing' and 'dropping' may have created the 'throwing' of a child/baby to land on the sand. Jackson has now been accused of child molestation. Physical child abuse includes throwing.

Thematic associations between Scene 1 and 2

Chapter 5 proposed that dream scenes are usually associated thematically rather than spatially. This was illustrated in A's dream but can also be seen in my quicksand dream.

The quicksand memory that emerges briefly in Scene 1 as a sand-death theme takes the dominant role in beach Scene 2. A child/baby is swallowed up by the sand. I fear another may meet the same fate.

The 'damaged hearing/ear' theme also continues into Scene 2 as the baby/child lands on his/her ear before disappearing into the sand.

Dreams as a Nexus of Associations

Scenes 1 and 2 are embedded in a complex nexus of associations. Immediately before I discern the house is covered in sand, I think it's covered by a piece of cloth. We all have a shared semantic association with cloth–death: the shroud. I also have a personal association: my fear that I may have covered Sam with too many blankets on the night of his death. Consequently the pattern could be extended to cover–sand–death–house. Also the house is under construction and may be too noisy for my middle son with the hearing problem. These associations produce: sand–construction–house–noise–damaged ear. Already the set of associations is not well reproduced in a linear fashion. Figure 6.1 is better but the dream images are better still. As discussed in Chapter 3, creating a visual image is the best way to merge and portray several non-obvious associations.[40] It's also clear that emotionally powerful and arresting dream images are so much more memorable than the nexus of associations for my quicksand dream, portrayed in Figure 6.1.

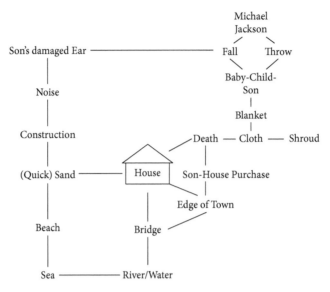

Figure 6.1 Nexus of association in 'quicksand'.

Enhancing Memory While Diminishing Emotional Charge or Reactivity

Chapter 5 focused on how REM sleep/dreams improve recollection through emotional association, i.e. personal emotional associations are mnemonic. Associations between my recent memories and remote memories already present in brain networks integrate new memory content with older memories, through making non-obvious associations among them. In my dream above, the phone call from my son (about the house someone had died in) is the to-be-integrated recent memory in Scene 2, and the Michael Jackson child molestation charge is the to-be-integrated recent memory in Scene 3. These associations identify non-obvious patterns between memories of experiences. In Scene 2 one pattern seems to be house–death–sand. In Scene 3 another related pattern is child/baby–death–throw/drop–sand.

As discussed earlier, the amygdala makes us afraid of risks we can't control. Across evolutionary time, we couldn't control the behaviour of predators, competitors, and mates. But identifying a pattern in their behaviour at a landmark junction would have increased abilities to manage risk. In a risky situation, for example, a flash of yellow in the vegetation around a waterhole that may indicate a lion, unconscious knowledge of any pattern in the behaviour of lions can trigger a fast, appropriate response. Discerning patterns in events increases control; in turn, more control reduces fear, anxiety, and reactivity. My proposal is that REM sleep/dreams identify these patterns. REM sleep/dreams reduce reactivity in the amygdala, which would be expected after pattern identification.

Knowledge of patterns also enables expectations about the future. For example, early humans would have been better able to predict when mates would be present at a landmark junction but competitors and predators would be absent. Pattern identification confers evolutionary advantage. So a reduction in reactivity to enable a rapid response, consequent upon pattern identification, would have been conserved through evolution.

Pattern identification in REM sleep would both increase memorability *and* reduce reactivity, so that negative emotional experiences have less ability to perturb and positive ones less power to elate. Think of separating the informational content of an experience from its emotional power to distress or excite, so that the former is strengthened in memory while the latter is diminished.[41] Another possibility, related to a reduction in reactivity, is that the dream brings or signals some resolution to a problem or concern (see earlier discussion).

My illustrative quicksand dream did awaken me—immediately after Scene 2. In terms of my sleep-dependent memory processing, Scene 1 would have been retained as a landmark junction in my cortex and indexed in my hippocampus (see Chapter 5) because, although I am becoming afraid, my sleep-dependent memory processes are not disturbed. By contrast, the traumatic associations in Scene 2 may not have been retained because, after this scene, I wake up terrified. This suggests that Scene 2 wasn't subsequently instantiated in my brain networks as a landmark junction, nor did indexation in the hippocampus occur.

Earlier, I suggested that the associative pattern in Scene 3 is child/baby–death–throw/drop–sand. I only awake terrified as the second child is thrown and I fear that this child may also be swallowed up by the sand. Perhaps, unsurprisingly, after the sudden death of one child, I had an intense fear of losing another child unexpectedly. This nightmare, portraying the death of a second child, provokes the terror that awakens me.

Nightmares, Reactivity, and REM Sleep

Nightmares happen primarily in late-night REM sleep; they generally result in abrupt awakenings with strong recollection of fear-inducing dream content and they prevent any subsequent reduction in reactivity.[42] Despite this, most nightmares follow normal dreaming processes—in the sense of associating elements of different experiences—as in my quicksand nightmare. I do not dream of what actually happened—my youngest son dying suddenly and unexpectedly in his cot at the foot of my bed. Rather this memory is associated with my childish fear of death in quicksand, my fear about my middle son's hearing problem, and the fear-inducing incident where Michael Jackson appears to be about to drop his son from a balcony.

Some nightmares do replicate or, are highly similar to, actual traumatic experiences. This happens most often for people suffering from post-traumatic stress disorder (PTSD), where REM sleep/dreams fail to relieve their distress.[43] Drawing on the evidence, I propose three possibilities:

1. Normal, highly associative REM dreaming that reduces emotional reactivity while improving memory for the informational content.
2. Highly associative REM dreaming that begins normally but the dream associations induce so much fear that the dreamer awakens. Consequently, emotional reactivity isn't reduced.
3. REM nightmares that closely replicate, rather than associate, an actual threatening experience. Consequently, emotional reactivity isn't reduced.

Associating a new negative experience with previous experiences, followed by integration into brain networks, seems to be therapeutic—in the sense of reducing subsequent reactivity during waking hours. But the strengthening of the informational content of negative experiences while reducing their reactivity is likely to be a delicate balance. If the emotional, associational strengthening within the dream generates too much fear, awakening will occur preventing any reduction in reactivity. For nightmares that closely replicate a severe trauma, the mind-brain may resist association with past events because the event is uniquely terrifying.

For PTSD, if dream association doesn't occur naturally during sleep, one approach is to train the dreamer to dream lucidly (see Chapter 1). With control over dream content, the frequency of nightmares can be reduced.[44] Creating new associations with the traumatic events during waking hours can be an effective therapeutic substitute, if undertaken over a period of time.[45] Also effective, while awake, is eye movement desensitization and reprocessing (EMDR), which mimics the rapid eye movements of REM dreaming and acts to integrate traumatic memories into brain networks.[46]

If emotional reactivity to fear-inducing experiences isn't reduced, undue fear and anxiety would be expected during waking hours, particularly on exposure to events that are, in any way, similar to the original experience, even if these events are, themselves, non-threatening.

This makes the brain-mind emphasis on the retention of negative memories appear dysfunctional. But if people are sleep-deprived, the amygdala biases the brain towards negative, aversive memories;[47] contemporarily, this seems inappropriate[48] but its evolutionary origins are clear. Negative, especially potentially life-threatening experiences, at landmark junctions, would have been of greater significance for survival than positive memories of rewards. Learning that occurred on the basis of the informational content of negative memories would have enhanced fitness. This learning, through associating negative memories during REM sleep and dreaming and retaining them in an unconscious image, may prime the mind/brain to recognize negative stimuli faster than positive ones during waking hours. At an unconscious level, negative stimuli are detected more quickly than positive ones.[49]

Briefly...

REM sleep and dreaming amplify emotional memories, particularly negative ones, through association but also reduce the emotional impact of the memories during subsequent waking hours. This sounds contradictory. The apparent paradox is resolved if we think of strengthening the informational content of the memory while separating this informational content from its power to disturb and distress or elate and uplift. REM sleep's unique neurochemistry both enhances memory and decreases tension, so our dreams can, usually, associate and integrate memories into a pattern within a safe neurochemical environment. Once identified this unconscious pattern can be mobilized in wake to reduce risk, increase control, and, therefore, reduce fear and anxiety.

This balancing act seems to break down when the dream associations engender a scene that is, personally, highly emotional and negatively potent for the dreamer; for example, the throwing of a baby/child in Scene 2 of 'quicksand'. In contrast, dreaming of hanging on to the top of a double decker bus while it careers around Edinburgh would be terrifying during my waking hours yet poses no problems for me in a dream because it isn't constructed from making highly negatively charged personal associations.

Next

This chapter has been about emotions. We feel elated or happy when anticipating rewards. In evolutionary time, this elation prompted a decision to approach a waterhole or food source. Fear or disgust triggers a decision to avoid or withdraw. The next chapter looks at how retained dreams may activate unconscious decision making.

Notes

1. See p. 195 in Walker, M. (2018). *Why We Sleep: The New Science of Sleep and Dreams*. Penguin, London.
2. Maquet, P., Péters, J. M., Aerts, J., Delfiore, G., Degueldre, C., Luxen, A., & Franck, G. (1996). Functional neuroanatomy of human rapid-eye-movement sleep and dreaming. *Nature*, *383*(6596), 163–166; Nofzinger, E. A., Mintun, M. A., Wiseman, M., Kupfer, D. J., & Moore, R. Y. (1997). Forebrain activation in REM sleep: an FDG PET study. *Brain*

Research, 770(1), 192–201; and Ruby, P., & Decety, J. (2004). How would you feel versus how do you think she would feel? A neuroimaging study of perspective-taking with social emotions. *Journal of Cognitive Neuroscience, 16*(6), 988–999.

3. See pp. 110–111 in Hobson, A. (2002). Dreaming: An Introduction to the Science of Sleep. Oxford University Press, Oxford; and https://www.psychologytoday.com/blog/dream-catcher/201410/dreams-more-accurately-track-thought-and-emotion-waking

4. Hall, C. S., & Van de Castle, R. L. (1966). *The Content Analysis of Dream.* Appleton-Century-Crofts, New York.

5. Kramer, M., Winget, C., & Whitman, R. M. (1971). A city dream: a survey approach to normative dream content. *American Journal of Psychiatry, 127*, 1350–1356.

6. Merritt, J. M., Stickgold, R., Pace-Schott, E., Williams, J., & Hobson, J. A. (1994). Emotion profiles in the dreams of men and women. *Consciousness and Cognition, 3*(1), 46–60.

7. Schredl, M., & Doll, E. (1998). Emotions in diary dreams. *Consciousness and Cognition, 7*(4), 634–646.

8. Sikka, P., Valli, K., Virta, T., & Revonsuo, A. (2014). I know how you felt last night, or do I? Self-and external ratings of emotions in REM sleep dreams. *Consciousness and Cognition, 25*, 51–66.

9. Sikka, P., Feilhauer, D., Valli, K., & Revonsuo, A. (2017). How you measure is what you get: differences in self-and external ratings of emotional experiences in home dreams. *American Journal of Psychology, 130*(3), 367–384.

10. Nielsen, T. A., Deslauriers, D., & Baylor, G. W. (1991). Emotions in dream and waking event reports. *Dreaming, 1*(4), 287.

11. Revonsuo, A. (2000). The reinterpretation of dreams: an evolutionary hypothesis of the function of dreaming. *Behavioral and Brain Sciences, 23*(6), 877–901.

12. McNamara, P., McLaren, D., Smith, D., Brown, A., & Stickgold, R. (2005). A 'Jekyll and Hyde' within: aggressive versus friendly interactions in REM and non-REM dreams. *Psychological Science, 16*(2), 130–136.

13. Domhoff, G. W. (2013). *Finding Meaning in Dreams: A Quantitative Approach.* Springer, New York.

14. Smith, M. R., Antrobus, J. S., Gordon, E., Tucker, M. A., Hirota, Y., Wamsley, E. J., . . . & Emery, R. N. (2004). Motivation and affect in REM sleep and the mentation reporting process. *Consciousness and Cognition, 13*(3), 501–511; and see p. 139 in Hartmann, E. (2010). *The Nature and Functions of Dreaming.* Oxford University Press, Oxford.

15. Zadra, A. L., & Nielsen, T. A. (1999). The 55 typical dream questionnaire: consistency across three student samples. *Sleep, 22*(Supplement 1), S175.

16. Lang, P. J., & Bradley, M. M. (2010). Emotion and the motivational brain. *Biological Psychology, 84*(3), 437–450.

17. Lang, P. J., & Bradley, M. M. (2010). Emotion and the motivational brain. *Biological Psychology, 84*(3), 437–450.

18. Walker, M. (2018). *Why We Sleep: The New Science of Sleep and Dreams.* Penguin, London.

19. See http://bigthink.com/ideafeed/how-sleep-helps-us-deal-with-stress

20. Desseilles, M., & Duclos, C. (2013). Dream and emotion regulation: insight from the ancient art of memory. *Behavioral and Brain Sciences, 36*(6), 614–614.

21. Walker, M. P., & Stickgold, R. (2006). Sleep, memory, and plasticity. *Annual Review of Psychology, 57*, 139–166; Walker, M. P. (2008). Cognitive consequences of sleep and sleep loss. *Sleep Medicine, 9*, S29–S34; and Yoo, S. S., Gujar, N., Hu, P., Jolesz, F. A., & Walker, M. P. (2007). The human emotional brain without sleep—a prefrontal amygdala disconnect. *Current Biology, 17*(20), R877–R878.

22. Popa, D., Duvarci, S., Popescu, A. T., Léna, C., & Paré, D. (2010). Coherent amygdalocortical theta promotes fear memory consolidation during paradoxical sleep. *Proceedings of the National Academy of Sciences, 107*(14), 6516–6519.

23. Fischer, S., Diekelmann, S., & Born, J. (2011). Sleep's role in the processing of unwanted memories. *Journal of Sleep Research, 20*(2), 267–274.

24. Desseilles, M., Sterpenich, V., Dang-Vu, T. T., & Schwartz, S. (2011). REM sleep and emotion regulation. In B. N. Mallick, S. R. Pandi-Perumal, R. W. McCarley, &A. R. Morrison (Eds) *Rapid Eye Movement Sleep: Regulation and Function*(pp. 427–436). Cambridge University Press, New York.

25. Cartwright, R. D. (1991). Dreams that work: the relation of dream incorporation to adaptation to stressful events. *Dreaming, 1*(1), 3.

26. Sterpenich, V., Perogamvros, L.,Tononi, G., & Schwartz, S. (2020). Fear in dreams and in wakefulness: evidence for day/night affective homeostasis. *Human Brain Mapping, 41*, 840–850. https://doi.org/10.1002/hbm.24843

27. Vallat, R., Chatard, B., Blagrove, M., & Ruby, P. (2017). Characteristics of the memory sources of dreams: a new version of the content-matching paradigm to take mundane and remote memories into account. *PloS One, 12*(10), e0185262.

28. Gujar, N., McDonald, S. A., Nishida, M., & Walker, M. P. (2010). A role for REM sleep in recalibrating the sensitivity of the human brain to specific emotions. *Cerebral Cortex, 21*(1), 115–123; and van der Helm, E., Yao, J., Dutt, S., Rao, V., Saletin, J. M., & Walker, M. P. (2011). REM sleep depotentiates amygdala activity to previous emotional experiences. *Current Biology, 21*(23), 2029–2032.

29. Rosales-Lagarde, A., Armony, J. L., del Río-Portilla, Y., Trejo-Martínez, D., Conde, R., & Corsi-Cabrera, M. (2012). Enhanced emotional reactivity after selective REM sleep deprivation in humans: an fMRI study. *Frontiers in Behavioral Neuroscience, 6*, 25. doi:10.3389/fnbeh.2012.00025.

30. Wassing, R., Benjamins, J. S., Talamini, L. M., Schalkwijk, F., & Van Someren, E. J. (2018). Overnight worsening of emotional distress indicates maladaptive sleep in insomnia. *Sleep, 42*(4), 1–8.

31. Amygdala (2019). Available at: http://brainmadesimple.com/amygdala.html

32. Dolcos, F., LaBar, K. S., & Cabeza, R. (2004). Interaction between the amygdala and the medial temporal lobe memory system predicts better memory for emotional events. *Neuron, 42*(5), 855–863.

33. Maquet, P., Péters, J. M., Aerts, J., Delfiore, G., Degueldre, C., Luxen, A., & Franck, G. (1996). Functional neuroanatomy of human rapid-eye-movement sleep and dreaming. *Nature, 383*(6596), 163–166.

34. Genzel, L., Spoormaker, V. I., Konrad, B. N., & Dresler, M. (2015). The role of rapid eye movement sleep for amygdala-related memory processing. *Neurobiology of Learning and Memory, 122*, 110–121.

35. Why you're more afraid of flying than driving to the supermarket. Available at: https://io9.gizmodo.com/5846218/why-youre-more-afraid-of-flying-than-driving-to-the-supermarket

36. Kramer, M. (2011). REM sleep and dreaming: the nature of the relationship. In B. N. Mallick, S. R. Pandi-Perumal, R. W. McCarley, &A. R. Morrison (Eds) *Rapid Eye Movement Sleep. Regulation and Function* (pp. 40–48). Cambridge University Press, New York.

37. See p. 212 in Walker, M. (2018). *Why We Sleep: The New Science of Sleep and Dreams.* Penguin, London; and Werner, G. G., Schabus, M., Blechert, J., Kolodyazhniy, V., & Wilhelm, F. H. (2015). Pre-to postsleep change in psychophysiological reactivity to emotional films: late-night REM sleep is associated with attenuated emotional processing. *Psychophysiology, 52*(6), 813–825.

38. Baran, B., Pace-Schott, E. F., Ericson, C., & Spencer, R. M. (2012). Processing of emotional reactivity and emotional memory over sleep. *Journal of Neuroscience, 32*(3), 1035–1042.

39. Llewellyn, S. (2013). Such stuff as dreams are made on? Elaborative encoding, the ancient art of memory, and the hippocampus. *Behavioral and Brain Sciences*, 36, 589–659.

40. Paivio, A. (1990). *Mental Representations: A Dual Coding Approach*. Oxford University Press, Oxford.

41. See p. 208 in Walker, M. (2018). *Why We Sleep: The New Science of Sleep and Dreams.* Penguin, London.

42. Levin, R., & Nielsen, T.A. (2007). Disturbed dreaming, posttraumatic stress disorder, and affect distress: a review and neurocognitive model, *Psychological Bulletin*, 133(3), 482–528.

43. Mellman, T. A., & Pigeon, W. R. (2016). Dreams and nightmares in posttraumatic stress disorder. In M. H. Kryger, T. Roth, & W. C. Dement (eds) *Principles and Practice of Sleep Medicine* (sixth edition) (pp. 561–566).

44. Spoormaker, V. I., & Van Den Bout, J. (2006). Lucid dreaming treatment for nightmares: a pilot study. *Psychotherapy and Psychosomatics, 75*(6), 389–394; and Gavie, J., & Revonsuo, A. (2010). The future of lucid dreaming treatment. *International Journal of Dream Research*, 3(1), 13–15.

45. Foa, E. B. (1997). Psychological processes related to recovery from a trauma and an effective treatment for PTSD. *Annals of the New York Academy of Sciences, 821*(1), 410–424.

46. Stickgold, R. (2002). EMDR: a putative neurobiological mechanism of action. *Journal of Clinical Psychology, 58*(1), 61–75.

47. Sterpenich, V., Albouy, G., Boly, M., Vandewalle, G., Darsaud, A., Balteau, E., … & Rauchs, G. (2007). Sleep-related hippocampo-cortical interplay during emotional memory recollection. *PLoS Biology, 5*(11), e282; Walker, M. P. (2008). Cognitive consequences of sleep and sleep loss. *Sleep Medicine*, 9, S29–S34; Walker, M. P., & Stickgold, R. (2006). Sleep, memory, and plasticity. *Annual Review of Psychology*, 57, 139–166.

48. Yoo, S. S., Gujar, N., Hu, P., Jolesz, F. A., & Walker, M. P. (2007). The human emotional brain without sleep—a prefrontal amygdala disconnect. *Current Biology, 17*(20), R877–R878.

49. Dijksterhuis, A., & Aarts, H. (2003). On wildebeests and humans: the preferential detection of negative stimuli. *Psychological Science, 14*(1), 14–18.

7

Dream to Decide (and to Act)

Introduction

I argue rapid eye movement (REM) dreaming provides image-based associations, based on extracting a probabilistic pattern from our past experiences. These image-based patterns are then retained at an unconscious level. In this chapter I propose that, during wake, these unconscious images influence our decisions and actions. When are our decisions unconscious? We tend to think of decisions, almost by definition, as the result of conscious reasoning. When faced with an important choice our first reaction is 'to think about it'. We're also inclined to believe that conscious deliberation, carefully considering alternatives, improves our decision making but this isn't always the case.[1] To quote Freud, 'When making a decision of minor importance, I have always found it advantageous to consider all the pros and cons, in vital matters, however, such as the choice of a mate or a profession, the decision should come from the unconscious, from somewhere within ourselves.'[2]

Perhaps, surprisingly, experimental evidence supports Freud. Conscious thought turns out to be most useful for simple decisions, when there are only a few things to consider. When you face a complex, personally significant decision with many alternatives, unconscious thought is better.

Consequently, in this chapter, we look at two types of decision making and consequent action: first, fast, associative, unconscious and driven by basic emotions; and, second, slow, sometimes rule-based, sequential, conscious and driven by complex emotions.[3] Our language and thought expresses these two types. In the first mode, we speak of 'intuition', an instinctive, gut feeling of something being the right thing to do, and 'unconscious motivation', being driven by desires without any awareness of them. For example, 'love at first sight', an instant attraction to a stranger, is fast and intuitive, driven by basic emotions, and reflects unconscious associations. In contrast, the conscious, rule-based, sequential mode is reflected in 'thinking things through', 'setting goals', and 'following principles'. The adage 'marry in haste, repent at leisure' is a rule-based response to 'love at first sight'.

This first type of decision making evolved early, is shared with animals, and based on unconscious knowledge. The second evolved late, may not be shared with animals—at least in the sense of 'thinking about thinking'—and relies on conscious knowledge.[4] An associative image, formed during dreaming, would result in the first type of decision: fast, associative, unconscious and driven by basic

What Do Dreams Do? Sue Llewellyn, Oxford University Press (2020). © Oxford University Press.
DOI: 10.1093/oso/9780198818953.001.0001.

emotions. Conscious, reflective thought during waking hours would engender the second type of decision.

Unconscious Decisions and Actions

Unconscious decision making emphasizes the close link between decisions and actions. Chapter 4 identified movement as the evolutionary driver for human brain development. We evolved in a world where 'deciding' was overwhelmingly 'deciding to act quickly to obtain food and avoid predators'. Consequently, decision-making processes are embedded in motor processes.[5] If we want to understand how decision making evolved we need to understand voluntary action. Most of our decisions to act use the 95% of the brain that operates unconsciously. Life would be impossible if all of our decisions were conscious.

Just now I don't have to decide how to move to lift my coffee mug, so that I don't spill the coffee when I drink. I move to lift and drink unconsciously. These unconscious drinking actions are informed by unconscious motor imagery. I use internal image-based simulations to plan how to grasp the mug.[6] This motor imagery associates movements with outcomes, in the sense that there are several different ways to successfully grasp the mug; for example, I could grab the mug or take hold of the handle. Through mental imagery, I decide unconsciously between these different ways and act.

The image-based nature of unconscious thought is becoming more widely accepted (see Chapter 4). Both movement and spatial information are processed through the image-based system, which can handle complex associations, whereas sequential, simpler, 'what follows what' associations rely on the verbal, language-based system.[7] Unconscious decisions result from image-based associations. When we decide unconsciously, based on influences from the past, where do these image-based associations come from?

Chapter 4 argued REM dreams identify image-based associative patterns in past events, for example, in evolutionary time, 'lion–waterhole–visit–night' and 'lion–waterhole–dry season–visit–day'. These associative patterns were portrayed and retained in unconscious images that improved the survival chances of early humans through using prior experience to enable them to act.

In a dangerous situation an unconscious image has four substantive advantages for action. First, an unconscious image *doesn't interfere* with visual perception and attention. In contrast, a conscious image does. Conscious imagery would be particularly detrimental in perilous conditions that require close, continuous visual monitoring of the environment. Second, as mentioned in previous chapters, an unconscious image enables *fast* flight, fight, or freeze actions. In evolutionary time, speed could make the difference between a life or death outcome. An early human couldn't wait to think in words: 'Hey, it's during the day in the dry season, which means the chances of the flash of yellow being a lion is higher than in the wet season, so should I run or take a chance on it being a butterfly?' Immediate danger offers no time for thought-based deliberation. Third, unconscious images can *incorporate complex associations*. Fourth, and relatedly, if unconscious knowledge is transferred to consciousness, *information loss* results[8] because the complexity inherent in the image isn't retained.

Next, we return to the daily tour in the home range to see how fast, associative, unconscious decision making, driven by basic emotions and slow, reflective, sometimes rule-based, sequential, conscious decisions, driven by complex emotions, may have arisen.

Dream to Decide or Time to Decide?
Returning to the Daily Tour

On the daily tour, early humans walked along pathways to reach a series of landmarks. In evolutionary terms, slow, reflective conscious decision making may have emerged whenever there were no immediate dangers requiring fast responses, thus giving time for deliberation about possible action.[9] As discussed in Chapter 4, early humans would have had time to think on the pathways between landmark junctions. They could use this time to, for example, logically plan the sequence of routes to take on any particular day: first, walk to the clump of trees, then to the bush to gather some blackberries, and next to the waterhole. In contrast, at the landmarks themselves, for example, the waterhole, unconscious fast, associative decisions were essential because these places attracted predators and competitors. Fast, unconscious decision making, through mental images, would have had primacy across evolutionary time.[10]

Although this unconscious processing was fast, it was informed. In evolutionary terms, a flash of yellow seen on approach to a waterhole may be a lion or a hyena but could just be a butterfly. Water is essential for humans. Early humans could not always retreat when they glimpsed a yellow flash near a waterhole. We make sense of what is perceived through relating it to prior experience. I gave the example of a retained dream image that used past experience to associate the presence of a lion or a hyena at a waterhole during the day with the dry season. Lions get thirstier in the dry season so they sometimes switch to daytime visits rather than their usual night visits in the wet season. In consequence, a yellow flash during the day in the wet season is more likely to be a butterfly than a lion or hyena, as compared with during the dry season, when the chances of a glimpse of yellow being a lion or a hyena are increased. Any intuitive, fast response to a glimpse of yellow may be called a gut response, but it's an informed one based on integrating perception with past experience.

We tend to venerate our consciousness over our unconsciousness, which is why it's unsettling to discover that unconscious decision making is better at making complex decisions. Surely we need to be conscious to handle complex decisions? But this reasoning neglects the evolutionary context for unconscious decisions: these were image-based decisions to act quickly using complex, multiple associations between past experiences and current information from the environment. The evolutionary setting for unconscious decisions was a place—a landmark junction—which offered vital rewards but harboured dangers.

As mentioned above, walking along a pathway to a place not yet reached may have engendered reflective consciousness. This evolutionary context would explain why our episodic memories, derived from associated, sequential experiences along a pathway, are conscious and we can reflect on them. In contrast, the associations *between* elements of our episodic memories, derived from patterns in our past landmark junction experiences s, would be retained unconsciously. We cannot reflect upon them unless we remember our dreams and ponder on the associations that drive them.

Back to the Quicksand Dream

For example, my remembered Quicksand dream (described in Chapter 6) is driven by my house–threat–death–sand association. My mind/brain has identified this pattern based on my previous experiences. In the dream, the recent memory that seems to trigger Scene 1 is the phone call from my eldest son. He and his then-girlfriend, now-wife, are thinking of buying a house; it's located on the edge of town and someone has died in it. I have two reactions to this.

Driven by the basic emotion of fear, I immediately want to say 'Don't buy that house.' But I suppress this instantaneous, default, gut decision. I don't want my son to think I'm irrational. I don't say anything. I listen carefully. After I put the phone down I still feel afraid but switch to the second type of reasoning: conscious, reflective, and driven by complex emotions. I decide on a strategy: I will try to persuade my son not to buy the house through stressing its inconvenient position on the edge of town. But this isn't actually why I don't want him to buy it. My reason is an unconscious house–threat–death association. The knowledge that someone has already died in the house has triggered it.

Why would I have a house–threat–death association? Most people's association with 'house' is 'safe'. The phase 'safe as houses' is usually taken to mean completely safe.[11]

Unsafe houses: illustrative dreams

But, in evolutionary time, refuges are only safe if predators can't get in. If they can, you are trapped—your flight response is blocked. I often dream of being in a house, when some menacing presence tries to get in or somehow has already entered.

Sometimes the threatening presence takes a specific form, but this is not usually the case.

For these dreams, I'm not going to report the memory sources in detail. My intention is merely to give readers a sense of these 'unsafe house dreams' with house–threat–death associations.

The Red Room, 2 June 2012

I am in a large house or it could be a hotel. I enter a room. It's completely red. Shiny red material covers everything including a large dais against the wall to the right. There are red curtains, bunched up. I approach them, feeling afraid. Suddenly a vampire-like man steps out of the curtains, towards me. His face is wide and white. He has very blue, wide-spaced eyes.

I wake up, very afraid.

The day before this dream I had been reading a research paper that mentions vampires and discusses how wearing red goggles during the day results in red images during dreams.[12]

The Cold Door, 14 November 2013

J (my partner) is in bed. It's very dark. I am lying on the floor near the bed. I may be holding J's hand. I hear a noise outside of the room. Then the noise starts to sound like people talking. R, my sister, may be there. I move to close the door. The handle feels cold. I can't get the door closed quickly enough. The people are pulling on the other side. J comes to help me but it's no good. They are going to get in.

I wake up terrified.

At the time of the dream we are staying in a very large house in Japan. It's November and bitterly cold. Immediately before going to bed on the night before the dream, I ask J if I may shut the bedroom door but he wants it open. During the day before the dream I was going from the kitchen to the bedroom when I was struck by the coldness of the round brass handle on the bedroom door. While J is gone during the day, I am working in the house writing a paper. I often think I couldn't stay here alone at night. It's just too scary.

The Axe Break-in, 19 June 2017

I'm in a room. I hear a noise. I must secure the door. Someone is on the other side trying to get in. They are trying to break the door panel with an axe. The axe is very close to my face. It's no good: the wood of the upper door panel is splintering right in front of my eyes. They are going to get in. I can't stop them.
  I wake up terrified.

I usually avoid watching horror movies, but my sons watched them as teenagers. I remember years ago coming in to the sitting room where they were viewing the axe scene from *The Shining* (https://www.youtube.com/watch?v=d-ABIIZV3vA).

The Power of Unconscious Decision Making

This house–threat–death association has plagued me for most of my life. Not just in my dreams. Awake, alone, it's very hard for me to be in a house overnight. I obsess about doors and corridors. I could never live in a house with a cellar. Just as if I'd had a close encounter with a predator, my amygdala won't let go of this association. (The amygdala is the brain's fear centre; it controls reactions to threatening and dangerous events, see Chapter 6.) My mother used to say: 'Better safe than sorry.' The amygdala seems to work this way too. For people like me, unconscious associations can be powerfully disturbing. They can drive seemingly irrational reactions to a house someone has died in: 'Don't buy that house!'—although refusing to buy such a house wouldn't be irrational for me because living in it would provoke too much fear. As discussed earlier, for complex choices, unconscious decisions are usually better, but what if there is relevant information consciously available?

For example, take another buying decision—not to buy a house but a statue. Malcolm Gladwell, the Canadian journalist and author, relates how, based on specialist evidence and letters of provenance, the J. Paul Getty Museum decided to buy a marble statue, reputed to be Greek and 2,000 years old, its price tag: US$10 million.[13] Their decision making was slow, taking 14 months. The Getty's lawyers were given documents confirming a 50-year history of ownership. Expert, rule-based analysis found the marble to be old.

But, when the Getty invited several art professionals to view, their immediate reaction was the statue 'didn't look right'. One said the first thing that went through his head was the word 'fresh'. Another felt 'intuitive repulsion'. A 2,000-year-old statue shouldn't look fresh. Experts shouldn't be repelled on viewing. Just like early humans seeing a yellow flash on approach to a waterhole, these experts assimilated what they saw with their unconscious expert experience of ancient statues. Their fast, unconscious decisions, driven by the basic emotion of disgust, turned out to be right. The provenance documents were forgeries. The marble analysis overlooked that potato mould had been used to age the statue. Eventually, the Getty concluded the statue was a modern fake.

But the Getty museum story is just anecdotal and the consciously available information turned out to be fake or misleading. What is the experimental evidence for unconscious decision making?

Experimental Evidence for Unconscious Decision Making

Ap Dijksterhuis, a psychologist at Radboud University, Nijmegen, The Netherlands, has, along with others, produced considerable experimental evidence for unconscious decision making. For example, the results of five experiments show when a complex decision involves weighing up many different features, unconscious decision making results in better decisions than conscious decision making. His inferred reasons for this are: first, unconscious processing is better at associating and integrating disparate information; and second, conscious processing tends to give too much attention to a few features while neglecting others, so meaningful mental associations are made between some features but other relevant features are not incorporated.[14]

Take the decision to buy a car. We have to take many, complex attributes into account: price, age, size, colour, make, design, safety, comfort, functionality, economy to run, and in-car entertainment. For complex decisions, when we have to weigh many aspects, unconscious decisions seem to be best.[15] Colour, comfort, and safety would be very important to me when buying a car so I would place more weight on these than many other people would. The limits of conscious thought for decision making are reached when about seven attributes have to be considered.[16] In the car example, above, I've reckoned on 11 important attributes. It looks as though unconscious thought will be better for car purchases.

Unconscious decisions seem to result from 'deliberation-without-attention', i.e. we are thinking or deliberating unconsciously about the relevant, important issues (e.g. price, size and so on, when buying a car) while our conscious attention is directed elsewhere.[17] To be able to assess many different attributes we have to associate and integrate them; for example, a big car is likely to be more expensive and have better functionality, including in-car entertainment. Big–price–functionality–entertainment are associated so if you buy a big car you are likely to get the other three attributes too, including having to pay more, whereas colour is not associated with any of these. Ap Dijksterhuis's experiments found unconscious thought is better than conscious thought at association and integration.

What about decisions where expert judgement comes into play? There isn't much research on this, but unconscious thought outperforms conscious thought in clinical decision making over psychiatric diagnosis.[18] In deciding what is just, unconscious decisions over the justice of complex job application procedures were more accurate than conscious ones.[19]

The power of unconscious association for decision making is, sadly, perhaps best demonstrated for suicide. An unconscious association between the self and death/suicide predicts suicide, being associated with around six times the risk of making a subsequent suicide attempt within the following 6 months and having more predictive power than known risk factors such as a history of suicide attempts and depression.[20] This finding is understandable in the context of unconscious associations driving decisions and actions.

We tend to think we know when we have made a decision and when we are still undecided. But this isn't always the case. People who, consciously, think that they haven't made up their minds may have actually already decided at an unconscious level. Unconscious mental associations, formed through past experiences, drive these unconscious choices. For example, residents of Vicenza in Italy were asked whether they were in favour of, undecided, or against the enlargement of the US base in their city.[21] Their unconscious associations about the US base were inferred from their performance on various trials where participants had to categorize images of the US base along with negative and positive words as quickly as possible. For participants who said they were undecided when first asked, researchers could predict their later conscious choices through their unconscious associations as revealed during the trials. A gambling task produced similar results. Participants chose an advantageous strategy unconsciously before they consciously realized which strategy worked best.[22]

More generally, although we assume we make a conscious decision to act before acting, experiments show we have an unconscious will that can initiate actions outside of conscious awareness.[23] You can have decided even though you don't yet know you have. Also you can decide to act in pursuit of a goal even though you aren't consciously aware of the goal.

These experiments indicate that unconscious associations, formed through past experience, can prompt decisions and choices outside of conscious awareness. This raises the question of where the unconscious associations come from and whether they are forged during the highly associative state of dreaming. The experiments described above did not include a period of sleep but the next section looks at research which does. Folk wisdom tells us to 'sleep on it'. Is this right?

Should You 'Sleep on It' Before Making Decisions?

The experiments described in the previous section show that unconscious decisions are best in complex situations where there are many aspects to be taken into account. Similarly, when people sleep on it they perform better on difficult problems, but, when the problems are easy, sleeping on it doesn't make any difference.[24]

Similarly sleeping on it improves people's performance on difficult tasks but doesn't make as much difference for easy ones.[25] Conversely, sleep deprivation reduces people's abilities to integrate thinking with emotion when making complex moral decisions.[26]

The above studies suggest that 'sleeping on it' does improve performance on difficult issues. These sleep-dependent benefits for difficult problems, tasks, and decisions would follow from the way that REM sleep and dreaming enables us to make non-obvious, complex associations between different aspects of a problem or decision. What is the evidence for this? REM sleep can extract associative patterns from memories of episodic events.[27] During REM dreams non-obvious, complex associations are identified and strengthened.[28] REM sleep improves performance on complex tasks.[29]

Where the associations are simpler we can solve the problem, complete the task, or make the decision consciously while we are awake, using our slow, sometimes rule-based, sequential logic, but to make complex associations we need REM sleep. In *Macbeth*, Shakespeare says 'Sleep that knits up the ravell'd sleave of care'. We should 'REM sleep on it' to 'knit up' or associate things that are 'ravell'd', or not clearly associated, using our waking minds.

Sleep improves people's decisions about risk and reward.[30] Conversely, when you are sleep deprived your judgement is impaired. In uncertain situations, when sleep deprived, you are more likely to take high risks,[31] because your expectations of rewards are increased while your responses to losses are attenuated.[32] Also sleep-deprived individuals cannot cope with the unexpected and with changing circumstances because they don't properly update their knowledge based on feedback from the environment.[33]

Briefly...

I argue associative dream images can trigger unconscious decisions; these retained images stem from knowledge of a complex pattern in past experience. An evolutionary example is using knowledge of a probabilistic pattern in past experience to gauge how likely, for example, a flash of yellow in the undergrowth around a waterhole is indicative of a lion. In the contemporary Getty museum example, this patterned knowledge produces the expertise that can assess the authenticity of antiquities just by looking at them.

These perceptually based decisions may be driven by basic emotions but reflect distilled experience. We call unconscious decisions 'gut feelings', 'intuitions', and 'hunches', but they are rooted in experiential knowledge. Unconscious decisions are fast but informed, although this distilled knowledge isn't consciously accessed at the time.

Associative dream images would have been mobilized unconsciously, while conscious attention is directed towards monitoring the environment. Across evolutionary time, in an environment that afforded both high rewards and high risks, integrating past experience of the probability of dangers would have enabled a substantial weighting to the possibility of a predator. As discussed in the chapter, research shows that sleep is essential for optimally balancing risks and rewards when deciding how to act.

The experimental evidence (cited in the chapter) is that sleep improves performance on difficult, complex decisions but doesn't make a difference for easy ones. When people make decisions in new situations, they are motivated by unconscious associations from the past.[34] Unconscious influence is one of Freud's basic premises. When my partner and I decided to buy a house, we saw one that seemed to meet almost all of our criteria. I was enthusiastic. I liked its 1920s Art Deco features. But my partner didn't want to buy. Months later he suddenly remembered his father had been scathing about houses built in the 1920s—in his view, they weren't built to last. But, when house-viewing, my partner wasn't consciously aware of his father's influence that led him to associate 1920s houses with 'not built to last'. When my son was thinking about buying a house that someone had died in, I immediately wanted to say 'Don't buy that house' based on an unconscious (at the time) association between 'house–threat–death', as illustrated in my unsafe house dreams.

When are unconscious decisions influenced by REM dream associations? REM dream associations identify a non-obvious or complex pattern in episodic memories. This would translate to retained REM dream associations influencing complex decisions that involve unconscious weighting of elements of different personal experiences in deciding what to do. These decisions are fast; we call them 'intuitive' but they use unconscious, distilled knowledge of a probabilistic pattern in events.

Next

In the next chapter I show how unconscious knowledge of a probabilistic pattern in events enables prediction. When early humans approached a waterhole they could anticipate what was likely to happen there. They didn't know for sure but they had expectations about the presence and behaviour of competitors, potential mates, and predators. Visual cues from the environment—a flash of yellow— would trigger unconscious knowledge of a probabilistic pattern to enable fast action if the decision was to flee—a high probability of a predator. Experience of the world enables unconscious decision making but it also makes prediction possible.

Notes

1. Our unconscious brain makes the best decisions possible. Available at: http://www. rochester.edu/news/show.php?id=3295

2. Reik, T. (1948). *Listening with the Third Ear: The Inner Experience of a Psychoanalyst.* Farrar, Straus & Co., New York, p. vii. Theodor Reik had asked his mentor, Freud, about deciding to follow a career in psychoanalysis.

3. See, for example, Evans, J. S. B., & Stanovich, K. E. (2013). Dual-process theories of higher cognition: advancing the debate. *Perspectives on Psychological Science, 8*(3), 223–241. For popular accounts of dual process theories, see Kahneman, D. (2011). *Thinking, Fast and Slow.* Macmillan, London; and Gladwell, M. (2007). *Blink: The Power of Thinking Without Thinking.* Back Bay Books, New York.

4. Evans, J. S. B., & Stanovich, K. E. (2013). Dual-process theories of higher cognition: advancing the debate. *Perspectives on Psychological Science, 8*(3), 223–241.

5. Cisek, P., & Kalaska, J. F. (2005). Neural correlates of reaching decisions in dorsal premotor cortex: specification of multiple direction choices and final selection of action. *Neuron, 45*(5), 801–814.

6. Johnson, S. H. (2000). Thinking ahead: the case for motor imagery in prospective judgements of prehension. *Cognition, 74*(1), 33–70.

7. Paivio, A. (1990). *Mental Representations: A Dual Coding Approach.* Oxford University Press, Oxford.

8. Connell, L., & Lynott, D. (2016). Do we know what we're simulating? Information loss on transferring unconscious perceptual simulation to conscious imagery. *Journal of Experimental Psychology: Learning, Memory, and Cognition, 42*(8), 1218.

9. See p. 62 in Tucker, D. M. (2007). *Mind from Body: Experience from Neural Structure.* Oxford University Press, New York.

10. Paivio, A. (1990). *Mental Representations: A Dual Coding Approach.* Oxford University Press, Oxford; Paivio, A. (2014). *Mind and Its Evolution: A Dual Coding Theoretical Approach.* Psychology Press, Hove; and Reber, A. S. (1996). *Implicit Learning and Tacit Knowledge.* Oxford University Press, Oxford.

11. See Safe as houses. Available at: https://www.collinsdictionary.com/dictionary/english/ safe-as-houses

12. Roffwarg, H. P., Herman, J. S., Bowe-Anders, C., & Tauber, E. S. (1978). The effects of sustained alterations of waking visual input on dream content. In A. M. Arkin, J. S. Antrobus, & S. J. Ellman (Eds) *The Mind in Sleep: Psychology and Psychophysiology* (pp. 295–349). Erlbaum, Hillsdale, NJ.

13. See pp. 3–8 in Gladwell, M. (2007). *Blink: The Power of Thinking Without Thinking.* Back Bay Books, New York.

14. Dijksterhuis, A. (2004). Think different: the merits of unconscious thought in preference development and decision making. *Journal of Personality and Social Psychology, 87*(5), 586.

15. See Conscious vs. unconscious thought in making complicated decisions. Available at: https://www.psychologicalscience.org/news/releases/conscious-vs-unconscious-thought-in-making-complicated-decisions.html

16. Dijksterhuis, A. (2004). Think different: the merits of unconscious thought in preference development and decision making. *Journal of Personality and Social Psychology*, *87*(5), 586.

17. Dijksterhuis, A., Bos, M. W., Nordgren, L. F., & Van Baaren, R. B. (2006). On making the right choice: the deliberation-without-attention effect. *Science*, *311*(5763), 1005–1007.

18. de Vries, M., Witteman, C. L., Holland, R. W., & Dijksterhuis, A. (2010). The unconscious thought effect in clinical decision making: an example in diagnosis. *Medical Decision Making*, *30*(5), 578–581.

19. Ham, J., van den Bos, K., & Van Doorn, E. A. (2009). Lady Justice thinks unconsciously: unconscious thought can lead to more accurate justice judgments. *Social Cognition*, *27*(4), 509–521.

20. Nock, M. K., Park, J. M., Finn, C. T., Deliberto, T. L., Dour, H. J., & Banaji, M. R. (2010). Measuring the suicidal mind: implicit cognition predicts suicidal behavior. *Psychological Science*, *21*(4), 511–517.

21. Galdi, S., Arcuri, L., & Gawronski, B. (2008). Automatic mental associations predict future choices of undecided decision-makers. *Science*, *321*(5892), 1100–1102.

22. Bechara, A., Damasio, H., Tranel, D., & Damasio, A. R. (1997). Deciding advantageously before knowing the advantageous strategy. *Science*, *275*(5304), 1293–1295.

23. Custers, R., & Aarts, H. (2010). The unconscious will: how the pursuit of goals operates outside of conscious awareness. *Science*, *329*(5987), 47–50.

24. Sio, U. N., Monaghan, P., & Ormerod, T. (2013). Sleep on it, but only if it is difficult: effects of sleep on problem solving. *Memory & Cognition*, *41*(2), 159–166.

25. Kuriyama, K., Stickgold, R., & Walker, M. P. (2004). Sleep-dependent learning and motor-skill complexity. *Learning & Memory*, *11*(6), 705–713.

26. Killgore, W. D., Killgore, D. B., Day, L. M., Li, C., Kamimori, G. H., & Balkin, T. J. (2007). The effects of 53 hours of sleep deprivation on moral judgment. *Sleep*, *30*(3), 345–352.

27. Peigneux, P., Laureys, S., Fuchs, S., Destrebecqz, A., Collette, F., Delbeuck, X., ... & Luxen, A. (2003). Learned material content and acquisition level modulate cerebral reactivation during posttraining rapid-eye-movements sleep. *Neuroimage*, *20*(1), 125–134; and Chow, H. M., Horovitz, S. G., Carr, W. S., Picchioni, D., Coddington, N., Fukunaga, M., ... & Braun, A. R. (2013). Rhythmic alternating patterns of brain activity distinguish rapid eye movement sleep from other states of consciousness. *Proceedings of the National Academy of Sciences*, *110*(25), 10300–10305.

28. Sterpenich, V., Schmidt, C., Albouy, G., Matarazzo, L., Vanhaudenhuyse, A., Boveroux, P., ... & Luxen, A. (2014). Memory reactivation during rapid eye movement sleep promotes its generalization and integration in cortical stores. *Sleep*, *37*(6), 1061–1075.

29. Smith, C. (2001). Sleep states and memory processes in humans: procedural versus declarative memory systems. *Sleep Medicine Reviews*, *5*(6), 491–506; and Fogel, S. M., Smith, C. T., & Cote, K. A. (2007). Dissociable learning-dependent changes in REM and non-REM sleep in declarative and procedural memory systems. *Behavioural Brain Research*, *180*(1), 48–61.

30. Pace-Schott, E. F., Nave, G., Morgan, A., & Spencer, R. (2012). Sleep-dependent modulation of affectively guided decision-making. *Journal of Sleep Research*, *21*(1), 30–39.

31. Killgore, W. D., Balkin, T. J., & Wesensten, N. J. (2006). Impaired decision making following 49 h of sleep deprivation. *Journal of Sleep Research*, *15*(1), 7–13.

32. Venkatraman, V., Chuah, Y. L., Huettel, S. A., & Chee, M. W. (2007). Sleep deprivation elevates expectation of gains and attenuates response to losses following risky decisions. *Sleep*, *30*(5), 603–609.

33. Whitney, P., Hinson, J. M., Jackson, M. L., & Van Dongen, H. P. (2015). Feedback blunting: total sleep deprivation impairs decision making that requires updating based on feedback. *Sleep*, *38*(5), 745–754.

34. Galdi, S., Arcuri, L., & Gawronski, B. (2008). Automatic mental associations predict future choices of undecided decision-makers. *Science*, *321*(5892), 1100–1102.

8

Dream to Predict

Introduction

In *The Tempest*, Shakespeare has Antonio say 'What's past is prologue'. What's happened gives an idea of what will happen next. But this only works if there is a pattern or order in events. If events were random the past wouldn't be prologue so you couldn't predict. You can only anticipate your future by discerning an associative pattern in your experience. Associative patterns were discussed in Chapters 2 and 3 but it's worth a recap here because they're integral to prediction.

Some associative patterns are logical and determined. We can easily work them out during our waking hours. For example, night follows day. Night and day are, therefore, associated, as a sequence, in the human mind. We can predict that day will follow night because, across evolutionary time, we have been continually exposed to this tight, 'what happens next' associative pattern. 'What–where' is another associative pattern that would have been highly significant for early humans. For example, fruit–blackberry bush and water–waterhole would have been important co-occurrence patterns. These associations are not as predictable as 'day–night'. The waterhole may dry up in the dry season. Blackberries may be out of season. Also to access berries and water it's necessary to remember the locations of the bush and the waterhole, i.e. not only do you need to know that berries are on bushes and water is at the waterhole, you need to know where the bushes and waterhole are. Nevertheless, these simple what–where associations are readily observable during our waking hours.

What about predicting the behaviour of our fellow humans and animals? This is more difficult: based on their past behaviour you know it's likely they will do certain things or be at certain locations at particular times but you don't know for sure. Their behaviour is not random but neither is it determined. We call these patterns 'probabilistic' because they're based on events that only have a *tendency* to co-occur, so we can't be as confident in predicting them. Living beings can always surprise you because their patterned behaviour is non-obvious. Across evolutionary time, survival would have depended on minimizing predatory surprises.

Significantly, it may take the co-occurrence of several events for a tendency to arise. For a lion to visit the waterhole during the day (their usual pattern is to visit at night) it may take the dry season *and* being thirsty *and* the expectation of prey being present, so they can satisfy both their thirst and hunger in this single visit. The most important driver here is 'being thirsty'. So to make a better prediction

What Do Dreams Do? Sue Llewellyn, Oxford University Press (2020). © Oxford University Press.
DOI: 10.1093/oso/9780198818953.001.0001.

the associative pattern should also include associations to 'when are lions most thirsty?' This is usually midday, which, in turn, is associated with the sun being high in the sky.[1] Being thirsty is also associated with being hot. Nearly all lions still live in sub-Saharan Africa, where the dry season is generally cooler than the wet season.

This complexity means the question of when lions are most thirsty isn't easy to work out. The availability of water is less in the dry season but it's hotter in the wet season. In consequence, if trying to predict when lions will be at the waterhole, the best guess would still be at night. But when it happens to be hot in dry season, when water availability is very limited and the sun is high in the sky at midday, when lions are dehydrated and thirsty, *and* when there is an expectation of prey being present, lions may visit the waterhole during the day. Another association with thirst, for female lions, is likely to be when they are suckling cubs. Being thirsty is also associated with time since the last kill because lions can absorb moisture from the stomach contents of prey. Another useful association is knowledge that elephants chase lions away from places with rewards.

These associations aren't obvious. In a dangerous situation of possible predation there wouldn't be time to consider them all. Sometimes we can work out what animals and humans will tend do by observing them during waking hours but, if their behaviour is driven by these multiple, non-obvious associations (see Figure 4.4 in Chapter 4), the evidence indicates we need sleep and rapid eye movement (REM) dreams to identify these remote connections.

Associations are also much less obvious when we cannot observe them all together. It's very unlikely that any early human ever saw a dehydrated, thirsty female lion suckling cubs in the vegetation around a crowded waterhole in the dry season, when water availability was very limited, elephants were absent, and it was very hot with the sun high in the sky at midday. Although this scenario wouldn't have happened (in particular, lions wouldn't bring young cubs along when they were sitting in wait for prey), it brings together many of the variables that predict the likelihood of a lion being present at a waterhole. These variables may all have been observed but at different time periods and in varying places—the point is they were never experienced together.

During REM sleep and dreaming we are better at spotting the less obvious, 'remote', or complex associations that help predict the probabilistic behaviour of other humans and animals.[2] Also a dream brings together these elements of different experiences that happened at different time periods during wake. Dreams are timeless. But dreams aren't placeless—they always happen somewhere. The dream events, however, didn't all occur at the same place. These issues of time and place render dreams counterfactual, meaning the events in dreams are traceable to elements of past experience but these elements almost never actually occurred together. The unreal nature of dreams may be because they portray these associations across time and place. Retaining an unconscious REM dream image that depicts a probabilistic pattern across elements of different past experiences means you can have a better guess at what will happen next. So, across evolutionary time, at the first sign of possible danger or reward, you can act quickly to flee a predator or obtain food or water, through being faster than competitors. We think of prediction as foretelling the future, but acting on accurate expectations can preclude possible futures.[3] For example, by escaping from a predator I preclude being eaten. This shows that I, at least partially, create my own futures by acting in the world (e.g. escaping the predator), which changes the world (e.g. the predator becomes hungrier and more dangerous).

At this point I hope it's becoming clear this chapter is complementary to the last. The previous chapter argued that fast, intuitive, unconscious decisions to act are derived from retained REM dream associations based on a complex pattern in personally significant past experience. The reason why such decisions are fast and intuitive is that they are based on past experience—we aren't deciding 'from scratch', but we aren't consciously aware of our use of past experience to make the decision. In the same way that unconscious knowledge of what to expect informs decision making, it also enables prediction.

Predictive Brains

Our brains take in stimuli from the environment through the senses: vision, hearing, touch, taste, and smell. The traditional view sees this process as essentially passive—the brain creates a 'picture' of what's happening in the world through building a 'Lego-like' representation of increasing complexity as more and more stimuli are registered.[4] In contrast, the increasingly accepted active and predictive model of the brain emphasizes that this sensory input is used in the context of what we already know. Prior knowledge gives us expectations of what we will see, hear, touch, taste, and smell. More than that, in the predictive view of the brain, prior knowledge dominates in what we see, but we aren't conscious of this dependence on prior knowledge when we take in sensory stimuli. This is best illustrated by examples. The following ones are personal and all depend on the visual sense.

The man–bush and other predictions

I am sitting with my partner on the terrace at the back of a ground floor apartment in Barcelona, Spain. It's evening; the light's fading somewhat. Everything is quiet and still. Suddenly, our attention is caught by movement on the balcony of a fourth-floor apartment opposite. We both make the same comment at the same time 'There's a man—a large man—moving about on that balcony', i.e. we both see a man. But then after a few seconds we both say 'It's not a man, it's a bush!' We made the same error. Initially we saw a man but what was actually moving, presumably caught in higher air currents, was a bush. We both made the same error because we both had the same expectations. Our best guess at the identity of a large, moving object on a balcony was a man—so we saw a man.

It's easy to see how two Brits made this error. Anyone with a balcony in the UK would be unlikely plant a bush—they would want to maximize the sun. In contrast, in sunny Barcelona it is common to use bushes to provide shade on balconies. We sun-deprived Brits didn't expect to see a moving bush so we didn't see one. This exemplifies how the predictive brain works. We use our experience of patterns to interpret and, therefore, identify sensory input. Our prior expectations are usually fulfilled so we see what we expect to see.

A surprising discovery is that the retina suppresses the predictable features of the vista (the apartment block and balcony that we have seen before). These have already been anticipated by the brain and so are seen as predicted. The retina and brain enhance what is novel, unexpected, or ambiguous (the moving shape) because this is the most 'newsworthy'.[5] The incident illuminates how 'top-down' guesses based on memories of experience (if not man, then bush) meet 'bottom-up' raw data from the senses, which requires explanation (odd, moving large shape on a balcony).

Good predictions lessen the time required to consciously experience the world.[6] Our prior UK experience wasn't useful in Barcelona. We had to iterate 'man' before deciding on 'bush', which slowed the process down. Secure conscious perception results after iterating guesses until top-down expectations are consistent with 'bottom-up' sensory input. Or at least any discrepancies between top-down predictions and incoming sensory data are minimized.

Sometimes top-down expectations are so strong as to cause hallucinations.[7] Expectations override 'bottom-up' sensory stimuli. This happened to me when I was living in a flat with two of my sons, T and D. I was very stressed at the time, working at the kitchen table in the afternoon while T and D were at school. I strongly expected T to return from school before D because this was the usual pattern. I heard the front door open, looked up, and clearly saw T at the kitchen door. But then, before my eyes, the image of T dissolved and I saw it was D—a very disconcerting experience.

It also feels very strange when an explanation is called for but the brain can't interpret what you see. Travelling into work one morning I saw something on the road. My first guess was a piece of litter, but it was too substantial. My second guess was a dead bird or small animal, but it was too bright and multi-coloured. My third guess was a children's toy, but it wasn't the right shape. I still don't know what it was.

What did I use to make these predictions?

Unconscious Imagery in Prediction

Stephen Kosslyn, an American psychologist, formerly at Harvard University, is an expert on mental imagery. He argues its primary function is to enable us to make predictions, based on our past experience.[8] But what do we mean by unconscious mental imagery? We need to get to grips with this question before we can work out how unconscious images, formed from past experience, enable prediction.

We retain experiences as memories. These memories aren't passive reminiscences—we use them to gauge what will happen next. Our conscious predictions in wake are familiar territory. For example, based on my experience with balls, I can predict if I throw a ball to this height and with this force it will end up in next door's garden. We call this a simulation.

But here we are concerned with the unconscious use of memories for prediction. As argued in Chapter 3, your brain unconsciously simulates your past experience in an image because unconscious visual simulation is fast and doesn't interfere with visual perception. Archetypically, this image anticipates what is happening (this yellow flash is a predator), its probable consequences (being eaten), and/ or performing a certain action (fleeing to avoid being eaten). These unconscious simulations are *inferences*. They may not be right—just like any conscious simula- tion. Although I threw the ball high and with force it did not end up in next door's garden but in our apple tree. The yellow flash wasn't a predator so I didn't need to flee. Motor or action memories of experiences are the most basic. Hermann von Helmholtz (1821–1894), a German physicist, first suggested that the brain must use unconscious inference to predict the consequences of actions.[9] Contemporarily Karl Friston, a neuroscientist at University College London, and others have devel- oped and extended these ideas on the predictive brain.[10]

Chapter 7 discussed how, when I reach out to grasp a coffee mug to drink, I use unconscious, internal, image-based simulations to simulate my actions and their consequences, based on my past experience with mugs. Clearly acting to grasp a mug to drink coffee involves the prediction of bodily sensations like seeing the mug, touching the mug, and tasting/smelling the coffee. We think of imagery as being quintessentially visual but scientists use the concept of image for simulating all the senses. This generic use brings the scientific concept of 'image' close to the idea of 'imagining', which is usually more associated with artistic creativity. It is also easier to extend the concept of 'imagining' (rather than 'image') to under- standing prediction in relation to senses other than the visual.

Most people can readily imagine 'hearing a tune in your head' in the absence of its sound. Auditory imagining is central to musical abilities.[11] The unconscious na- ture of predictive auditory imagining is demonstrated by our surprise when a note is missing from a known musical sequence.[12] My taste experiences enable me to imagine and, therefore, anticipate, food pleasures. The 'perceptual strangeness'[13] that results when sensory experiences are anticipated but thwarted is, perhaps, most strikingly illustrated by taste. For example, I served roast parsnip to someone expecting a roast potato—he experienced a peculiar taste as his strong top-down anticipation of potato-ness met a bottom-up, surprisingly sweet sensation. Taste is strongly tied to smell. Rather more romantic than root vegetables is Proust's famous reflection on the power of the taste and smell of madeleines to conjure up a vision of his childhood experiences. The relevant extract begins 'When nothing else subsists from the past, after the people are dead, after the things are broken and scattered … the smell and taste of things remain … [in] the immense edifice of memory.' Smell and taste remain so we can recognize and anticipate what we have inhaled or consumed in the past. Equally, anticipating touch enables the prediction of a range of phenomena (e.g. pain, temperature, roughness or smoothness, and pressure) when my body comes into contact with another body or object.

All of these imaging or imagining examples demonstrate that the brain can generate sensory-like states (i.e. seeing, hearing, touching, tasting, and smelling) for itself without sensory input from the environment. Scientists use the term 'offline' for these states—this metaphor captures how these brain-generated states manifest themselves without being 'plugged into' the world. Against this background, dreaming shouldn't come as a surprise. It's a brain-generated offline state. During dreaming, sensory input from the environment is blocked, so the brain turns inwards to 'stored', potentially predictive, information, i.e. memories.

Dream Imagery and Prediction

With sensory input gated during sleep, the brain is free to explore and associate internal inputs, in the form of memories of experiences. Elements of experiences that occurred during the previous day feature in dreams. Freud called these 'day-residues'. Access to remote memories is enhanced during dreaming, as compared to being awake.[14] As discussed earlier, during REM dreaming the brain is hyperassociative, meaning the brain can spot non-obvious associations between elements of recent and remote memories. This is exactly the modus operandi needed to identify non-obvious patterns in past experience.

Going back to predicting when lions will visit a waterhole: this is usually in the evening and at night but in the dry season they sometimes visit during the day. Suppose also there are two waterholes in my home range: waterholes A and B. During the day, in the dry season, the chances of a lion at waterhole A are higher when water availability is very limited because waterhole B has dried up, when it's very hot and the sun is high in the sky at midday, when lions are dehydrated and thirsty, when female lions are suckling cubs, *and* when there is an expectation of prey being present. Let's say an early human had a dream that portrayed all these associations—this would produce a dream I've called 'the lion at the waterhole'.

> ### 'The lion at the waterhole'
>
> #### Scene 1
> *The sun is very high in the sky. I am walking along towards a pond. There are several wildebeest near the water. There is another pond in the distance but all its water has dried up. I am getting closer to the pond when suddenly a lion comes out from behind some bushes along the edge of the water.*
>
> #### Scene 2
> *The lion starts drinking from the pond. Now I can see that there are lion cubs in the bushes. I feel very afraid. I turn and run.*

Dreams are what scientists call 'sensorimotor'—they combine sensory input or data (I see a lion come from behind some bushes) and actions (I turn and run). Of course real life is sensorimotor too—I see my coffee mug and act to reach out for it. Earlier, I emphasized that our actions are quicker and more skilful because our predictive brains, in advance of any action, unconsciously simulate sensorimotor images of what we are going to do. I also argued that the ability to simulate actions is probably the evolutionary basis for sensory simulation, and, therefore, anticipation of sensory input in advance of the sensory experience. These simulations are unconscious so they are most readily apparent when we are in error. For example, I simulate and, therefore, anticipate a moving object on a balcony to be a man, so I see a man, but actually it's a bush. On seeing what my partner thinks is a roast potato on his plate he simulates its taste in advance, so he's surprised and confused at a sweet sensation—it's really a parsnip.

Simulations do not only function unconsciously to anticipate an action or sensation. Generally, they can consciously simulate our previous experiences in their absence. For example, right now I can hear (simulate) the first four notes of Beethoven's Fifth Symphony 'in my head'. I can see (simulate) the sitting room in my partner's flat in Edinburgh. We have to have experienced something in order to simulate it. I can't simulate Beethoven's Fifth Symphony if I have never had the experience of hearing it. I can't simulate my partner's flat if I've never been there or had it described.

The last section ended by noting that dreaming is an 'offline' state but dreams don't simulate experiences because they don't replicate them. Instead I argue that a dream identifies a pattern through associating elements of past experiences. This associative pattern is retained as an image so that it can be simulated unconsciously. But if a dream is only going to be used at an unconscious level, why are my dreams conscious? Why do I live through my dream events without ever doubting their reality? Well, as argued above, I have to have consciously experienced something to be able to unconsciously simulate it. Maybe I have to consciously experience a dream so that I can unconsciously simulate it, to predict what will happen next and act quickly. In waking life, behavioural adaptation (anticipate and act) to faces depends on actually seeing the face, i.e. the face must have been consciously experienced.[15] If the evolutionary driver for dreaming was to predict the behaviour of other living beings (with faces), this may also explain why dreams are conscious.

When Are Predictions Based on Dreams?

Given the above discussion, the archetypical evolutionary forerunner for dream-based prediction is predicting the presence of opportunities (e.g. mates) and threats (e.g. competitors and predators) at landmark junctions. For example, given ambiguous sensory input, what are the chances of a predator? Specifically, is the flash of yellow in the undergrowth around the waterhole a lion or just a butterfly?

My dream-based predictions will arise from emotionally charged, personally significant, complex probabilistic patterns in my past experience. In contrast, we can discern simple patterns between elements of events during our waking hours. For example, although I was wrong first time around in the man–bush case, the associations were simple, binary co-occurrence ones. When I saw something large move on a balcony in Barcelona I guessed 'man'. Based on my previous experience of British balconies, I associated 'balcony' with 'man'. If I'd been a Spaniard, with a different past experience in a hotter climate, I may well have associated 'balcony' with 'bush'.

Equally, my hallucinatory example was a simple pattern of 'what follows what'. My expectation of T before D was so strong it prevailed over my sensory input—given that I was in a stressed and emotionally charged state. But the associative pattern 'T usually comes home before D' is simple and could easily be observed during my waking hours.

I need a dream-based predication when the associative pattern is complex and difficult to discern during waking hours because the associations are non-obvious. These remote associations are between elements of events that occurred at different times and, sometimes, at different places. Although any dream scene is timeless it will happen at one place—the evolutionary archetype for this place is a landmark junction. In the dream image example given earlier, the landmark junction is the waterhole that attracts predators (e.g. lions) and prey (e.g. wildebeest). Actually, when sitting in wait for prey, female lions would not bring suckling cubs to the waterhole. Suckling cubs live in a den[16] and would be left there if their mother went to the waterhole. In the dream the lion cubs are portrayed as being at the waterhole because they are relevant to predicting the presence of lions there but their appearance at the waterhole is counterfactual. Lions don't suckle cubs at the waterhole; this happens back at the den.

As argued in Chapter 4 the most dangerous time for early humans on their daily tour would have been on approach to a landmark junction such as the waterhole. What's the evidence that, on approach to a landmark junction during waking hours, REM dreams may be used to predict events at that landmark?

REM Dreams and 'Preplay'

Clearly, contemporary humans do not make the same daily tours in search of food and water as their ancestors did. In any case, although landmarks junctions in human brain networks may still represent 'places'—in the sense of place-associated elements of emotionally, significant events—investigating their brain networks for evidence of this during REM dreaming is clearly not feasible, at least in the present state of scientific research, although a start has been made. In a recent study people slept inside a brain scanner. They were then woken up and asked to recount their dreams. When people dreamt of specific things, like a key, a chair, or a bed, their brain activity matched that recorded when shown the same things while they were awake.[17] But this is still a far cry from discerning a pattern of associated elements of events that was used to predict on approach to a place previously visited or, contemporarily, when anticipating a situation similar to one encountered in the past.

But, as argued in Chapter 4, animals do make tours in search of food and water and omnidirectional place cells fire at landmark junctions. When an animal advances along a path it has used before it can anticipate up to five or six events that occurred at an upcoming place.[18] On such an approach, the animal can form a prediction, termed 'preplay' in this animal-based research, of events not previously experienced.[19] The same preplay/prediction occurs regardless of which directional path the animal uses on approach.[20] The preplay/prediction phenomenon suggests that the animal may be able to associate elements of previous experiences to anticipate future events at a landmark junction.[21] As argued in this chapter, such predictions are based on inference. Animals are capable of inference[22] to generate not just simple binary pairings but also more complex associations.[23]

We have known for some time that mammals dream and other animals may do too.[24] More recently, it was found that lizards have REM sleep and so may dream.[25] After rats ran in a maze with a food reward at the end of one route but not another, their brain cells firing during sleep showed the same pattern as that recorded when going along the route with the food—as if they were dreaming about going along to get the food.[26] We can't ask rats if they dream about approaching places with rewards, but we can ask humans. As mentioned in Chapter 4, approach behaviours featured in 73% of human dreams.

Updating Dreams and Predictions

Earlier we discussed a pattern of associations that could predict when lions are *more* likely be present at a particular waterhole during the day, i.e. dry season–other waterholes dried up–hot–sun high in the sky–thirsty–dehydrated–suckling cubs–expectation of prey being present. An early human will visit a waterhole frequently—if not every day—so there is always a potential opportunity to add a new association to the predictive pattern.

I discussed the example of elephants chasing lions away from trees in Chapter 4. Here I use a related example. One day, on approach to the waterhole in the dry season, an early human sees an unusual event. Lions are lying in wait for prey near the water when a young, trumpeting bull elephant chases them away.[27] When dreaming the following night, would an element of this scenario get incorporated into a nexus of associations that help predict the chances of lions *not* being at the waterhole during the day in the dry season? In other words, would the presence of an elephant at the waterhole lower the chances of lions being around? On the basis of only a single observation, this seems uncertain, but suppose a few days later an early human observes a herd of elephants chasing lions away, but not at a waterhole.[28] This makes the 'elephants chase lions' observation more compelling and may be enough to indicate that seeing elephants at the waterhole makes the presence of lions less probable and therefore the chances of being attacked less likely. The point being that the personal relevance of any experience may not be immediately apparent. The significance of some events only becomes clear over time as subsequent, related events unfold.

Events from waking life are incorporated in dreams over a distinct timescale. Incorporation follows a 7-day U-shaped curve. On any particular night, during REM dreams, memories of waking-life experiences are more likely to be present from the prior day (the day-residue effect) or from the prior 5–7 days, incorporation from the intermediate 2–4 days is less likely.[29] This timescale implies that elements of waking-life events that have clear personal significance for pattern formation will be incorporated the following night. Otherwise the brain may 'store' the experience for up to 7 days. During these 7 days if further events confirm the pattern significance of any element, then this appears in a dream. The updated dream image is then retained at an unconscious level for prediction during waking hours.

Can Dreams Come True?

Can dreams ever predict the future? Many dreams incorporate bizarre or even impossible events that can never happen: last night I dreamt about my mother but she died years ago. I don't believe she will suddenly turn up again, but my mother's actions can clearly be a part of a pattern in my past experience.

Can dreams ever come true? Some people believe they can. Carlyle Smith, a psychologist and dream researcher wrote a book called *Heads-up Dreaming*.[30] He thinks some dreams could come true. Which ones?

If you look back at 'the lion at the waterhole' dream in this chapter, this portrays associated elements of past events in the life of an early human that make the presence of a lion at the waterhole more likely. In other words it brings together many factors that predict when lions will be at the waterhole during the day in the dry season. Could this dream come true? It's very unlikely because one element—the presence of the suckling cubs at the waterhole—is highly improbable. The mother would have left them back in the den. I could have introduced an element that would have made the dream not only unlikely but impossible. As mentioned in Chapter 4, if an early human sees a flash of yellow in the undergrowth by a waterhole this could be the fur of a lion or a hyena. A REM dream could associate these two animals in a fused image (the 'liena') because, for an early human, they are alike—both have the same significance (e.g. they are predators) and would trigger the same reaction (e.g. fleeing). With a liena, the dream couldn't predict the future.

But without a liena and the cubs all the events in the dream are possible and predictive of the presence of a lion at the waterhole in the dry season during the day. This dream could come true!

Briefly. . .

'The lion at the waterhole' dream portrays the associated factors in the experience of an early human that make the presence of a lion at the waterhole more likely. Any one of these could act as a trigger for the lion to visit the waterhole or, maybe, there was some other reason, unknown to the early human. In terms of the known reasons, it's unlikely they would all occur together. which makes dreams coming true improbable.

If an early human thinks 'I dreamt of a lion at the waterhole and my dream came true', this sounds impressive but actually may signal a failure of the predictive function of dreaming. Used unconsciously on approach to the waterhole, the purpose of the dream is to avoid an encounter with a lion. Also a more valuable dream, in this predation context, would be to include a liena. Better to avoid two predators than only one. Maybe the best dreams can't come true!

Next

To predict we have to have insight into the pattern a dream portrays. The next chapter looks at how dreams reveal associative patterns in our experience, i.e. at what dreams mean.

Notes

1. Adigun, B. Stand-in li-on: thirsty pride of lions queue up for a drink. Available at: http://animals.barcroft.tv/pride-lions-kruger-national-park-south-africa-water-hole-thirsty-drought

2. Llewellyn, S. (2016). Dream to predict? REM dreaming as prospective coding. *Frontiers in Psychology*, 6, 1961.

3. Gilbert, D. T., & Wilson, T. D. (2011). Previews, premotions, and predictions. In M. Bar (Ed.) *Predictions in the Brain: Using Our Past to Generate a Future* (pp. 159–169). Oxford University Press, Oxford.

4. See p. 51, Clark, A. (2015). *Surfing Uncertainty: Prediction, Action, and the Embodied Mind*. Oxford University Press, Oxford.

5. Hosoya, T., Baccus, S. A., & Meister, M. (2005). Dynamic predictive coding by the retina. *Nature*, 436(7047), 71.

6. Melloni, L., Schwiedrzik, C. M., Müller, N., Rodriguez, E., & Singer, W. (2011). Expectations change the signatures and timing of electrophysiological correlates of perceptual awareness. *Journal of Neuroscience*, 31(4), 1386–1396.

7. Fessenden, M. (2015). Where do hallucinations come from? It may just be what you've seen. Available at: https://www.smithsonianmag.com/smart-news/hallucinations-could-come-memories-what-people-have-

8. Moulton, S. T., & Kosslyn, S. M. (2009). Imagining predictions: mental imagery as mental emulation. *Philosophical Transactions of the Royal Society B: Biological Sciences*, 364(1521), 1273–1280.

9. Helmholtz, H. (1866/1962). Concerning the perceptions in general. In: *Treatise on Physiological Optics* (3rd edition), J. Southall, Trans., III, Dover, New York.

10. Friston, K. (2012). Prediction, perception and agency. *International Journal of Psychophysiology*, 83(2), 248–252.

11. Halpern, A. R., & Zatorre, R. J. (2005). Mental concerts: musical imagery and auditory cortex. *Neuron*, 47, 9–12.

12. See p. 3, Clark, A. (2015). *Surfing Uncertainty: Prediction, Action, and the Embodied Mind*. Oxford University Press, Oxford.

13. See p. 3, Clark, A. (2015). *Surfing Uncertainty: Prediction, Action, and the Embodied Mind*. Oxford University Press, Oxford.

14. See p. 27 in Hobson, J. A. (2003). *Dreaming: An Introduction to the Science of Sleep*. Oxford University Press, New York.

15. Moradi, F., Koch, C., & Shimojo, S. (2005). Face adaptation depends on seeing the face. *Neuron*, 45(1), 169–175.

16. Think you know where lions live? Available at: https://animalsake.com/lion-habitat-where-do-lions-live

17. Horikawa, T., Tamaki, M., Miyawaki, Y., & Kamitani, Y. (2013). Neural decoding of visual imagery during sleep. *Science*, 340(6132), 639–642.

18. Jensen, O., & Lisman, J. E. (1996). Hippocampal CA3 region predicts memory sequences: accounting for the phase precession of place cells. *Learning & Memory*, 3(2–3), 279–287.

19. Dragoi, G., & Tonegawa, S. (2011). Preplay of future place cell sequences by hippocampal cellular assemblies. *Nature*, *469*(7330), 397.

20. Lisman, J., & Redish, A. D. (2009). Prediction, sequences and the hippocampus. *Philosophical Transactions of the Royal Society of London B: Biological Sciences*, *364*(1521), 1193–1201.

21. Llewellyn, S., & Hobson, J. A. (2015). Not only … but also: REM sleep creates and NREM Stage 2 instantiates landmark junctions in cortical memory networks. *Neurobiology of Learning and Memory*, *122*, 69–87.

22. Tolman, E. C. (1948). Cognitive maps in rats and men. *Psychological Review*, *55*(4), 189; and Pfeiffer, B. E., & Foster, D. J. (2013). Hippocampal place-cell sequences depict future paths to remembered goals. *Nature*, *497*(7447), 74.

23. Honey, R. C., Iordanova, M. D., & Good, M. (2014). Associative structures in animal learning: dissociating elemental and configural processes. *Neurobiology of Learning and Memory*, *108*, 96–103.

24. Bekoff, M. (2012). Do animals dream? Science shows of course they do, rats too. Psychology Today. Available at: https://www.psychologytoday.com/gb/blog/animal-emotions/201212/do-animals-dream-science-shows-course-they-do-rats-too

25. Underwood, E. (2016). Do sleeping dragons dream? *Science*. Available at: http://www.sciencemag.org/news/2016/04/do-sleeping-dragons-dream

26. Wilson, C. (2015). Rats dream about the places they wish to go. *New Scientist*. Available at: https://www.newscientist.com/article/dn27788-rats-dream-about-the-places-they-wish-to-go/

27. Elephant chases lions from waterhole. Available at: https://www.newsflare.com/video/140186/animals/elephant-chases-lions-from-waterhole

28. Elephants chasing lions at Tembe Elephant Park. Available at: https://www.youtube.com/watch?v=Xz4Uhg7nKTE

29. Nielsen, T. A., & Powell, R. A. (1989). The 'dream-lag' effect: a 6-day temporal delay in dream content incorporation. *Psychiatric Journal of the University of Ottawa*, 14, 561–565; Powell, R. A., Cheung, J. S., Nielsen, T. A., & Cervenka, T. M. (1995). Temporal delays in incorporation of events into dreams. *Perceptual and Motor Skills*, *81*(1), 95–104; and Van Rijn, E., Eichenlaub, J. B., Lewis, P. A., Walker, M. P., Gaskell, M. G., Malinowski, J. E., & Blagrove, M. (2015). The dream-lag effect: selective processing of personally significant events during rapid eye movement sleep, but not during slow wave sleep. *Neurobiology of Learning and Memory*, *122*, 98–109.

30. Smith, C. T. (2014). *Heads-up Dreaming: How your Dreams Can Predict Your Future and Change Your Life*. Turning Stone Press, San Francisco, CA.

9

Dream to Reveal

Introduction

After Freud, many believe dreams have personally important hidden meanings that interpretation can reveal. For example, researchers asked participants which of four prominent dream theories they considered most true: first, dreams provide useful insights on how to solve problems; second, dreams are a by-product of unrelated brain activity; third, dreams reveal hidden truths; and, fourth, dreams assist learning. Fifty-six per cent endorsed the Freudian view of dreams as revealing hidden truths, with only 8% for problem-solving, 18% for by-product, and 18% for learning.[1]

In a second related study by the same research team, 182 US commuters were asked how likely they would be to avoid flying on a scheduled trip if on the night before their flight the US Department of Homeland Security raised the national threat level, warning of a high risk of terrorism; or they consciously thought about their plane crashing; or they dreamt about their plane crashing; or a real plane crashed on their intended route.[2] The commuters were more likely to report avoiding flying after dreaming of their plane crashing than after either a conscious thought of a crash or a government warning. Even the scenario of an actual plane crash on the intended route did not make people more likely to avoid flying than a dream indicating a plane crash. Remarkably, those who endorsed a Freudian theory of dreams having hidden meanings considered distilled information from a dream about their plane crashing even more influential on a decision not to fly than a real plane crash on their intended route.

My central argument in Chapter 4 was that originally we dreamed to survive; so, perhaps, it's not so surprising that many still report avoiding a planned flight after dream indications of their plane crashing. But how to interpret a dream so that any hidden meanings are revealed?

Is the Meaning of Dreams Revealed Through Symbols?

To reveal any covert meanings, some see symbols as the language of dreams. They think the meaning of a dream can be read off against a universal dream symbol 'dictionary', in a similar way to looking up the meaning of a word.[3] This isn't surprising because, contemporarily, we tend to think of meaning as expressed in language.

What Do Dreams Do? Sue Llewellyn, Oxford University Press (2020). © Oxford University Press.
DOI: 10.1093/oso/9780198818953.001.0001.

For example, the word 'bark' has two meanings: it can mean either the outer part of a tree or the sound a dog makes. Similarly, if you put 'white butterfly symbol dream meaning' into Google, three meanings come up. 'White butterfly' means 'the pure soul' or 'joy' or 'transformation'.

A question for those who believe dreams have universal symbolic meanings is: if a white butterfly means the pure soul or joy or transformation, why not dream of pure souls or joy or transformation directly? Why use these indirect symbolic routes to meaning? Most answers rely on the idea of the 'dream as message'. This message may come either from an external source, like the gods, or an internal one, like the unconscious. This implies that the gods and the unconscious speak through universal symbols. For those who believe in universal symbols, a dream symbol dictionary can reveal hidden meanings.

I think dreams present an image of a complex associative pattern in experience. For me, interpreting a dream means identifying and revealing its visual, associative pattern. The reason why I do not directly and immediately comprehend this pattern is simply because, physiologically, my mind/brain in wake is not attuned to detecting visual, associative non-obvious patterns. But my dreaming minds/brains is—as evidenced in the three experiments on non-obvious associations discussed in Chapter 3.

My dream patterns are derived from making associations between elements of *my experience*. Meaning is revealed in association, nothing means anything on its own—to ask about the meaning of my dream is to ask how things are associated with other things[4] *for me*. Dream meanings are, quintessentially, personal meanings.

I think dreams are retained unconsciously but, during wake, we can reveal the personal meanings the dream expresses, if a dream, first, becomes conscious after waking; second, is remembered in some detail; and, third, the dreamer is able to access the memory elements and identify the associations. This implies recording and working with the dream soon after experiencing it.

Personal Meanings, Metaphors and Dreams

For example, in Chapter 3, my Swedish friend and colleague, A, identified the associative pattern in 'the white paper kite and the butterfly'. Butterflies and kites both mean embarrassment for A because both are associated with mistakes. But butterflies and kites don't mean embarrassment for me, or, probably, you either. Dreams are deeply personal—they are tied to individual experience. That's why I don't think dreams are composed of universal symbols.

Are there any associations in our dreams that aren't wholly personal? Well, clearly there are because, as argued in Chapter 3, dreams incorporate some semantic knowledge. We all know that butterflies and kites both fly in the air—they are associated in this sense in A's dream. Equally, they are associated in this sense for all of us. But I think most dream associations are profoundly personal. They reveal private meanings.

Are some dream images personally metaphorical? Chapter 4 argues dreaming evolved in our pre-linguistic days, when we thought in images. Over time, as we acquired language and our world became more complex, it would have become increasingly difficult to represent our personal experiences and concerns in associative visual images. Concrete things (kites, butterflies, and husbands) are easily cast into images, but abstractions (release and freedom) and concerns (wondering whether to leave academia but not being able to because of supervising a PhD) are not. During wake, language can elaborate abstractions and concerns. I propose dreaming, as a primarily visual modality, remained constrained to represent them through concrete images.

Using concrete images to represent abstractions and concerns may have generated what we now call metaphors. Metaphors are thought of as linguistic in nature but, in essence, they use a concrete thing to refer to an abstract one, where the abstraction is associated in some way (or ways) with the concrete entity.[5] For example, the metaphor 'life is a journey' directs us to understand the abstract concept of 'life' through the concrete experience of a 'journey'. Life is associated with a journey because it moves forward in time, has a distinct beginning/ending, and involves a series of, often challenging, experiences.

But our use of metaphor may predate our acquisition of language. Metaphor may have arisen through thinking in associative images during dreaming. If so, it's just a special instance of the associative picturing that goes on in dreaming. For example, in the second scene in A's dream, when the kite flies away she says, 'The white paper kite flying away may relate to the issue that I have thought of leaving the academy so many times. . . But I couldn't leave because I was a supervisor on a PhD. When this suddenly finished [the recently awarded PhD] I was both surprised and satisfied because it meant I was released.'

Given A's proposal here it's hard to resist the idea that the kite flying away is a metaphor for release. But unlike 'life is a journey', which has universal resonance in wake, the kite release in A's dream remains associated with her personal memories and concerns. In consequence, the metaphor 'kite flying away is release' is an aspect of the personally associative, picturing which suffuses her dreaming.

Does the universal 'life is a journey' metaphor permeate our dreams? Given my proposal that dreaming evolved to detect patterns in our experiences at landmark junctions on daily journeys in the home range, it would be odd if it didn't. Dreaming is sensorimotor in character, meaning we are typically moving: walking, running, climbing, cycling, driving, or flying as we perceive the world. Moving forward on a journey does seem to be a universal dream metaphor for our lives, but I contend that most dream metaphors are quintessentially personal.

Personal Associations and Affordances

Personal associations may have evolved from the 'affordances' that link animals and humans to their world.[6] The concept of affordances captures the *relations or associations* between the abilities or capacities of animals and humans, and features of their environment. Affordances aren't properties of either animals or the world. Rather they arise from the associations between the two. For example, fruit only means and is associated with food *for* fruit-eating animals.[7] If an animal's digestive system can't cope with fruit, then fruit isn't food for those animals. Some affordances, like those associated with foods, are universal for humans, but some people are allergic to certain foods. Proteins in foods like shellfish can trigger reactions that mean life-threatening events for some, but are fine for others.

Affordances between me and the world are mine—they are *for me*. Through experiences, affordances forge associations, which create meanings. Kites are aspects of our contemporary environment. They don't afford much for me or mean much to me except perhaps ineptitude because I could never get them to fly properly, despite much running up and down the beach. But, for A, they have a rich set of associations: they mean presents, family, and fun, but also embarrassment, and release. Butterflies have a semantic association with kites for all of us because both fly in the air. But, for A, butterflies are also associated with mistakes. These associations construct her dream.

A very important aspect of our world, both contemporarily and across evolutionary time, is other people. For A, the butterfly only means and is associated with embarrassment in the presence of other people who hear A's mistake over butterflies. The personal association between butterfly and embarrassment arises out of an affordance between A's capacity to feel discomfited by mistakes and the presence of her colleagues in her world. Personal meaning also implies tangible significance for needs, desires, and goals.[8] Clearly, one contemporary desire is not to feel embarrassed in front of colleagues.

When we talk about the meaning of a dream, this isn't analogous to the universal meaning of word within a culture. We should think 'What does this dream mean *for the dreamer*?' If we can't reveal the meaning of dreams in universal symbols, where does the meaning come from? The question of dream meanings is linked to how dreams are represented in memory networks.

Landmark Junctions and the Meaning of Dreams

You will recall from Chapters 3 and 4 that memories of experiences—episodic memories—are represented along pathways in brain networks. These pathways meet, overlap, and are associated at landmark junctions both in the world and in the brain. Chapter 4 described how, across evolutionary time, landmark junctions came to identify the patterns of behaviour associated with the presence of, archetypically, predators, competitors, and potential mates.

György Buzsáki argues the brain cells that make up an omnidirectional landmark junction collectively convey its meaning or significance.[9] For early humans, the meaning or significance of a landmark junction, like a waterhole, would have been how the place either met their needs, satisfied their desires, and furthered their goals, or, alternatively, left their needs unmet, frustrated their desires, and thwarted their goals. In a natural environment, a lion at a landmark junction, like a waterhole, means 'fundamental threat to my goal of survival'. The presence of a competitor means 'rivalry with me for scarce resources'. An encounter with a mate means 'sexual satisfaction and possible reproduction for me'.

In consequence, in evolutionary terms, the meaning of a landmark junction, as portrayed in a dream scene, would have been its associated patterns of rewards and risks. As argued earlier, these dream patterns derive from associating those elements of past experiences that happened at the landmark junction or, sometimes, occurred away from the junction but were significant for landmark events. Archetypically, for early humans, those elements of past experiences would relate to predators, competitors, and potential mates who also frequented the landmark, who represented threats or opportunities, and whose behaviour was non-obvious.

Dream associations and personal meanings seem a far cry from discerning a pattern in predator behaviour. Actually, they aren't. Much of our contemporary sense of personal meaning comes from our interpersonal lives with partners, relatives, and friends. Their behaviour is still non-obvious. We can discern any complex, non-obvious patterns in this behaviour through associating elements of previous experiences with our partners, relatives, and friends. If the complex, associative pattern in a dream image is represented at an omnidirectional landmark junction, the meaning of a dream is revealed there because, as argued above, interpreting a dream is equivalent to identifying its associative pattern.

Being able to detect non-obvious associative patterns is termed insight. Insights reveal something that was previously obscure or difficult to understand. Do sleep and dreaming result in insight? We look at personal insights first. Then we consider some knowledge-based insights from famous dreams.

Personal Insights and Dreams

I have already discussed A's dream, 'the white paper kite and the butterfly', at some length. Some dream researchers distinguish two ways in which personal insight can be gained from dreams: first, the identification of elements of waking life experiences; and, second, the ability to gain greater self-understanding.[10] In A's case these two insight possibilities were expressed through, first, her discovery of the memory sources for her dream associations, and, second, her enhanced ability to connect with her concerns, emotions, and memories through seeing them in a new light. How to define psychological insight? Robert Elliott, a psychotherapist and psychologist at the University of Strathclyde, UK, suggests four elements[11]:

> The first element is metaphorical vision, or seeing with figurative eyes (e.g. 'It made me see I have a tremendous conflict there'). This element also includes the metaphorical illumination that makes the 'seeing into' possible ('The light went on'). This visual metaphor is in keeping with the etymology of the word insight as 'internal seeing' (The Compact Edition of the Oxford English Dictionary, 1971).
>
> The second element is connection, including both the perception of patterns or links ('He really put together all the pieces'). These connections may involve reasons, causes, categorizations, or parallels.
>
> The third element is suddenness: Clients may describe something 'clicking' or may report feeling surprised ('I was sort of amazed. Wow!').
>
> The fourth element is newness, the sense of discovering something not previously known ('It was just something I never thought of').

In relation to dreaming of past personal experience, the first two aspects of psychological insight are immediately relevant. Dreaming is certainly internal seeing, and metaphors in dreaming are visual. My core proposal is that dreaming constructs complex, non-obvious patterns in my past experience, so, 'connection', the second aspect of psychological insight, is the most apt in this sense.

We'll discuss the third and fourth aspects next in relation to famous dreams, which can go beyond solely personal resonance and meaning. Although suddenness and newness can characterize personal insights, these aspects are perhaps heightened in famous dreams.

We noted earlier that although dreams are generally constructed from elements of episodic memories, they do include semantic knowledge also. Struggling with knowledge-based problems makes them concerns, so we would expect knowledge-based problems to appear in dreams. In the same way that dreams reveal personal insights they may also reveal knowledge-based ones. Next we discuss three famous dreams thought to generate scientific knowledge, which takes the dream beyond the purely personal.

Famous Dreams and Scientific Insights

Chapter 3 pointed out that upon wakening a period of inertia occurs when the mind/brain is still in a more dream-like state. This is when most dreams are recalled and when instances of insight into knowledge, derived from specific dreams, can occur.

Perhaps the most famous scientific example is Friedrich August Kekulé's insight into the structure of the benzene ring through association with a dream image of a snake biting its own tail. Kekulé is said to have first mentioned his self-devouring snake dream at a benzene symposium in 1890.[12] Carbon can link with itself to form long molecular chains. The benzene molecule is made of six carbon atoms connected in a ring with one hydrogen atom attached to each. Therefore, through association, the structure of benzene could be pictured as a snake biting its own tail.

Chapter 1 outlined chemical transmission between neurons. Otto Loewi dreamt of two frogs' hearts as a way of testing the theory of chemical transmission. Upon awakening from the frogs' hearts dream in the dead of night, he immediately undertook a successful demonstration of chemical transmission. The results of this eventually won him a Nobel prize.

Elias Howe's invention of the sewing machine was dream-inspired. It went like this: 'I was in Africa and was being chased by wild cannibals. They caught me and placed me in a huge pot. I kept trying to get out but they kept forcing me back in with spears.' Howe had been struggling with the problem of how to automate the sewing process. When he pondered the dream he realized that the spears all had holes in them near their tips. This insight solved the automation problem because the sewing machine needle was forced back into the garment (in his dream Howe was forced back into the pot with spears) whenever a stitch was made.

We can only surmise there were events in the lives of Kekulé, Loewi, and Howe that led them to dream of snakes, frogs, and spears, respectively. But, in each case, associative dream imagery engendered an insight that was new and came suddenly upon awakening.

Famous Dreams and Artistic Insights

These three artistic insights were also new and sudden but they present as metaphorical illumination. They all came about when the artist was in a dream-like state.

The most celebrated arts case is probably Coleridge's epic poem 'Kubla Khan' or 'A Vision in a Dream: A Fragment'. Before falling asleep he had been reading Samuel Purchas's *Pilgrimage* in which Kubla Khan ordered a new marble palace to be built. Coleridge said the poem came to him while asleep. In emphasizing its involuntary, dream-like nature, he remarked on its composition, 'if that indeed can be called composition in which all the images rose up before him as things, with a parallel production of the correspondent expressions, without any sensation or conscious effort'.[13] Coleridge was a regular user of opium—known to engender vivid dreams.

Another well-known dream creation is Mary Shelley's *Frankenstein*. One evening she listened to a lengthy conversation between her husband, Percy Shelley, and Lord Byron. They discussed the possibility of making a creature of manufactured components, assembling them and, then, freakishly bringing the monster alive. Mary Shelley described her experience on going to bed:

> I did not sleep. . . My imagination, unbidden, possessed and guided me, gifting the successive images that arose in my mind with a vividness far beyond the usual bounds of reverie. . . I saw the hideous phantasm of a man stretched out, and then, on the working of some powerful engine, show signs of life and stir with an uneasy, half vital motion . . . behold the horrid thing.[14]

Mary Shelley did not think herself asleep but *Frankenstein* probably arose through hypnogogic hallucination at sleep onset (see Chapter 1). Like Coleridge, she emphasizes *Frankenstein*'s uncontrolled appearance in the theatre of her dreamy imagination.

Dreams are essentially visual experiences—it would be odd if painters didn't depict them. The Surrealists are known for their dream-like art with strange juxtapositions that defy rationality. While the young Max Ernst was ill with a measles-induced fever, he had dream-like hallucinations, including a menacing nightingale. This experience was the source for his painting: *Two Children Threatened by a Nightingale*. In the third person, Ernst recalled his dream as 'provoked by an imitation-mahogany panel opposite his bed, the grooves of the wood taking successively the aspect of an eye, a nose, a bird's head, a menacing nightingale, a spinning top, and so on'. A poem Ernst penned shortly before he undertook the painting begins, 'At nightfall, at the outskirts of the village, two children are threatened by a nightingale'.[15]

These artistic dream exemplars demonstrate that insight is incubated in prior experiences. Max Ernst had had a menacing nightingale hallucination during wake—what's more his alter ego was a bird-like character named Loplop. One might say he obsessed over threatening birds—this concern in wake permeated the dream that provoked his painting. Mary Shelley had listened to Percy Shelley and Lord Byron talk of making a creature of manufactured components and bringing it alive. Coleridge had read of the Kubla Khan's order for a new marble palace.

Although the dreams portray something new, they are rooted in preceding formative events during wake. Insights cannot emerge from a void. In other words, as Shakespeare has King Lear say, 'Nothing will come of nothing.'

Insights During Sleep and Dreaming: Experimental Work

The dreams of Kekulé, Loewi, and Howe seemed to give insights into patterns, which led to scientific discoveries. For example, Kekulé saw the patterned structure of benzene as a snake biting its own tail.

Sleep and insights: experiments

Several experiments show that sleep, and particularly rapid eye movement (REM) sleep, enables insights into hidden patterns, i.e. patterns that are non-obvious during wake are revealed after sleep. The first study of this kind demonstrated that sleep (as compared with the same time awake) more than doubled insight into a hidden, complex pattern in digit sequences.[16]

You will recall from Chapter 3 two other experiments that we can now see as showing better insight into patterns after REM sleep. The first, called the Remote Associates Test (RAT), led by Denise Cai, asked participants for remotely associated words.[17] For example, what word is associated with 'falling', 'actor', and 'dust'? After REM sleep participants were better able (than a group who stayed awake) to identify the word associated with all three words: in this case, 'star'. This can be seen as a hidden pattern because the words 'falling', 'actor', and 'dust' seem unrelated. Adding the word star reveals they can form a star pattern, e.g. falling–star, actor–star, and stardust. The second experiment, in 2015, led by Murray Barsky, asked participants to predict one of two probabilities—'sun' or 'rain'—based on multiple associations between 'sun' or 'rain' and eight other things.[18] These associations formed a complex pattern. The group with REM sleep showed improved insight into the pattern that predicted the weather; the group without did not.

Solving anagrams reveals a word pattern. For example, OSEOG is a nonsense word until rearrangement reveals GOOSE. An experiment gave participants 32 such anagrams to solve before sleep; they were tested again after awakening from non-rapid eye movement (NREM) and REM sleep, and there was a 32% improvement (compared with wake) in the number solved after REM sleep but no improvement after NREM sleep.[19]

A very different kind of pattern, but one that would have been crucial across evolutionary time, is visual detection of objects camouflaged against their background. In my example of avoiding predators, like lions and hyenas, at the waterhole, I have stressed insight into their visiting patterns, but also very relevant is the ability to distinguish a lion shape against the camouflage afforded by the undergrowth around the waterhole. REM sleep enhanced this visual pattern recognition especially for super-detectors—defined as in those in the top-performing quartile.[20] You will recall from Chapter 1 that REM sleep periods are associated with the highest percentage of dreams: a recent study reported that 96.4% of awakenings from REM sleep came with a dream report.

Dreams and insights: experiments

Is there research into dreams revealing insights into patterns? Two researchers at different sites used dream-sharing techniques to work with about 10 participants, one of whom, in turn, reported a recent dream. The other group members then worked with the dream reporter to try to gain insight into, first, any waking-life sources for the dream events, and, second, the personal significance of the dream. At the end of the sessions, all participants answered questions about any insight gains. For example, 'I learnt more from the session about how past events influence my present behaviour' or 'I learnt more about issues in my waking life from working with the dream.' These dream-sharing techniques revealed significant personal insights for the dreamer, even if they had no previous conscious awareness of them.[21]

Any personal insights are likely to be similar to what A experienced when she realized that the PhD completion meant release from her responsibilities at her current university so she was free to seek work elsewhere. In her dream, the personal metaphor of the kite flying away seems to portray this new sense of freedom. Notably, in her waking life, A experienced significant personal embarrassment at the kite loss because it had been an expensive present. As we already know dreaming does not replicate experiences in waking life; rather it associates elements of different experiences to produce something new. My proposal is that REM dreams reveal complex, patterns through associating elements in past experience. This makes it difficult to design experiments to reveal past experiences in dream content because, first, they only incorporate elements, and, second, which elements will be incorporated is not easy to predict. But, as Freud said, most, perhaps all, dreams do seem to incorporate at least one element from the previous day.[22]

One experiment showed dream imagery incorporated elements of a maze navigation task performed before sleep, i.e. on the previous day.[23] But this study was on NREM sleep. As argued in Chapters 3 and 5, NREM sleep can also reveal insights into patterns. These NREM patterns, consisting archetypically of what–where associations, aren't as complex as those in REM sleep. However, they would be relevant to maze navigation, as demonstrated by the 10-fold improved performance after sleep that incorporated task-based dream imagery. Also because NREM task incorporations would be less complex, involving fewer associations, they would be easier for researchers to identify in dream imagery.

This maze navigation experiment was later replicated but with awakenings from all sleep stages. During REM dreaming one participant reported, '...we were just like walking through it but it was like a formal maze ... one of those outdoor like ones made out of like hedges and bushes'.[24] This report illustrates what we already expect: dreams do not rehearse the maze navigation task rather they associate elements of the task with previous experience or knowledge. This indicates that insight into a pattern of associations between maze experiences (or knowledge of them) accounts for the performance improvement on the maze navigation task.

Briefly. . .

Usually dream insights into associative patterns are only into personal meanings and of only personal interest and relevance. For example, for A, butterflies and kites are associated with mistakes but these associations aren't universal ones. However, sometimes, we are personally concerned with a problem that has universal significance or appeal. For example, Elias Howe's dream-inspired invention of the sewing machine was important for all of those, like me, who enjoy sewing, and his discovery made money for the subsequent manufacturers of automated sewing machines. Equally, Mary Shelley's dream of Frankenstein's monster—a creature of manufactured components who came alive—appealed to all horror fans.

This personal versus universal significance may relate to the origin of dreams revealing complex patterns in the behaviour of predators, competitors, and potential mates at landmark junctions. Although my dreams would have detected their behavioural patterns in *my* past experience, another early human would have had similar concerns vis-à-vis predators, competitors, and potential mates, and may have had similar landmark experiences. This correspondence would render my experiential pattern relevant to her/him also. In this way personal insights would have had universal resonance. But without sophisticated language skills and secondary consciousness our ability to communicate our insights to others is very limited.

Next

Some of the insights in this chapter were contingent on dream recall after awakening, but others depended on being in a more dream-like state during wake. Chapter 10 probes the creative potential inherent in dream-like consciousness during wake. A recurring question is whether, when we create, we reveal something that was there all along but remained hidden, or do we actually create something new?

Notes

1. Morewedge, C. K., & Norton, M. I. (2009). When dreaming is believing: the (motivated) interpretation of dreams. *Journal of Personality and Social Psychology, 96*(2), 249.
2. Morewedge, C. K., & Norton, M. I. (2009). When dreaming is believing: the (motivated) interpretation of dreams. *Journal of Personality and Social Psychology, 96*(2), 249.
3. What's in your dream? Available at: http://www.dreammoods.com/dreamdictionary/
4. See pp. 4–10 Polkinghorne, D. E. (1988). *Narrative Knowing and the Human Sciences.* Suny Press, New York. For a formal account of how meaning emerges in a narrative, see Barthes, R., & Duisit, L. (1975). An introduction to the structural analysis of narrative.

New Literary History, 6(2), 237–272. Available at: https://rosswolfe.files.wordpress.com/2015/04/roland-barthes-an-introduction-to-the-structuralist-analysis-of-narrative.pdf

5. Lakoff, G., & Johnson, M. (1980). *Metaphors We Live By.* University of Chicago Press, Chicago, IL.
6. Chemero, A. (2003). An outline of a theory of affordances. *Ecological Psychology, 15*(2), 181–195.
7. Turvey, M. T. (1992). Affordances and prospective control: an outline of the ontology. *Ecological Psychology, 4*(3), 173–187.
8. Clore, G. L., & Ortony, A. (2000). Cognition in emotion: Always, sometimes, or never. In R. D. Lane & L. Nadel. (Eds) *Cognitive Neuroscience of Emotion* (pp. 24–61). Oxford University Press, New York.
9. Buzsáki, G. (2005). Theta rhythm of navigation: link between path integration and landmark navigation, episodic and semantic memory. *Hippocampus, 15*(7), 827–840.
10. Edwards, C. L., Ruby, P. M., Malinowski, J. E., Bennett, P. D., & Blagrove, M. T. (2013). Dreaming and insight. *Frontiers in Psychology, 4,* 979.
11. Elliott, R., Shapiro, D. A., Firth-Cozens, J., Stiles, W. B., Hardy, G. E., Llewelyn, S. P., & Margison, F. R. (1994). Comprehensive process analysis of insight events in cognitive-behavioral and psychodynamic-interpersonal psychotherapies. *Journal of Counseling Psychology, 41*(4), 449.
12. The benzene ring: dream analysis. Available at: https://www.nytimes.com/1988/08/16/science/the-benzene-ring-dream-analysis.html
13. Coleridge's poetry. Available at: https://www.sparknotes.com/poetry/coleridge/section5/
14. Martin, P. (2002). Counting sleep, Flamingo, London, p. 201.
15. Max Ernst: paintings, biography and quotes. Available at: http://www.max-ernst.com/two-children-are-threatened-by-a-nightingale.jsp
16. Wagner, U., Gais, S., Haider, H., Verleger, R., & Born, J. (2004). Sleep inspires insight. *Nature, 427*(6972), 352.
17. Cai, D. J., Mednick, S. A., Harrison, E. M., Kanady, J. C., & Mednick, S. C. (2009). REM, not incubation, improves creativity by priming associative networks. *Proceedings of the National Academy of Sciences, 106*(25), 10130–10134.
18. Barsky, M. M., Tucker, M. A., & Stickgold, R. (2015). REM sleep enhancement of probabilistic classification learning is sensitive to subsequent interference. *Neurobiology of Learning and Memory, 122,* 63–68.
19. Walker, M. P., Liston, C., Hobson, J. A., & Stickgold, R. (2002). Cognitive flexibility across the sleep–wake cycle: REM-sleep enhancement of anagram problem solving. *Cognitive Brain Research, 14*(3), 317–324.
20. McDevitt, E. A., Rowe, K. M., Brady, M., Duggan, K. A., & Mednick, S. C. (2014). The benefit of offline sleep and wake for novel object recognition. *Experimental Brain Research, 232*(5), 1487–1496.
21. Carr, M. Proven methods to gain insight into your dreams. Psychology Today. Available at: https://www.psychologytoday.com/gb/blog/dream-factory/201603/proven-methods-gain-insight-your-dreams

22. Nielsen, T. A., & Powell, R. A. (1992). The day-residue and dream-lag effects: A literature review and limited replication of two temporal effects in dream formation. *Dreaming, 2*(2), 67.

23. Wamsley, E. J., Tucker, M., Payne, J. D., Benavides, J. A., & Stickgold, R. (2010). Dreaming of a learning task is associated with enhanced sleep-dependent memory consolidation. *Current Biology, 20*(9), 850–855.

24. Wamsley, E. J., & Stickgold, R. (2019). Dreaming of a learning task is associated with enhanced memory consolidation: Replication in an overnight sleep study. *Journal of Sleep Research, 28*(1), e12749.

PART III

DREAM CREATIVITY
AND CRAZINESS

10

Dream to Create

Introduction

Chapter 7 introduced two modes of thought: first, fast, associative, unconscious, and driven by basic emotions; and, second, slow, sometimes rule-based, sequential, conscious, and driven by complex emotions. I've argued this duality derives from our basic evolutionary experiences: the fast, non-obvious associativity needed to spot experiential patterns at landmark junctions; along with the sequential, step-by-step, linear logic of walking along pathways.

Here we map this distinction onto creativity in wake engendering two types of creative mind/brain activity: type 1 based on unconscious, non-obvious, remote associations among memory (or knowledge) elements engendering sudden recognition of something previously unknown; and type 2 based on deliberate, incremental, linear-logical, analytic reasoning over a period of time.[1] The literature calls these two types insight and non-insight creativity, the former recognizing the visual nature of insight.

In Chapter 9 insight was defined using Robert Elliott's four aspects: metaphorical vision, connection, suddenness, and newness. In this chapter the focus is on suddenness and newness. I also use another definition of insight from two cognitive psychologists, John Kounios at Dexel University, USA and Mark Beeman at Northwestern University, USA. They define insight creativity in the following way, 'the ability to reinterpret something by breaking it down into its elements and recombining those elements in a surprising way to achieve some goal.'[2] You will see that their definition of insight creativity resembles rapid eye movement (REM) dreaming processes excepting that, for REM dreaming, the 'something' is past experience and/or knowledge. Also a dream doesn't use all elements but only those that make up the pattern.

Kounios and Beeman suggest the game of Scrabble to contrast insight with non-insight creativity, saying that if you look at the letters 'A-E-H-I-P-N-Y-P' and suddenly realize they can make the word EPIPHANY, this is a creative insight. Whereas if you try possible combinations of the letters in a step-by-step manner until you come across EPIPHANY, you are using a non-insight analytic approach.

In this chapter we explore how dreaming may stimulate insight creativity during wake. In Chapter 9 we saw how insights can happen through dream recall but also noted that creativity is fostered through being in a more dream-like state of mind. This chapter concentrates on how creative people may be in a

What Do Dreams Do? Sue Llewellyn, Oxford University Press (2020). © Oxford University Press.
DOI: 10.1093/oso/9780198818953.001.0001.

state of mind closer to REM dreaming during wake. We all daydream (discussed in Chapter 1) but daydreaming may be more vivid, more absorbing, and last longer in creative people. Insight creativity can produce something new, imaginative, or innovative, which makes us look at the world, or act within the world, differently.

The Shock (and Pleasure) of the New (and Unreal)

The critic Robert Hughes wrote about the impact of modern art in *The Shock of the New*.[3] But the new is not just surprising or shocking, it's also absorbing, interesting, and pleasurable, particularly when it's *not* real. We all enjoy viewing (through films), hearing (through stories we tell each other), and reading (through books) unusual and dramatic experiences rather than boring everyday events. Imaginary worlds are much more enchanting than real ones. The English film director and producer Alfred Hitchcock once said 'What is drama but life with the dull bits cut out.' We love drama. In his book *How Pleasure Works*, the Canadian-American psychologist Paul Bloom points out that the average American devotes most of their leisure time to imaginary worlds—books, movies, television. and video games along with daydreaming and fantasizing; more time is given to consuming fiction, the unreal, than real-life eating, sexual activities, socializing, playing sports, or just relaxing.[4] Why?

Does the explanation for our deep-seated devotion to the unreal derive from the evolutionary importance of unreal dreams for our survival? I think it does. Our lives depended on believing in patterns—which hadn't actually happened— during REM dreaming. In a dream you never question the reality of the unfolding events—even if they're impossible. Likewise, when reading fiction or viewing a movie, the best ones make you forget it's just a story and stop thinking about your everyday concerns, you are immersed in the narrative. Likewise dreams are single-minded[5]—as we move through the dream world we don't get diverted, we never think other things, like did I lock the front door when I left this morning, or I wonder if Tom is having a good holiday?

Across evolutionary time, we had to be convinced by (and absorbed in) our dream narratives because avoiding predators or competitors and meeting mates depended on detecting and remembering patterns in their movements. Once remembered, we accepted these patterns as true, unless new events in the world led to an update—as explained in Chapter 5.

As discussed earlier, narratives are the brain's way of organizing experiences in both wake and dreaming. Also a visual narrative that associates individual experiential elements is much easier to remember than the separate individual items. The drama of dreams also emerges through serial, narrative construction. Once engaged by an ongoing narrative, we long to know what happens next.

The lives of early humans must have been much more dramatic, dangerous, and thrilling than contemporary existence. But, on many days, there would have been no distant glimpse of a predator on approach to the waterhole, no fight with a competitor, and no meeting with a mate—just a quick drink, a watchful walk around, and on to the blackberry bush. When the day was eventful and worth remembering, perhaps because of a meeting with a mate, only the 'meeting the mate-related' elements would have been retained. The usual quick drink and watchful walk around were left out—they weren't relevant to the pattern of experiential elements that predicted when mates were likely to be at the waterhole. Any events that were associated with *all* waterhole visits were habitual and mundane. We leave the dull associations out of REM dreams. To prevent our stories being boring, we do this too in wake when we relate our experiences to friends, pen a novel for a wider audience, or even tell a joke. Jokes work when you get them: the surprise or shock when what you thought the story was about—the obvious—is subverted as the non-obvious breaks through and makes you laugh.[6]

As discussed in Chapter 3, during REM dreaming your mind/brain is primed to detect associations between things that don't always go together but only sometimes do. Clearly there wasn't always a lion at the waterhole, but sometimes one was sitting, waiting in the undergrowth. Key to survival for early humans was detecting the pattern that predicted the likelihood of a lion at the waterhole. These associations went like this: lion at the waterhole–night; lion at the waterhole–thirsty; lion at the waterhole–length of time since last kill; lion at the waterhole–day–dry season; lion at the waterhole–no elephants; lion at the waterhole–suckling cubs. The reason we worry about not getting jokes—not anticipating the punchline— may be rooted in the ancient fear of not spotting non-obvious associations.

You may object that lion at the waterhole–thirsty is an obvious association but the key issue is: it wouldn't have been easily detected by early humans. Lions will drink water daily, if available, but can go 4–5 days without water through absorbing moisture from the stomach contents of prey. So the best visual indicator of lion thirstiness is length of time since last drink and/or prey kill. Clearly, this wouldn't have been easy to observe, or infer, which is why non-obvious associations are creative—not everyone can work them out.

Many of these associations are cumulative vis-à-vis prediction. For example, the chances of a lioness at the waterhole during the day increase with thirstiness, the length of time since the last kill, the absence of elephants, and the existence of suckling cubs. So an early human may have dreamt of a hungry, thirsty lioness at the waterhole, suckling cubs, with elephants on the far horizon. REM dreams embed multiple, rather than binary, associations; they are also fictional in the sense that there never was a hungry, thirsty lioness at the waterhole, suckling cubs with elephants on the far horizon. These associations are all relevant to working out when lions will be at the waterhole but, as mentioned earlier, a lioness would never suckle her cubs at the waterhole because it would be too dangerous.

Chapter 4 noted that, across evolutionary time, throughout the 2.5 million years when we lived as animals, we retained dream insights into non-obvious patterns in experiences unconsciously. On approach to a waterhole where a predator may be lurking, there wasn't time to think; instant action was key to survival. Unconscious retention of dream images enabled vitally important fast responses. Few dreams are consciously recalled. But if most dreams never reach consciousness how can we, as a society, benefit from their creativity?

Creative Dream Insights and Secondary Consciousness

Chapter 4 argues that consciousness evolved during times of relative safety, arche-typically, when walking along the pathways between landmark junctions. It also distinguished between primary and secondary consciousness. The famous dreams described in Chapter 9 were recalled in the transitional zone between dreaming and wake when the mind/brain is still in a dream-like state but will soon regain wake-like secondary consciousness. Without secondary consciousness any dream-inspired creative insight, whether painting, poem, or sewing machine cannot be expressed as an artefact, communicated as an idea, or shared with others as a social product. Unconscious retention of dream insights into patterns served us well in the past to deal with immediate personal dangers but, to meet the exigencies of contemporary societies, creative insights must reach secondary consciousness.

But more than this, although dreams are conscious experiences, dreamers only have primary consciousness. There is no secondary awareness. Consequently, while dreaming the dreamer cannot know if the pattern identified in dreams is a creative insight that can translate into an artefact or an idea that will be socially useful. The hallmark of a creative insight in wake is the so-called Aha! moment—the sudden realization of a breakthrough idea or solution.[7] But when Elias Howe dreamt of cannibals forcing him back into the pot using spears with holes in their tips, he couldn't think during the dream: 'Aha!, this gives me insight into my problem over automating sewing!' Only dream recall into waking consciousness, with its associated secondary awareness, can trigger an Aha! moment.

As one might expect from the celebrated dreams reported in the Chapter 9, cre-ative people have better dream recall than less creative ones.[8] Creative traits, such as absorption, imagination, and fantasy are positively linked to dream recall.[9] Also recalling dreams through keeping a dream diary improves scores on a test of cre-ativity,[10] so the relationship between dream recall and creativity is bidirectional. Nevertheless, content analysis of dreams generally uncovers only personally rele-vant associations between experiences rather than socially beneficial creative in-sights, as the illustrative dreams in this book show. This is what we would expect, given my proposal that dreams derive from the elements of personal experiences that, across evolutionary time, predicted the presence of a predator, competitor, or mate at a landmark junction. But a dream-like state of mind/brain during wake may engender a creative insight that results in an artistic artefact or solves a socially relevant issue.

Several studies link dreaming and creativity: first, brain imaging and dream reports show that dreaming is an intensified form of the mind-wandering that enables creativity during wake[11]; second, the reported impact of dreams on behaviour in wake (e.g. on relationships, decision making, and planning for the future) correlates with creativity; and, third, when subjects were asked to report complex problems and dreams related to them, two-thirds had dreams that creatively addressed their problem and one-third had dreams that offered a solution. In this study independent judges rated only a few less dreams as addressing or offering solutions to problems than the dreamers themselves.[12]

The next section explores how a more dream-like state of mind during wake may engender creative insights.

Creative Insights in Wake

Do creative insights in wake derive from a dream-like state of mind/brain? You will recall the research reported in Chapter 4 showing that during REM we make new associations (i.e. ones we hadn't made during wake), which we retain unconsciously. Creative people often report that their associative insights arise suddenly from their unconscious minds while awake, but in a relaxed, dreamy state of mind.[13] An oft-cited instance is that of ancient Greek mathematician and philosopher, Archimedes. This is how the story goes.

The reputed tyrant, King Hieron of Syracuse (at the time a Greek colony) suspected his goldsmith of cheating him by making a golden crown that actually contained silver. He passed the problem to Archimedes to solve, who felt under some pressure to find an answer. Gold weighs more than silver. Archimedes reasoned that a golden crown with some silver would have to be of greater volume to reach the same weight as one of pure gold. But, at that time in ancient Greece, it wasn't known how to measure the volume of an irregular object like a crown. Archimedes had been pondering this for some time, as he tried to solve Hieron's problem.

Then he visited the public baths. While relaxing in the water he noticed the further he sank into the bath, the more water his body displaced. He unconsciously associated the bath experience with the problem of measuring the volume of an irregular object. The result was that he suddenly and consciously realized the solution: water displacement. If the crown was adulterated with silver it would displace more water than the same weight of pure gold. As the story goes, Archimedes was so elated by his insight he jumped from the bath and ran naked around Syracuse, shouting 'Eureka!'—another epithet for the Aha! moment.

Archimedes wasn't dreaming when in the bath but more than likely he was in a restful state of mind, probably even daydreaming. During wake, creative insights are more likely to arise when people aren't consciously thinking of the issue or problem; instead they are engaged in relaxed activities like bathing or showering or undemanding tasks that engender mind-wandering.[14] On the other hand, Archimedes had been pondering the problem of working out if the golden crown (an irregular object) had been adulterated with silver for some time. He had made some progress but became stuck on how to measure the volume of an irregular object. In the Archimedes case, sensory input (the bathing experience) triggered the associations between water displacement, his body as an irregular object, and the volume of the golden crown adulterated with silver. Similarly at the archetypal waterhole it would be sensory input (a flash of yellow in the undergrowth) that activates an unconscious pattern that predicts the likelihood of this flash being a liena. But at the waterhole the pattern remains unconscious, whereas Archimedes had a conscious insight. Why? I think it's because Archimedes was a creative person whose state of mind in wake was more dream-like than a non-creative person but he had sufficient wake-like secondary consciousness to realize he had solved his problem of how to measure the volume of an irregular object, like a crown.

In his 1926 book *The Art of Thought*,[15] Graham Wallas, a social psychologist, outlined four stages to the creative process during wake. I will map these stages on to the Archimedes example. Wallas' first stage, *preparation*, equates to Archimedes' initial conscious analysis of the complex problem of discerning the volume of an irregular object like a golden crown. Archimedes already knew that gold weighs more than silver so he had used logical, sequential, step-by-step reasoning to work out that a golden crown adulterated with silver must have a greater volume than a pure gold one of the same weight. The second stage is *incubation, a* period of unconscious, associational activity. Several nexuses of unconscious associations may be formed before one nexus makes associations that appear to solve the problem. In Archimedes' case the associational nexus must have been something like: bathing displaces water–the water displaced equals the volume of the body in the water–the body is an irregular object–the golden crown is an irregular object–if the golden crown is submerged, the water displaced will be equal to its volume. The non-obvious association here is between bathing and the adulterated golden crown. These two phenomena seem unrelated until Archimedes associates his body and the golden crown—they are both irregular objects. The third stage of the creative process is the *sudden conscious insight* of the solution, when Archimedes jumped from the bath with such abandon that he forgot his nakedness and ran around Syracuse shouting 'Eureka!' or 'I have found it'. Wallas's fourth stage is *verification*—another conscious process that can only happen during wake. Archimedes would have tested his insight through checking that a pure golden crown would displace less water than one of the same weight that was tainted with silver.

Only one of four stages, incubation, is unconscious. To what extent is unconscious incubation during wake similar to REM dreaming? You will recall from Chapter 4 that dream construction is thought to be unconscious, although the subsequent constructed dream is conscious. Several studies indicate that incubation involves an unconscious period of spreading neural activation to construct non-obvious, remote associations among memory (or knowledge) elements; as already mentioned, this kind of diffuse neural activation is thought to precede creative insights in wake.[16] The mind/brain generates spreading neural activation to make non-obvious, remote associations among memory elements more readily during REM sleep than either in wake or non-rapid eye movement (NREM) sleep.[17] Consequently, being in a dreamy state of mind during wake would enable creativity—through unconscious incubation (similar to unconscious dream construction) followed by a conscious, creative insight (similar to a conscious dream scene).

At the same time, dreamy wake is a somewhat different state of mind from REM dreaming. In dreamy wake, as opposed to REM dreaming proper, any creative insights can be recognized through secondary consciousness. As discussed earlier, the lack of secondary consciousness in REM dreaming means that creative insights can't be identified as such, so Aha! or Eureka! moments don't occur.

A research team led by Kounios and Beeman demonstrated the brain processes that accompany Aha! moments in wake. After a period during which the brain makes unconscious, non-obvious associations between problem elements, there is a sudden burst of brainwaves at gamma frequency beginning 0.3 seconds before a creative insight reaches consciousness and an Aha! moment happens.[18] You will recall from Chapter 1 that brainwaves occur across a continuous spectrum of different frequencies. Gamma brainwaves are the fastest; they spike (or fire) to bind (or associate) neurons. Commenting on gamma waves and Aha! moments, Kounios and Beeman said:

> Gamma activity indicates a constellation of neurons binding together for the first time in the brain to create a new neural network pathway. This is the creation of a new idea. Immediately following that gamma spike, the new idea pops into our consciousness, which we identify as the Aha! moment.[19]

These sudden bursts of gamma activity are observed more frequently in REM sleep than during wake[20]—another indication that REM sleep is our most creative state of mind. Consequently, shifting to a mind/brain state more similar to REM sleep/ dreaming while awake would enable creative insights to reach consciousness and so boost Aha! moments.

How Could Creatives Be in a More Enduring
Dreamy State During Wake?

But how can you be in state of mind more like REM sleep while awake? We tend to think of our wake, sleep, and dream states as distinct and discrete. When in one state, we assume we can't also be in another. But this assumption isn't quite right. You will recall from Chapter 1 that when not engaged in some pressing task we all frequently daydream. As its name suggests, the daydreaming state of mind/brain resembles dreaming.[21] We are all more creative while daydreaming! Also, while REM dreaming some people can become lucid—a state that is more like the mind/brain in wake. In normal or 'neurotypical' people daydreaming and lucidity are transient states, but creatives may be in a more enduring, de-differentiated state where the boundaries between REM dreaming and the wake state become permeable. Creatives may be so because they are in a more REM dream-like state during most of their waking hours.

At the level of the brain, what's going on if you are in a more REM dream-like state during wake? Well, REM dreaming and wake are different states because of two brain processes. The first is chemical. You will recall from Chapter 1 that brain cells (neurons) communicate with each other through chemical messengers (or, more formally, neurotransmitters) that can bridge the tiny gap between neurons. These chemical neurotransmitters move in the intercellular fluid between one neuron and another to transfer information, but they also impact on what your brain does with the information. During wake your brain state is mediated by two neurotransmitters (among others), serotonin and noradrenaline, but in REM sleep/dreaming these two neurotransmitters are more or less shut off. One linked result is that the brain region responsible for logical reasoning (the lateral, prefrontal cortex) is deactivated. Without these two neurotransmitters and the lateral, prefrontal cortex the mind/brain cannot control its thoughts, engage in step-by-step, analytical reasoning, and remember what is happening from minute to minute.[22] These changes sound like big losses. They are, but there are gains too. For a difficult insight task 82% of patients with damage to the lateral prefrontal cortex solved the task, whereas only 43% of normal participants did so, showing that although prefrontal areas are crucial for step-by-step, logical reasoning, they actually hinder difficult, creative insights. When the mind/brain changes its state from wake to REM dreaming, it becomes better at creative insight tasks while worse at logical ones.

Another important neurotransmitter, acetylcholine, which is crucial for learning and memory, is present during both wake and REM sleep. In the absence of serotonin and noradrenaline, the power of acetylcholine is enhanced. It goes into overdrive. During REM dreams we cannot remember what is happening from minute to minute but we have better access to remote memories. In short, the loss of serotonin and noradrenaline, along with the heightened power of acetylcholine puts the mind/brain in a hyperassociative, rather than a linear-logical mode, when processing memories. Also without serotonin, noradrenaline, and the prefrontal cortex, our dreaming narratives, based on associating memory elements, are freed from logical constraints. We can dream of impossibilities, like flying or lienas. Finally we suspect that dopamine (another neurotransmitter that occurs during both REM sleep and wake) takes a different pathway through the brain in the two different states: instead of taking a main route through the cortex, it courses freely through the limbic system.[23] You will recall the limbic system from Chapter 6: it's the brain's emotional centre. While the prefrontal cortex is the rational, step-by-step, thinking centre. The upshot of dopamine mainly flowing through the limbic system, rather than the prefrontal cortex, is that the mind/brain becomes much more instinctive, prone to emotional storms, and much less realistic in making choices about what to do and who to do it with. With dopamine flooding your limbic systems you believe you can scale high mountains, dance until dawn, or sleep with your favourite movie star!

A second brain process, aside from brain chemistry, which makes wake and REM sleep/dreaming unalike is input–output 'gating'. For example, before going to sleep but while awake in bed, your sensory gates are still open, you can see your bedroom, hear any sounds from your house, feel the bed sheets on your body, taste that lingering late-night curry, and smell your bed partner.) In contrast, your sensory gates are closed during REM dreaming. Instead the mind/brain turns inwards to memories, specifically to associate elements of different experiences.

But, during sleep, this gating isn't absolute. If a loud, unexpected noise occurs in your house (a burglar?), this will probably wake you up. Alternatively, if your bladder is getting full you may dream of looking for a lavatory. Along with the gating of external input, output is also blocked during REM dreaming. As discussed in Chapter 1, movement is ubiquitous during REM dreaming. Your brain generates these movements and you feel you are moving, but you don't move because your muscles are paralysed. The output from the movements made in REM dreaming is *gated*.

But knowing the differences between REM dreaming and wake doesn't explain how these states could become 'mixed-up', 'in-between', or de-differentiated—for this we turn to chaos theory.

Brain States, Chaos Theory, and Creativity

There is no central controller in the brain to dictate its state. Rather, like an ant colony or the solar system, brain states are self-organized and driven by chaos. But this 'chaos' doesn't mean brain states are completely disorderly and unpredictable. Indeed, although a lay person may think of dreams as disorderly and unpredictable, chaos theory indicates that dreams disclose underlying patterns.[24]

In the language of chaos theory, the human brain is poised at the 'edge of chaos', i.e. unstable on the border between order and disorder.[25] We are accustomed to thinking that systems need to reach an orderly equilibrium. Within this mind-set, an edge of chaos positioning sounds precarious, even hazardous, but it's actually optimal for information processing in all complex, adaptive systems including, of course, the brain.

The brain is not unusual in balancing order and disorder to optimize its performance. Across other complex and adaptive systems in both the natural and social worlds, 'in-betweenness' is advantageous:

> Nothing novel can emerge from systems with high degrees of order and stability—for example, crystals, incestuous communities, or regulated industries. On the other hand, complete chaotic systems, such as stampedes, riots, rage, or the early year of the French Revolution, are too formless to coalesce. Generative complexity takes place in the boundary between regularity and randomness.[26]

Too much order stops anything new, novel and creative arising in a system. On the other hand, excessive disorder disrupts normal, everyday operations. Being on 'the edge of chaos' is best.

This 'edge' of chaos metaphor is misleading in one sense, however, because the edge is understood better as a transitional zone. Being within this transitional zone is called self-organized criticality. What have chaos theory and self-organized criticality got to do with creativity? Well, within this zone in-between order and disorder, brain states are more creative when they lean towards the disorderly, whereas brain states are more constrained when they tend more towards order. A rigid separation between dreaming and wake results in constrained order. Some intermingling enables creativity, but a breakdown of the differentiation between wake and dreaming brings disorder.[27] Creative people who tend towards disorder are at super-criticality. This results in maximum information processing because more neurons are recruited across a wider and longer network. In this supercritical state, activation spreads throughout the network; the danger is that the network is overwhelmed. Whereas, in constrained order, the activation dies out quickly; if the environment is dynamic, the danger is that the individual fails to react and adapt.

You will recall from earlier in this chapter that you have more creative insights when daydreaming, which is a state in-between dreaming and wake. But for neurotypical people, daydreaming is transient. Whereas, I propose, for creatives, a dreamy in-between state is more enduring. How can we understand creative dreaminess in wake in terms of chaos theory?

A key concept in chaos theory is the phase transition. For any complex adaptive system, including the brain, a phase transition occurs when the system shifts from one position to another. Creative people at super-criticality will make more phase transitions. This is equivalent to saying that creatives will have more Aha! moments because such insights are a manifestation of discontinuity and phase transition in the brain. Before an Aha! moment there is chaotic exploration of memories in a search for non-obvious associations. After an Aha! moment, a chaotic process integrates the new associations and modifies thinking, so the mind/brain shifts position.

Relatedly, how does chaos theory relate to the mechanisms (neurotransmitter systems and input–output gating) that control the differentiation between dreaming and wake? Brain states arise out of many spontaneous local interactions. For example, as described above, the differences between wake and dreaming depend on neurotransmitter systems and input–output gating. In any chaotic system, small changes (here, neurotransmitters and input–output gating) can have far-reaching and substantial impact. The large impact of small events in complex adaptive systems is commonly known as the 'butterfly effect'. This concept overturned the conventional wisdom that small events can only have a small impact and, relatedly, it takes big events to bring about big consequences.[28] The butterfly effect means a small disruption to the interacting effects of the different neurotransmitter systems (outlined in the previous section) can have a big impact. In this case, producing a dreamy state in-between wake and dreaming. But what would cause a small disruption to the interacting effects of neurotransmitters?

You will recall from Chapter 1 that there are tiny gaps between neurons (brain cells). To communicate across these tiny gaps (called synapses) electrical messages, called action potentials, which can only propagate within the neuron, are replaced by chemical messages. These chemical messages are 'carried' in small sacs (or vesicles) that store neurotransmitters. When an action potential reaches and excites the cell membrane, neurotransmitters are released from the neuron, which initiates the communication (the presynaptic neuron). Having travelled across the synapse, the neurotransmitters dock at receptor sites in the neuron that is receiving the message (the postsynaptic neuron). Different neurotransmitters have different receptors in the postsynaptic neuron. Neurotransmitters act like keys, with receptor sites acting like gates with locks. The right key is needed to open the right lock. If the neurotransmitter is the right key for the lock in the gate, it can transmit the message and an action potential travels across the receiving, postsynaptic neuron. The chemical messaging process is called neurotransmission. For a guide to neurotransmission, see YouTube.[29] Figure 10.1 shows a simplified version of neurotransmission.

But where is the message coming from? During dreaming, input–output gating ensures the message content is almost totally from memories of experiences. In contrast, during wake, the gates are open for sensory input from the external world. Indeed, while you are awake, except during daydreaming, the external world usually has priority over the internal one. Neurotransmission is also involved in

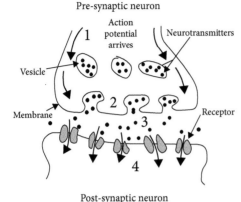

Figure 10.1 Neurotransmission across the synapse.

Adapted from "The Synapse", under a CC BY-SA 3.0 license. Available at: https://www.khanacademy.org/science/biology/human-biology/neuron-nervous-system/a/the-synapse

input–output gating. In the external world, gates are always at a boundary. This is also the case when transmitting messages between brain cells. All neurons have a membrane boundary at which there are gates with locks for neurotransmission.

The integrity of neuronal cell membranes is essential to neurotransmission and so is crucial for both the process of messaging and whether the message comes from the external world, the internal world, or combines input from both. Neuronal cell membranes are themselves poised at the edge of chaos in-between solid and liquid states.[30] This particular in-betweenness enables effective neurotransmission. I don't suppose you have thought too much about the integrity of your neuronal cell membranes but you should because they are crucial to the effectiveness of your brain states. A host of factors determines their integrity, some of which are genetic and so outside of your control but others are environmental, like diet, and so within your control.

Small changes in the solid–liquid composition of neuronal cell membranes can have positive or negative effects on your mind/brain states. Specifically, and in line with chaos theory, a small change can have substantial impact on neuromodulation (the impact of the neurotransmitters, serotonin, noradrenaline, acetylcholine, and dopamine that control the distinctiveness of dreaming and wake) and, hence, result in some de-differentiation between dreaming and wake. As discussed above, in terms of the changes in neuromodulation, de-differentiation to an in-between state during wake would involve some loss of serotonin and noradrenaline, along with an increase in the power of acetylcholine and more dopamine flooding into the limbic system. This would put the mind/brain into a more instinctive, more emotional, more associative, and less linear-logical mode during wake. Also, with gates to the outside world partially closed and neuromodulation shifting towards a more REM dream-like state, the mind/brain would turn inward to associate memories in a narrative, sometimes incorporating bizarre, even impossible characters and events. Chapter 9 mentioned how Mary Shelley and Coleridge were in a more dream-like state when creating *Frankenstein* and *Kubla Khan*. We now turn to the work of a contemporary writer.

Creative Writing and Writers

In 2016 the English writer Ian McEwan published *Nutshell,* a book in which the narrator is a foetus who listens to his mother and uncle plotting to kill his father. The *Washington Post's* book critic described it as a 'preposterously weird little novel'. MacEwan spoke about his family's involvement in *Nutshell's* genesis in a *Times* interview, 'She [McEwan's daughter-in-law] was very advanced in her third trimester and talking about the baby all the time. We were aware that if it was a fully conscious being that it would be hearing all these conversations.' At the time of his daughter-in law's pregnancy he was rereading *Hamlet,* 'I periodically dip back into Shakespeare plays and Hamlet was on my mind at the same time, so at some point they [the foetus and Hamlet] fused.'

Being in a state in-between dreaming and wake may have driven McEwan to creatively associate (to fuse, in his words) his thinking about what a foetus may overhear with his knowledge of *Hamlet*. Hamlet's uncle has killed his father and married his mother. But why connect *Hamlet* and the foetus? What is the non-obvious association? McEwan says, 'The lack of agency, Hamlet's inability to act was the joining point'. Clearly, a foetus cannot intervene in the course of events. Similarly, indecision paralyses Hamlet as he contemplates killing his uncle. In another interview with *The Guardian* McEwan says the first line of *Nutshell* came to him as it from nowhere, 'Suddenly there appeared before me the opening sentence of the novel, which I don't think I've changed, apart from adding "So" in front of it: "So, here I am upside down in a woman." ' We've discussed the suddenness of creative insights earlier in this chapter in relation to Archimedes and science. In this case the insight was the first line of a narrative, which McEwan saw before him. Both prose and poetry conjure up (and are conjured up by) visual worlds.

Poems, as compared to prose, are, arguably, even closer to dreams in being hyperassociative—in the sense of driven purely through associations (from knowledge or personal experience). In W. H. Auden's poem, *Musée des Beaux Arts,* the second stanza is associated with a painting that, in Auden's time, was thought to be by Pieter Brueghel the Elder: *Landscape with the Fall of Icarus*.[31] Seeing this Old Master was an aspect of Auden's experience. He had visited the Musées Royaux des

Beaux-Arts de Belgique while staying with Christopher Isherwood in Brussels in December 1938. In the second verse, Auden writes:

> *In Breughel's Icarus, for instance: how everything turns away*
> *Quite leisurely from the disaster; the ploughman may*
> *Have heard the splash, the forsaken cry,*
> *But for him it was not an important failure; the sun shone*
> *As it had to on the white legs disappearing into the green*
> *Water, and the expensive delicate ship that must have seen*
> *Something amazing, a boy falling out of the sky,*
> *Had somewhere to get to and sailed calmly on.*

But art historians and Auden scholars now think the first stanza is also associated with other Bruegel paintings. In poems, like dreams, associations often require detection and are always open to revision, extension, and debate. Auden writes:

> *About suffering they were never wrong,*
> *The old Masters: how well they understood*
> *Its human position: how it takes place*
> *While someone else is eating or opening a window or just walking dully along;*
> *How, when the aged are reverently, passionately waiting*
> *For the miraculous birth, there always must be*
> *Children who did not specially want it to happen, skating*
> *On a pond at the edge of the wood:*
> *They never forgot*
> *That even the dreadful martyrdom must run its course*
> *Anyhow in a corner, some untidy spot*
> *Where the dogs go on with their doggy life and the torturer's horse*
> *Scratches its innocent behind on a tree.*

The Numbering (Census) at Bethlehem and *The Massacre of the Innocents* are works by Pieter Brueghel the Elder, which Auden would have seen in the same place as *Landscape with the Fall of Icarus*—the Musées Royaux des Beaux-Arts de Belgique.[32] Some of the adult figures in *The Numbering (Census) at Bethlehem* are thought to be depicted by Auden as 'someone else … eating or opening a window or just walking dully/along'. The painting also shows children 'On a pond at the edge of the wood'.[33]

The Massacre of the Innocents portrays the scene in Bethlehem after Herod's order to slaughter Jewish boys—on being told that a King would be born to the Jews. This introduces the martyrdom theme, prominent in Auden's poem, because the slain boys are traditionally considered the first of the Christian martyrs. Early Christians saw Jesus as the first and greatest martyr. His miraculous birth is anticipated in *The Numbering (Census) at Bethlehem* through the depiction of Mary and Joseph arriving for the census. Auden's enigmatic words 'Children who did not specially want it [the miraculous birth] to happen' are thought to refer to the associated massacre of the innocents. The eponymous painting also depicts five dogs pursuing their lives and a torturer's horse next to a tree.

Like dreams, poems feature strange juxtapositions, often have a timeless quality, and are frequently discontinuous. In *Musée des Beaux Arts*, people are just walking dully along and, then, immediately following this, the aged are passionately awaiting the miraculous birth. Although the poem is written, the associations Auden makes are visual—from Brueghel's paintings and, presumably, other related visual memories. Like dreams, poetic associations are based on personal experience and knowledge. Although, in the poem, this knowledge is often cultural (e.g. Auden knows Brueghel is an Old Master). Cultural awareness is much rarer in dreams than poems.

Maurice Halbwachs (1877–1945), a major figure in the history of sociology, remarked on how 'In dreams the mind is most removed from culture and society'.[34] This absence may reflect the origins of dreams in instinct and individual experience. On the other hand, art, like a REM dream, is deeply emotional. Hannah Ryggen, the Swedish textile artist, points out that 'Art is just a summarization of something one has felt with great intensity'. [35] The non-obvious emotional association in Auden's poem is between human suffering and its banal setting, reflecting the indifference of many to the fate of their fellows. Like McEwan's prose, Auden's poetry may be driven by an enduring state of mind/brain where the boundaries between dreaming and wake become more permeable, resulting in wake taking on some (but not all) of the characteristics of dreaming. Chapter 5 emphasizes that REM dreaming encodes memories through association. If creative writers like McEwan and Auden are in a de-differentiated state, in-between dreaming and wake, one way to think about their writing is the encoding of their memories during wake.

An Enduring Dreamy Condition During Wake is an In-between, Hybrid State

An enduring dreamy state of mind during wake must take a hybrid form, i.e. creative people are in a state of mind *in-between* wake and REM dreaming. Creatives are not actually REM dreaming during wake or, at any rate, only transitorily.

Chapter 4 looked at how the brain networks of early humans represented the tours they undertook to gather food. As we noted earlier, over time these experiences would have engendered the conscious, step-by-step, linear logic of walking along pathways, along with the unconscious, fast, creative associativity needed to spot experiential patterns at landmark junctions. To turn a creative insight into a creative product, in either science or the arts, unconscious insights must become conscious. I argue this happens through some de-differentiation of dreaming and wake to produce a hybrid form in the manner described above. Is this interpenetration apparent in creative people?

Chapter 1 pointed out that the large-scale default brain network operates when people are daydreaming and their minds wander; REM dreaming is an intensified form of this default-daydreaming network. Usually, if a demanding task comes along, the default network is suppressed by the executive or task-positive network required for cognitive control, focus, and concentration, i.e. these networks do not usually operate together, they are differentiated. But in creative people, the default and executive networks do work together, along with the salience network, which is needed for the identification of personally relevant stimuli.[36] Joint working of the default and salience networks would enable the generation of creative insights from personally relevant stimuli. These creative insights would be consciously recognized, evaluated, and disseminated through the executive network. Such joint working may also indicate the de-differentiation of dreaming and wake in creative people because the default and executive networks are differentiated in neurotypicals.

Also, when tested in wake, creative people can come up with many, both near and remote, associations with a stimulus. In contrast, less creative individuals can only think of more obvious associations and then dry up.[37] For example, when given the word 'table' and asked for associations, creatives may say 'chair' but also offer more remote associations like 'cloth', 'altar', 'food', and 'offering', whereas, less creative individuals will be likely to say 'chair' and then be unable to think of more remote associations. During REM dreaming we make more remote rather than more obvious associations. Some de-differentiation of dreaming and wake would result in more obvious *and* more remote associations, as is observed in creative people.

Linked to an ability to make more remote, novel associations, is the concept of 'leaky' sensory gating where a broader range of phenomena (including ones that look, initially, to be irrelevant) are considered for synthesis in relation to an issue or problem. Creative people exhibit this leaky sensory gating.[38] 'Lateral' thinking and 'thinking outside the box' are related popular ideas, promulgated in the 1960s and 1970s. If the dreaming state of mind partly invades wake, then attention would take on a wider horizon and things that initially appeared to be disparate may be associated.

Dreaming is, quintessentially, visual. Mental imagery is the only sense that readily integrates things that are only remotely associated, like a lion and a hyena. I can't hear, taste, touch, or smell a liena, but I can easily visualize one. If wake became more dream-like, more mental imagery would be expected. Mental imagery is crucial for creativity—as is pattern recognition. The food-gathering tours undertaken by pre-linguistic early humans would have relied on mental imagery, pattern recognition, and spatial ability. These abilities are thought to be related in creativity.[39] Visuospatial ability is a good predictor of outstanding achievement in science, technology, mathematics, and engineering.[40] Any de-differentiation of dreaming and wake would be expected to increase mental imagery, enhance pattern recognition, and boost visuospatial ability.

Finally, during REM dreaming we are in bed and cannot move. De-differentiation of dreaming and wake may promote a capacity for sustained, relatively immobile study. Many creative individuals preferred to write in bed. Proust, who stayed in bed for a decade to write *In Search of Lost Time* is the most famous example, but George Orwell, Winston Churchill, Edith Wharton, Colette and Mark Twain all wrote in bed.[41]

Briefly...

We are all more creative in our dreams but not all of us are outstandingly creative during wake. I argue sudden creative insights, as opposed to creativity after deliberate, incremental, linear-logical, analytic reasoning over a period of time, emerge either from dream recall in the carry-over, transitional state between REM dreaming and wake or from being in an enduring state of mind closer to REM dreaming during wake. This in-between state of mind/brain merges the primary, instinctive, emotional awareness of dreaming with the reflective, secondary consciousness of wake. Both the neurobiological brain basis of this in-between state and its associated mindfulness can be explained through neuromodulation and input–output gating. Being in a zone in-between order and disorder optimizes mind/brain function. Mind/brain states become more creative towards the disorderly realm, whereas mind/brain states are more constrained towards the orderliness sphere. A rigid separation between dreaming and wake produces constrained order. Some intermingling enables creative insights, but if the differentiation between wake and dreaming breaks down, the result is disorder. Creative people are in a supercritical state so they are more prone to disorder.

Next

The next chapter addresses the question of what disorder means in the minds/ brains of creative people. While I have proposed that a degree of de-differentiation enables creative insights in wake, in a more progressive and enduring form it may also engender various psychopathologies. Chapter 11 sets out my proposal, which is: we aren't crazy in our dreams. We are identifying non-obvious associations between past experiences. But creativity, craziness, or both can result if wake, sleep, and dreaming get 'mixed up'—dependent on the extent of the de-differentiation between the states.

Notes

1. Baird, B., Smallwood, J., Mrazek, M. D., Kam, J. W., Franklin, M. S., & Schooler, J. W. (2012). Inspired by distraction mind wandering facilitates creative incubation. *Psychological Science*, *23*(10), 1117–1122. 0956797612446024; Dijksterhuis, A., & Meurs, T. (2006). Where creativity resides: the generative power of unconscious thought. *Consciousness and Cognition*, *15*(1), 135–146, Dijksterhuis, A., & Nordgren, L. F. (2006). A theory of unconscious thought. *Perspectives on Psychological Science*, *1*(2), 95–109; Ritter, S. M., & Dijksterhuis, A. (2014). Creativity—the unconscious foundations of the incubation period. *Frontiers in Human Neuroscience*, *8*, 215; and Yaniv, I., & Meyer, D. E. (1987). Activation and metacognition of inaccessible stored information: potential bases for incubation effects in problem solving. *Journal of Experimental Psychology: Learning, Memory, and Cognition*, *13*(2), 187.
2. See pp. 9–10 in Kounios, J., & Beeman, M. (2015). *The Eureka Factor: Creative Insights and the Brain*. Heinemann: London.
3. Hughes, R. (1980). *The Shock of the New: Art and the Century of Change*. British Broadcasting Corporation London.
4. See pp. 155–156 in Bloom, P. (2011). *How Pleasure Works*. Vintage Books, London.
5. Rechtschaffen, A. (1978). The single-mindedness and isolation of dreams. *Sleep*, *1*, 97–109.
6. Erdelyi, M. H. (2013). Beware of being captured by an analogy: dreams are like many things. *Behavioral and Brain Sciences*, *36*(6), 617.
7. Kounios, J., & Beeman, M. (2009). The Aha! moment: the cognitive neuroscience of insight. *Current Directions in Psychological Science*, *18*(4), 210–216.
8. Schredl, M. (1995). Creativity and dream recall. *The Journal of Creative Behavior*, *29*(1), 16–24; and Brand, S., Beck, J., Kalak, N., Gerber, M., Kirov, R., Pühse, U., . . . & Holsboer-Trachsler, E. (2011). Dream recall and its relationship to sleep, perceived stress, and creativity among adolescents. *Journal of Adolescent Health*, *49*(5), 525–531.
9. Watson, D. (2003). To dream, perchance to remember: individual differences in dream recall. *Personality and Individual Differences*, *34*(7), 1271–1286.
10. Sierra-Siegert, M., Jay, E. L., Florez, C., & Garcia, A. E. (2019). Minding the dreamer within: an experimental study on the effects of enhanced dream recall on creative thinking. *The Journal of Creative Behavior*, *53*(1), 83–96.
11. Fox, K. C. R., Nijeboer, S., Solomonova, E., Domhoff, G. W., & Christoff, K. (2013). Dreaming as mind wandering: evidence from functional neuroimaging and first-person content reports. *Frontiers in Human Neuroscience*, *7*, 412. doi:10.3389/fnhum.2013.
12. Barrett, D. (2017). Dreams and creative problem-solving. *Annals of the New York Academy of Sciences*, *1406*(1), 64–67.
13. How to stimulate creative breakthroughs: the unconscious and creativity. Available at: https://academyofideas.com/2016/06/stimulating-creativity-unconscious/; Markman, A. (2012). Can you be unconsciously creative? *Psychology Today*. Available

at: https://www.psychologytoday.com/gb/blog/ulterior-motives/201210/can-you-be-unconsciously-creative; and Andreasen, N. C. (2011). A journey into chaos: creativity and the unconscious. *Mens Sana Monographs*, 9(1), 42.

14. Pinola, M. (2013). Science explains why our best ideas come in the shower. Available at: https://lifehacker.com/5987858/5987858/the-science-behind-creative-ideas.; and Baird, B., Smallwood, J., Mrazek, M. D., Kam, J. W., Franklin, M. S., & Schooler, J. W. (2012). Inspired by distraction: mind wandering facilitates creative incubation. *Psychological Science*, 23(10), 1117–1122.

15. Wallas, G. (1926). *The Art of Thought*. Harcourt Brace, San Diego, CA.

16. Baird, B., Smallwood, J., Mrazek, M. D., Kam, J. W., Franklin, M. S., & Schooler, J. W. (2012). Inspired by distraction mind wandering facilitates creative incubation. *Psychological Science*, 23(10), 1117–1122., Dijksterhuis, A., & Meurs, T. (2006). Where creativity resides: the generative power of unconscious thought. *Consciousness and Cognition*, 15(1), 135–146; Dijksterhuis, A., & Nordgren, L. F. (2006). A theory of unconscious thought. *Perspectives on Psychological Science*, 1(2), 95–109. Ritter, S. M., & Dijksterhuis, A. (2014). Creativity—the unconscious foundations of the incubation period. *Frontiers in Human Neuroscience*, 8, 215; and Yaniv, I., & Meyer, D. E. (1987). Activation and metacognition of inaccessible stored information: potential bases for incubation effects in problem solving. *Journal of Experimental Psychology: Learning, Memory, and Cognition*, 13(2), 187.

17. Cai, D. J., Mednick, S. A., Harrison, E. M., Kanady, J. C., & Mednick, S. C. (2009). REM, not incubation, improves creativity by priming associative networks. *Proceedings of the National Academy of Sciences*, 106(25), 10130–10134; Sterpenich, C., Schmidt, G., Albouy, L., Matarazzo, A., Vanhaudenhuyse, P., Boveroux, C., ... & Collette, F. (2014). Memory reactivation during rapid eye movement sleep promotes its generalization and integration in cortical stores. *Sleep*, 37(6), 1061; Stickgold, R., Scott, L., Rittenhouse, C., & Hobson, J. A. (1999). Sleep-induced changes in associative memory. *Journal of Cognitive Neuroscience*, 11(2), 182–193; Walker, M. P., Liston, C., Hobson, J. A., & Stickgold, R. (2002). Cognitive flexibility across the sleep–wake cycle: REM-sleep enhancement of anagram problem solving. *Cognitive Brain Research*, 14(3), 317–324; and Landmann, N., Kuhn, M., Maier, J. G., Spiegelhalder, K., Baglioni, C., Frase, L., ... & Nissen, C. (2015). REM sleep and memory reorganization: potential relevance for psychiatry and psychotherapy. *Neurobiology of Learning and Memory*, 122, 28–40.

18. Jung-Beeman, M., Bowden, E. M., Haberman, J., Frymiare, J. L., Arambel-Liu, S., Greenblatt, R., ... & Kounios, J. (2004). Neural activity when people solve verbal problems with insight. *PLoS Biology*, 2(4), 500–510.

19. Gamma waves and inspiration: How is your brain vibrating? Available at: https://www.theepochtimes.com/gamma-waves-and-inspiration-how-is-your-brain-vibrating_1975608.html

20. Montgomery, S. M., Sirota, A., & Buzsáki, G. (2008). Theta and gamma coordination of hippocampal networks during waking and rapid eye movement sleep. *The Journal of Neuroscience*, 28(26), 6731–6741.

21. Domhoff, G. W., & Fox, K. C. (2015). Dreaming and the default network: a review, synthesis, and counterintuitive research proposal. *Consciousness and Cognition*, 33,

342–353; and Wamsley, E. J., & Stickgold, R. (2010). Dreaming and offline memory processing. *Current Biology*, *20*(23), R1010–R1013.

22. See p. 162 in Hobson, A. (2002). Dreaming: An Introduction to the Science of Sleep. Oxford University Press, Oxford.

23. For more details on how neurotransmission shifts between wake and REM sleep, see chapter 4 in Hobson, A. (2002). *Dreaming: An Introduction to the Science of Sleep*. Oxford University Press, Oxford.; and Llewellyn, S. (2011). If waking and dreaming consciousness became de-differentiated, would schizophrenia result? *Consciousness and Cognition*, *20*(4), 1059–1083.

24. Combs, A., & Krippner, S. (2017). Walter Freeman III and the chaotic nature of dreams. *Nonlinear Dynamics, Psychology, and Life Sciences*, *21*(4), 475–484.

25. Explainer: what is chaos theory. Available at: http://theconversation.com/explainer-what-is-chaos-theory-10620; and Public Library of Science (2009). The human brain is on the edge of chaos. Available at: https://www.sciencedaily.com/releases/2009/03/090319224532.htm

26. See p. 67 in MacIntosh, R., Maclean, D., Griffin, D., & Stacey, R. (2013). *Complexity and Organization: Readings and Conversations*. Routledge, Abingdon.

27. Llewellyn, S. (2011). If waking and dreaming consciousness became de-differentiated, would schizophrenia result? *Consciousness and Cognition*, *20*(4), 1059–1083.

28. The butterfly effect in psychology. Available at: https://www.alleydog.com/glossary/definition.php?term=Butterfly+Effect

29. 2-minute neuroscience: synaptic transmission. Available at: https://www.youtube.com/watch?v=WhowH0kb7n0

30. See p. 51 in Lewin, R. (1993). *Complexity: Life at the Edge of Chaos*. Phoenix, London.

31. At the time of Auden's visit to Musées Royaux des Beaux-Arts de Belgique, the painting *Landscape with the Fall of Icarus* was attributed to Bruegel, but is now generally thought to be an early copy of a lost work.

32. Kinney, A. F. (1963). Auden, Bruegel, and Musée des Beaux Arts. *College English*, *24*(7), 529–531.

33. *Musée des Beaux Arts* (Poem). Available at: https://en.wikipedia.org/wiki/Mus%C3%A9e_des_Beaux_Arts_(poem)

34. See p. 42 in Halbwachs, M. (1992). *On Collective Memory*, L. A. Coser (Ed., transl) University of Chicago Press, Chicago, IL.

35. Hannah Ryggen's political tapestries are subject of Malmö exhibit. Available at: https://www.metropolismag.com/ideas/arts-culture/hannah-ryggens-political-tapestries-subject-malmo-exhibit/

36. Beaty, R. E., Kenett, Y. N., Christensen, A. P., Rosenberg, M. D., Benedek, M., Chen, Q., … & Silvia, P. J. (2018). Robust prediction of individual creative ability from brain functional connectivity. *Proceedings of the National Academy of Sciences*, 201713532.

37. Mednick, M. T., Mednick, S. A., & Jung, C. C. (1964). Continual association as a function of level of creativity and type of verbal stimulus. *The Journal of Abnormal and Social Psychology*, *69*(5), 511; and Mednick, S. (1962). The associative basis of the creative process. *Psychological Review*, *69*(3), 220.

38. Zabelina, D. L., O'Leary, D., Pornpattananangkul, N., Nusslock, R., & Beeman, M. (2015). Creativity and sensory gating indexed by the P50: selective versus leaky sensory gating in divergent thinkers and creative achievers. *Neuropsychologia, 69*, 77–84.

39. See pp. 21–22 in West, T. G. (1991). *In the Mind's Eye: Visual Thinkers, Gifted People with Learning Difficulties, Computer Images, and the Ironies of Creativity.* Prometheus Books, Buffalo, NY.

40. Kell, H. J., Lubinski, D., Benbow, C. P., & Steiger, J. H. (2013). Creativity and technical innovation spatial ability's unique role. *Psychological Science*, 24(9); and Wai, J., Lubinski, D., & Benbow, C. P. (2009). Spatial ability for STEM domains: Aligning over 50 years of cumulative psychological knowledge solidifies its importance. *Journal of Educational Psychology, 101*(4), 817, 1831–1836.

41. McCrum, R. (2011). The advantages of writing in bed. *The Guardian.* Available at: https://www.theguardian.com/books/booksblog/2011/apr/28/writing-in-bed-robert-mccrum

11

Dream to Go Crazy?

Introduction

This chapter has a question mark because I, and others, think dreaming is functional. Also in Chapter 10 I proposed a dream-like state of mind/brain in wake enables creative insights. On the other hand, an association between creativity and craziness is a long-standing idea, think of the saying, 'genius is akin to madness'. Another age-old suggestion is that if dreaming pervades wake, madness may result. Aristotle, Kant, Schopenhauer, Freud, Jung, and Bleuler all suggested this. Even contemporary scientists who think dreaming useful also say it's a model for madness.

Take Allan Hobson and Matt Walker, for example. They say you become routinely psychotic during dreams because you hallucinate (see things which aren't there), are delusional (believe things that are impossible), disoriented (confused about place and time), emotionally unstable (feel extreme ups and downs), and suffer from amnesia (you forget your dream experiences).[1]

I argue, during dreaming, you see things that aren't there because you are looking at a visual pattern in your experience, archetypically, across evolutionary time, elements of past events that predict the likelihood of a predator at the waterhole. During dreaming you believe in this pattern, even if it features impossibilities; for example, a lioness suckling young at the waterhole because the associations are correct. A lioness suckling young is associated with thirst, which is associated with her being at the waterhole. These patterned elements happened at different times so you appear disoriented in time. You appear confused about place because some things relevant to the landmark place happen away from it; for example, a lioness suckling young at home base is relevant to her appearance at the waterhole. You are emotionally unstable because you are dreaming about things that evoke extreme fear or strong elation; archetypically, avoiding predators/competitors or meeting mates at the waterhole. You usually forget your dreams, meaning they aren't accessed in waking consciousness, because, across evolutionary time, they were retained and used unconsciously. For example, there was no time to think at the waterhole, unconsciousness enables fast action, which was key to survival.

Chapter 10 proposed that creatives are in a disordered state in-between dreaming and wake. In this chapter I argue that if this in-between state becomes more severe and enduring, psychiatric disorders will result. The chapter explores, first, whether all creative people are somewhat crazy or disordered; second, what

What Do Dreams Do? Sue Llewellyn, Oxford University Press (2020). © Oxford University Press.
DOI: 10.1093/oso/9780198818953.001.0001.

being disordered implies from the perspective of chaos theory; and, third, how the single condition of being de-differentiated may result in the diverse range of conditions that we currently call psychiatric disorders.

Are All Highly Creative People Somewhat Crazy?

Popular stereotypes abound: the mad genius, eccentric scientist, absent-minded professor, tech wizard, and innovative geek. All imply creative insights come at a cost. And that varies from geekiness through absent-mindedness to madness. You will recall from Chapter 10 that in a highly associative dream-like state during wake your mind wanders, you lose concentration on analytic tasks, become more internally focused and, consequently, less aware of your surroundings. For creative people these losses are balanced by the ability to make the non-obvious associations that may stimulate creative insights and products—from discovering neural transmission to writing a novel. But if the dream-like state progresses and endures, hallucinations, delusions, disorientation, emotional instability, and amnesia may result. All of which signal madness. All of which we use to characterize dreaming. But, to be clear, I don't think you are crazy when dreaming. Madness can be the result when a progressive and enduring dream-like state invades wake *and a progressive and enduring wake-like state invades dreaming.*

What is the evidence that creativity and craziness are linked? To assess this we have to know what we mean by both. Chapter 10 proposed that insight creativity is linked to madness. What do we mean by madness? We call people mad if they seem to have lost contact with our reality. They are living in a different world. I think they are living in a world in-between wake and dreaming. John Keats captured the essence of this in-between waking dream state in *Ode to a Nightingale* with these last two lines, 'Was it a vision, or a waking dream? Fled is that music:—Do I wake or sleep?' Those we call mad can be distressed and unpredictable. We struggle to communicate with them. We are unnerved by them. If mad people are in waking dreams, our responses are hardly surprising.

What do psychiatrists mean by madness? Unlike Keats they generally don't think of waking dreams. They classify mental illness into two broad categories: first, severe, a category that includes psychosis, schizophrenia, bipolar disorder, and major depression; and, second, less severe, including obsessive-compulsive, attention deficit/hyperactivity, depressive, panic, and dissociative disorders. Distinctions between the different disorders aren't clear-cut. Consequently, many patients are diagnosed with more than one disorder or with different conditions at different times. Even the divide between severe and less severe is fuzzy. There is little evidence either of natural boundaries between psychiatric disorders or of a clear separation between mental illness and normality,[2] indicating that psychiatric classifications may not map onto any real, distinct psychiatric conditions. There is growing recognition of this in psychiatric practice through the concept of 'transdiagnostic'—defined as underlining psychological processes that exist across a range of mental disorders.[3]

It's better to think of, first, psychiatric disorders overlapping in a multidimensional space, and, second, that space extending into the normal population.[4] In terms of psychotic symptoms in the normal population, a survey of 52 countries found considerable disparity between reported levels in different countries. For example, for a specific symptom, between 0.8% in Vietnam and 31.4% of people in Nepal reported hallucinations; overall 12.52% of people reported at least one psychotic symptom.[5] Unlike psychosis, depression and anxiety are normal responses to many life events. We all sometimes have attention 'deficit', get obsessed about pet projects, and panicky in certain situations. So the origins of madness, like creativity, seem to lie in normal thinking and feeling. But how normality extends into creativity and craziness is not well understood. Maybe thinking about the links between creativity and craziness may shed some light on both?

There are biographical accounts of many creative people who suffered from what we call mental illness. Kay Redfield Jamison, an American psychiatrist, discusses the likelihood that Blake, Byron, Schumann, Van Gogh, and Woolf all had manic depression, now referred to as bipolar disorder, which has both depressive and manic phases. Her book begins with a comment from Byron, 'We of the craft are all crazy' he said of himself and fellow poets 'Some are affected by gaiety, others by melancholy but all are more or less touched.'[6] Focusing on writers and artists, Jamison found a 38% rate for mood disorders.[7] The US population rate is 9.5%.[8] The prevalence of mood disorders in creative people differs with the nature of their creativity. Writers, poets, and artists, who work through intuition, association, and emotional expression, have higher rates than literary critics, journalists, and designers, who depend more on analysis.[9] Also creative artists have higher rates of mental disorders than eminent scientists, who again may work mostly through analysis.[10] This is what we would expect given the two forms of creativity (insight and non-insight) discussed in Chapter 10. Creative insight works through non-obvious association and intuition, whereas non-insight creativity works through analysis.

Are poets the craziest? Byron seemed to think so. In a study of poets between 1600 and 1800, they were 20 times more likely than the general population to end up in an asylum.[11] Arguably, more than any other creative form, poetry depends on non-obvious associations, as illustrated by the Auden poem in Chapter 10. We know that dreaming makes non-obvious, remote associations. Do non-obvious, remote, or loose associations characterize mental disorders? Eugen Bleuler (1857–1939), the Swiss psychiatrist who coined the term 'schizophrenia', noted a core characteristic was a 'loosening' of associations. Similarly, 'schizotypy', which refers to a continuum ranging from imaginative states to 'mild' schizophrenia, engenders loose, non-obvious, or remote associations. 'Flight of ideas', 'racing thoughts', or 'loose associations' characterize both mania and psychosis. I propose that, in neurotypicals, loose or non-obvious associations characterize their retained REM dream images but remain unconscious, albeit influencing their thought, decisions, and actions, but in both creative people and, to use Byron's term, those touched by madness, these associations rise to the surface and become conscious.

So loose, non-obvious associations are fundamental to creative insights and also characterize mental illness, but are highly creative people crazy?

What's the Evidence That Highly Creative People Are Crazy?

Experimental studies show increased creativity in people with bipolar disorder, attention deficit hyperactivity disorder (ADHD), and dissociative disorders.[12] Long term research with large samples (epidemiological studies) also demonstrates a link with mental disorders; for example, a study of 300,000 people over 30 years showed people with bipolar disorder (and the healthy siblings of those with bipolar disorder or schizophrenia) were overrepresented in the creative professions. A study of the education and medical records of the entire Swedish population (almost 4.5 million people) found those studying a creative, artistic subject at university were (compared with the general population), later, 90% more likely to be hospitalized for schizophrenia, 62% more likely for bipolar disorder, and 39% more likely for depression.[13] The lead author comments on the associative nature of both creativity and delusions, 'Creativity often involves linking ideas or concepts in ways that other people wouldn't think of but that's similar to how delusions work—for example, seeing a connection between the color of someone's clothes and being part of an MI5 conspiracy.'[14]

Brain imaging techniques show that creative people and those with schizotypy think more broadly (known as divergent thinking) and, therefore, make more non-obvious associations than normal people.[15] Also, genetic risk scores for schizophrenia and bipolar disorder predict creativity. Specifically, creative people are 25% more likely to have genes that increase the risk of schizophrenia and bipolar disorder.[16] Or, more positively, the genetic profile associated with madness can also convey the advantage of creativity.[17] But not all creatives are nuts and not all mad people are creative.

There must be more to creativity than a bit of craziness. To begin with, there's a positive relationship between creativity and intelligence. The relationship exists up to IQs of about 120 (100 is average), when the two begin to diverge.[18] Intelligence is usually defined as the ability to acquire and use knowledge, whereas creativity comes from connecting up disparate bits of knowledge. Also creativity is linked to personality. Confidence, autonomy, and openness to new ideas and experiences are all important.[19] So intelligence and the requisite personality traits are necessary but not sufficient conditions for creativity at the highest levels. Does a modicum of madness add the additional magic?

Chapter 10 looked at the two types of creativity in some depth: Type 1 is based on unconscious, non-obvious associations among memory (or knowledge) elements resulting in sudden insight into something previously unknown; Type 2 is based on step-by-step, linear-logical reasoning over a period of time. To reiterate, I propose it is only Type 1, imaginative, creative insight, engendered by a dream-like state of mind/brain during wake that is linked to madness, and this is only if the dream-like state is progressive and enduring. Otherwise only eccentricity, geekiness, or absent-mindedness would be associated with creative insights. Such characteristics shade into what we consider a normal state of mind/brain.

Type 2 step-by-step, linear logic, which generally predominates during focused tasks in wake, can foster creativity, particularly in the sense of innovation, in science, technology, design, and engineering. Having said this, there are clearly times when creative insights drive discoveries in these areas. Chapter 10 discussed how dream associations led to identifying the benzene ring and the invention of the sewing machine. Famously, Einstein said imagination creates the new ideas that expand the boundaries of science, 'Imagination is more important than knowledge. For knowledge is limited to all we now know and understand, while imagination embraces the entire world, and all there ever will be to know and understand.'

This brief summary of the available evidence points to several conclusions. First, creativity is more likely to be linked to craziness in the arts than the sciences. But there are cases of eminent scientists with severe mental illness; for example, John Nash, the Nobel prize-winner who established the mathematics of game theory, was thought to have schizophrenia.

Second, the link may only hold across the mild to moderate end of the madness spectrum, i.e. creativity isn't positively associated with outright craziness. Anna Abraham, a psychologist and neuroscientist at Leeds Beckett University, UK, suggests an inverted U-shaped relationship between creativity and mental illness in the sense that creativity is linked to what we term mental illness up until the point when normal functioning in wake becomes severely impaired, after which creativity decreases. Bipolar disorder is categorized as severe mental illness, yet, as discussed earlier many creative people seem to have suffered from the condition. One possibility is that bipolar disorder can, to some extent, be accommodated within artistic work. Artists, writers, and poets may paint or write during periods of manic energy, then use the depressive episodes for editing or reworking.

Third, the link between creativity and madness may be apparent only in the relatives of the creative person. For example, one of Einstein's sons had schizophrenia, Bertram Russell also had a son with the condition, and James Joyce had a daughter.

Schizophrenia is highly disabling; most people with schizophrenia become socially isolated. The majority do not marry nor have children. So why does the condition persist? The link between craziness and creativity seems to have a genetic basis, at least in part. A shared genetic susceptibility to both mental illness, generally experienced as negative, and creativity, a positive attribute, would explain why a highly disabling and socially isolating mental illness like schizophrenia continues to be inherited.

Another puzzle is how a genetic predisposition to both creativity and craziness is expressed neurobiologically. There must be some shared, inherited characteristic or characteristics. A propensity for wake and dreaming to be de-differentiated (resulting in either creativity or mental illness or both) may be an inherited characteristic. As discussed in Chapter 10, other factors are environmental, i.e. a poor diet or severe stress may also contribute to mental illness through precipitating progressive and enduring de-differentiation that originates at the level of the cell.

Brain States, Chaos Theory, Creativity, and Mental Illness

You will recall from the previous chapter that brains work best at self-organized criticality within the zone between order and disorder. Brain states are more creative when they lean towards the disorderly. In line with their brain states, creative people work in a disorderly way![20] Photographed on the day he died, Einstein's desk was, famously, a mess of books, magazines, envelopes, a pipe, and what looks like a cookie jar. Allegedly he remarked 'If a cluttered desk is a sign of a cluttered mind, then what are we to think of an empty desk?' A disorderly desk can indicate creativity and productivity, whereas a highly organized desk may be the product of a sterile mind.

My proposal is that some limited de-differentiation between wake and dreaming brings enough disorder to enable creativity, but progressive and enduring de-differentiation, resulting in much less distinctiveness between wake and dreaming, engenders severe disorder. So psychiatric 'disorders' are exactly that. In terms of chaos theory, they are disorderly states. Also in line with chaos theory, the brain's self-organized critical positioning means that shifts towards less and less distinctiveness between wake and dreaming would have unpredictable and diverse effects, resulting in many disorders with no clear boundaries among them and no distinct separation between normality and disorder, which, as argued earlier, is just what we observe.

Another key point about complex chaotic systems, like brain states, is that they usually settle into a specific state called an attractor—albeit that this settling is dynamically unstable and liable to change. Brian Goodwin (1931–2009), a biologist and mathematician, remarked, 'For complex non-linear dynamic systems with rich networks of interacting elements, there is an attractor that lies between a region of chaotic behaviour and one that is "frozen" in the ordered regime, with little spontaneous activity'.[21] So settling into the zone between disorder and order is the result of an attractor. If the brain moves into the disordered state, it will tend to be attracted back into the in-between zone. Again Goodwin commented, 'Any such system, be it a developing organism, a brain, an insect colony, or an ecosystem will tend to settle dynamically at the edge of chaos. If it moves too far into the chaotic regime it will come out again of its own accord.'[22] But if the brain's de-differentiated state is progressive and enduring, the movement back to the attractor may fail. In effect, the brain becomes trapped in the chaotic, disorderly regime, in-between wake and dreaming.

However, within the disorderly realm there will still be attractors. The brain may settle into one of these engendering a mind/brain state like ADHD or, if the de-differentiation is more severe, schizophrenia. But sometimes, in accordance with chaos theory, the mind/brain state may swing between attractors—this phenomenon is called a strange attractor. Attractors may explain why there are many mental health conditions. Strange attractors may clarify why many patients are diagnosed with multiple conditions, with different conditions at different times, or have disorders that seem to transmute from one to another.

In the comment above, Goodwin observes that if the mind/brain 'moves too far into the chaotic regime it will come out again of its own accord'. This concept of self-healing is inherent in self-organizing. Two theoretical biologists, Humberto Maturana and Francisco Varela, speak of 'autopoiesis' to refer to systems like the brain that self-produce and can regenerate, i.e. maintain themselves in the face of perturbations.

The concepts of self-organizing, self-production, and autopoiesis may help explain some of the processes that underlie both creativity and mental disorders. To begin this discussion, we focus first on the loss of top-down control associated with the divergent thinking that underlies creativity and mental health disorders.

Understanding Craziness Through Loss of Top-down Control

From Chapter 10 you will recall the lateral prefrontal cortex. It has right and left parts. If you touch both sides of your forehead, these prefrontal areas are immediately beneath. They exert top-down control over your thoughts, actions, and emotions. The lateral prefrontal cortex is switched on in wake enabling a whole range of functions critical to our waking lives. Top-down control is crucial for: planning and decision making through logical, step-by-step reasoning; focused attention on tasks and the concentration required to complete them; the ability to control emotions; and working memory.

We haven't discussed working memory so far—it is essential for many activities. It gives you the ability to assess and integrate different items of information; for example, in planning and decision-making tasks. Take the decision to buy a car. If you are consciously contemplating a particular car you need to store information about its attributes in your working memory: price, size, colour, functionality, age, number of doors, and so on. The average number of things you can hold in working memory is seven. Some people can store nine, others only five.

As we know, during rapid eye movement (REM) dreaming, the lateral prefrontal cortex is deactivated. Without top-down control, a highly emotional mind/brain wanders to make divergent 'big picture', non-obvious complex associations. In earlier chapters I discussed the evolutionary advantages of this loss of top-down control because it enabled the identification of patterns in the behaviour of predators, competitors, and potential mates. In Chapter 10, I proposed that this highly associative, divergent thought boosts creativity in wake.

But we haven't thought yet about how, if a dream-like state invades wake, loss of top-down control impacts on the mind/brain. I argue thinking about this may help understand mental disorders. How many are there?

Dubbed 'The Psychiatrist's Bible' the latest, fifth edition of the Diagnostic and Statistical Manual (DSM-5) specifies around 300 mental disorders.[23] In the previous section, we discussed how multiple attractors may result in many disorders. The current proliferation means that almost 50% of Americans will have a diagnosable mental disorder in their lifetime, making abnormality the new normal![24] We will only consider a few, well-known disorders.

First, take ADHD.[25] This condition is usually first diagnosed in children, but the symptoms (difficulty paying attention, impulsiveness rather than planning, restlessness and poor working memory) persist into adulthood, when they result in lack of attention to tasks, difficulty with planning, and impaired Type 2 decision making. You will recall that Type 2 decision making is slow, sequential, conscious, sometimes rule-based, and driven by complex emotions. The loss of impulse and emotional control in ADHD can range from getting very impatient in queues to road rage over driving incidents. Mood swings and angry flare-ups make for unstable relationships. People with ADHD feel like their motor won't switch off. Their hyperactivity generates a longing to be moving and doing things; trying to suppress these impulses leads to restlessness.

During REM dreaming, the dreamer is usually much more active than they are in wake. In the daytime, I'm mostly sitting in front of my computer. In my dreams I don't recall ever doing this. Instead I'm doing things like hanging onto a double decker bus as it flies around Edinburgh. With the lateral frontal cortex switched off I don't try to sit still in my dreams, so I don't get restless. Without top-down control, I'm free to go with the flow. Likewise in REM dreams I don't plan or make decisions. Rather I constantly, seemingly impulsively, change what I'm doing: one minute I'm walking fearfully down a street to a bridge, the next I'm on a beach watching, horrified, as a child is thrown. In dreams my impulsivity, hyperactivity, and lack of emotional control don't result in any adverse consequences. Likewise attention deficit isn't an issue. As events are constantly changing I don't need sustained attention or the ability to store information in working memory. Top-down control is detrimental when I'm identifying a non-obvious, complex pattern in my experience.

But, in wake, the loss of top-down control could precipitate the kind of symptoms that typify ADHD: hyperactivity, inability to sustain attention or make decisions, lack of planning and emotional control, and loss of working memory. It is unusual for researchers to compare brain activation in REM sleep with that in people with psychiatric disorders but, for ADHD, one research team has done this. Roumen Kirov, a psychiatrist interested in sleep at the University of Sofia, Bulgaria, and Serge Brand, a research psychologist at the University of Basel, Switzerland, showed that during task performance in wake, the brain activation patterns of people with ADHD closely resemble those of healthy humans during REM sleep.[26] This may signal de-differentiation between REM sleep/dreaming and wake in ADHD.

Second, people with emotionally unstable personality disorder (EUPD), formerly termed borderline personality disorder, experience strong emotions like anger and distress or joy and elation, which rapidly change and they are unable to control. They can feel highly anxious, even paranoid. People with EUPD have panic attacks in situations when others would merely feel nervous. Or they feel humiliated instead of just embarrassed. The sense of self is disturbed, with uncertainty about work or relationship goals. Similar to ADHD, someone with EUPD has problems with impulse control. Also, one study found 43% of people with EUPD experience hallucinations, i.e. involuntary mental imagery.[27] In response to negative emotions, self-harming and suicide attempts are also common, although these decrease over time.[28] Indeed, EUPD itself gets better over time.[29]

You will recall from Chapter 6 that during REM dreams, you usually feel basic, strong emotions like fear, anxiety, elation, anger, and disgust rather than the evolutionarily later, socially related, less explosive emotions such as pride, shame, and embarrassment. These strong, primary emotions would have been appropriate when dreaming about an associative pattern to avoid predators while obtaining food and water or meeting mates. Chapter 6 emphasized that emotions motivate action through anticipating an experience. We feel elated when looking forward to rewards, prompting approach. Fear or disgust triggers avoidance or withdrawal. But elation, fear, and disgust, along with the elementary actions of approach or avoidance are out of step with most complex, contemporary work and social situations. Others can find people with EUPD threatening and, generally, out of control. Chapter 6 also emphasized a negative emotional bias in dreams. As reported above, negative emotions can lead people with EUPD to self-harm and attempt suicide. During REM dreaming my sense of self is shallow. I don't know my age, occupation, or whether I am in a relationship. Consequently, my personal identity is much diminished and I cannot form realistic work or social goals. In wake, the loss of top-down control could result in the symptoms that typify EUPD: strong, changeable emotions, a disturbed sense of self, and a propensity to self-harm.

Third, someone with obsessive-compulsive disorder (OCD) can't control their thoughts or behaviours. Thoughts or mental images may be dominated by proscribed subjects like sex or aggression towards others. Or thoughts/images constantly return to fear of harmful things, like germs, or fear of losing or misplacing valued items, like smartphones. Alternatively, thoughts/images may dwell on bad things that could happen, like intruders into the person's home (is the door locked?) or violence in the street (is that stranger threatening me?), however unlikely these dire events may be. The checking behaviours in OCD suggest problems with working memory: this is indeed the case.[30] The repeated thoughts/images become obsessions that result in urges to perform certain highly controlled rituals termed compulsions. Fear of disorganization leads to excessive cleaning and tidying. Fear of germs brings about excessive handwashing. Fear of lost items causes continual monitoring. Fear of intrusion triggers repeated checking of doors to ensure they are locked. The sufferer is highly anxious for most of the time. Although performing the compulsions may bring temporary relief, the obsessions rapidly return.

During REM dreaming you can't control your thoughts or behaviours, which are mostly expressed through mental images. Fear and anxiety are the dominant emotions. But we don't fear losing things like smartphones because, in dreams, we aren't surrounded and accompanied by our normal everyday paraphernalia. Our dream lives are quite sparse. Also in dreams, with the prefrontal cortex switched off, we don't anticipate losses—we live in the present. Aggression towards others is common in dreams as are aggressive acts on the dreamer. But we don't worry about aggression in advance, although we do feel fear when it happens. OCD sufferers do worry about aggression, germs, losing things, and unlocked doors. In wake, the loss of top-down control could trigger the symptoms that typify OCD: loss of control over thoughts and behaviours, an increased urge towards aggression, and other proscribed behaviours, and problems with working memory.

Although a dream-like, hybrid state in wake, with an associated decrease in top-down control, will enable creativity, if the hybrid state progresses and endures, some distinct problems, associated with loss of top-down control, would appear. The above discussion highlights these for ADHD, EUPD, and OCD. Brain imaging evidence indicates that loss of top-down control is apparent for ADHD, EUPD, and OCD, along with other psychiatric disorders. Frida Bayard and Charlotte Nymberg, neuroscientists at the Karolinska Institute in Sweden, noted the similarity between brain function associated with loss of top-down control in ADHD, EUPD, and other conduct disorders.[31] Claire Gillan, a psychologist at New York University, comments on her research,[32] 'It's not just OCD; there are a range of human behaviours that are now considered examples of compulsivity, including drug and alcohol abuse and binge-eating. What all these behaviours have in common is the loss of top-down control.'

These research studies raise the question of whether ADHD, EUPD, and OCD (and other disorders) are really distinct disorders or are they all the consequence of some loss of top-down control? Several symptomatic overlaps exist between disorders. Impulsivity characterizes ADHD, EUPD, and OCD—if, in OCD, the compulsions are understood as urges or impulses. Involuntary mental imagery is present in OCD and often occurs in EUPD. Mood swings typify ADHD and EUPD. Sufferers of ADHD and OCD both have problems with working memory and decision making. On the other hand, one could argue that the loss of top-down control is apparent mostly over actions in ADHD, mainly over emotions in EUPD, and predominately over thoughts and mental images in OCD—making them overlapping but with different predominant profiles. Such a situation would result from the strange attractors discussed in the previous section.

Another significant issue is whether people with these conditions become conscious of their loss of top-down control. The loss isn't absolute. It's a matter of degree. De-differentiation would exist across a continuum. In Chapter 4 we distinguished between primary and secondary consciousness. During REM dreaming you have primary consciousness so you are aware of what's happening, but you aren't aware of your own awareness—meaning you don't think thoughts like 'I am aware of being in a state of high alert'. You need the secondary consciousness of wake for such thoughts. Also with secondary consciousness you can assess your own state of mind. During wake I know I'm awake, but during dreaming, with only primary consciousness, I'm not aware I'm dreaming because I can't assess my own state of mind. Without the ability to assess my own state of mind, I can't become aware of any loss of control over my thoughts, mental images, emotions, and actions. But in the hybrid world of a more dream-like state in wake I could possibly become aware of a loss of control over my thoughts, actions, and emotions. Does this happen in ADHD, EUPD, and OCD?

In OCD the rituals of handwashing, checking, and monitoring can be interpreted as trying to gain some control over things that feel out of control. Handwashing controls the spread of germs. Checking to see if doors are locked controls intruders. Cleaning and tidying controls disorder in the home. Generally these compulsions focus on bringing order to things that seem out of control. In ADHD the urge to do things can be a form of control, through picking up on tasks that aren't done. In EUPD the change in emotions can be seen as controlling them. Elation controls or dispels depression. Anger can be a way of controlling fear.[33] I don't worry about control during dreaming but in a hybrid state I may have some awareness of loss of control and strive to achieve it. The previous section discussed autopoiesis: how the mind/brain tries to heal itself. A disordered mind/brain that has insight into its own loss of control may try to regain control as a form of self-healing.

Having said all of this, I don't think ADHD, EUPD, and OCD are fully explained through the intrusion of a dream-like state into wake. Indeed, if wake and sleep/dreaming become de-differentiated, the intrusion of more dream-like cognition into wake would only be 'one side' of the de-differentiation equation. We now look at the other side.

De-differentiation Has Two Sides

The other side of the de-differentiation equation is that a more wake-like state of mind/brain would suffuse sleep and dreaming. Consequently, impacting on both REM sleep/dreaming and non-rapid eye movement (NREM) sleep/dreaming. We will look at the impact on dreaming first, then the effect on sleep.

The phenomenon of lucid dreaming, mentioned in Chapter 1, shows that the brain can transition into a more wake-like state during REM sleep/dreaming. In my terms lucid dreaming would be one consequence of de-differentiation—the dreamer has some prefrontal top-down control. This is apparent in two different ways during lucid dreaming. First, some secondary consciousness is present so the dreamer becomes aware that they are dreaming and, while still asleep, can even communicate this to an observer through eye movement signalling. Second, some lucid dreamers can exercise top-down control over dream content, choosing to engage in pleasurable activities such as sex and flying. This sounds interesting and enjoyable.

If de-differentiation on both sides of the equation is mild we would expect this to be associated with creativity. But if de-differentiation is severe it may precipitate psychiatric disorders. One study shows that areas of the brain that are deficient in psychosis are mirrored during lucid dreaming when wake-like cognition suffuses sleep.[34] Another study, which compared the incidence of lucid dreaming in psychotic and non-psychotic subjects, found an association between lucid dreaming and psychosis.[35] Also lucid dreamers have higher scores on the creative personality scale.[36]

This book highlights the functions of REM dreaming. If prefrontal areas became active during sleep and dreaming resulting in greater top-down control, you would expect the functions of REM dreaming to be disturbed. What are these functions?

Chapter 5 says we dream to remember, arguing that REM dreaming encodes recent memories through visually associating them with memories already in the brain's memory networks. This association benefits memory retention and recollection. If these sleep-dependent memory processes are disrupted, then memory problems would emerge. Chapter 6 presents evidence that REM sleep and dreaming can reduce subsequent emotional reactivity during waking hours. If this function is disturbed, then stronger, over-reactive, inappropriate emotions would be expected during wake. Chapter 7 discusses how associative images, formed during REM dreams, would drive Type 1 decisions and actions, i.e. ones that are fast, associative, unconscious, and driven by basic emotions. The formation of the basis for Type 1 decisions and actions would be impeded by a more wake-like state during sleep and dreaming. Likewise, Chapter 8 explains how the associative mental images formed during REM dreaming, when retained at an unconscious level, enable predictions of what will happen next in wake based on past experience. This predictive function would also be disrupted through a more wake-like state of mind during REM dreaming. Is there evidence of problems with memory, emotional reactivity, unconscious, intuitive decision making, and prediction across psychiatric disorders?

It's hard to answer this question because these areas are so complex and, to my knowledge, there is little to no research that looks at disturbances to REM sleep/dreaming and possible impacts in these areas. Also if REM sleep/dreaming is disrupted, it seems that some of its functions can be transferred to NREM sleep.[37] We would anticipate this through autopoiesis or self-healing. Nevertheless, there is some relevant research.

To avoid an overlong section, I focus on OCD and only give a flavour of the research. People with OCD show problems with non-verbal, visual memory.[38] This is what you would expect, given that memory processes during REM dreaming are visually associative. Individuals with OCD symptoms (compared with those without) show heightened emotional reactivity to negatively toned films.[39] Again this would be anticipated if REM dreaming is not reducing emotional reactivity. Those with OCD make very slow decisions relying on extensive search for objective criteria including reviews, rating, and other people's choices.[40] This may indicate inability to use Type 1 decision making, which is fast, intuitive, associative, unconscious, and based on personal experiences. The associative images formed in REM dreaming form a basis for Type 1 decision making. OCD is also known as the 'doubting disorder'.[41] We doubt when we are uncertain what is happening and, consequently, what will happen next. The loss of the unconscious, associative mental images (created in REM dreaming), which are used with current sensory input to form expectations about what is happening and what will happen next, would lead to profound doubt.

If de-differentiation happens, the impact wouldn't only be on dreaming but on sleep itself. Although sleep disturbances are endemic to psychiatric disorders, only recently have researchers argued that altered sleep may trigger and sustain them. One exception is narcolepsy. This is classified as a severe sleep disorder with psychiatric symptoms. It has long been recognized as involving: REM sleep/dream intrusion into wake; excessive daytime sleepiness; and fragmented, disturbed sleep at night.[42] You will recall that during REM sleep the body is paralysed, which prevents the dreamer acting out their dreams. In narcolepsy, REM sleep/dream intrusion into wake can result in cataplexy, where the body goes limp and the person can fall to the ground; also narcoleptic patients hallucinate during wake. They cannot maintain the normal boundaries between wake, REM, and NREM sleep. Although psychiatrists don't use the term de-differentiation for narcolepsy patients, in effect they recognize this is happening. Narcolepsy causes problems for both wake and sleep. But are these equally severe on both sides of the de-differentiation equation? As with other psychiatric disorders, research has been much more concerned with problems in wake rather than during sleep and dreaming.

Would De-differentiation Be to the Same Extent on the Two Sides of the Equation?

Daydreaming, which results from less top-down control during wake, and lucid dreaming, which results from more top-down control during dreaming, can be seen as corresponding states. In my terms they both happen through de-differentiation of wake and sleep/dreaming. But daydreaming is a normal state of mind/brain, which emerges frequently in wake when people are not engaged in tasks requiring top-down control. You may recall from Chapter 1 that one survey found 50% of wake to be daydreaming. A dream-like state of mind in wake only becomes problematic when it's very intense and can't be switched off whenever top-down control is required. The frequency and normality of daydreaming contrasts with spontaneous lucid dreaming, which is rare. People can be trained to dream lucidly but even then lucidity is a fragile state—people tend to go back to normal dreaming or wake up.

This indicates that although there are two sides to the de-differentiation of sleep/dreaming and wake, sleep/dreaming may be more protected from the intrusion of a wake-like state of mind than wake is from a dream-like state of mind. If, as I propose, we originally dreamed to survive, evolutionary fitness would have driven the conservation of a pure dreaming state. This means that de-differentiation would not necessarily be to the same extent on both sides of the equation. Dream-like intrusion into wake may be less problematic for mental health, even when it causes hallucinations and delusions, than wake-like intrusion into REM sleep and dreaming. I think we may be able to see this through looking at the two most debilitating psychiatric disorders: schizophrenia and bipolar disorder.

Schizophrenia and Bipolar Disorder

We will consider schizophrenia first, followed by bipolar disorder.

Schizophrenia

Schizophrenia is a heterogeneous condition, meaning its symptoms can be broadly described but its manifestation differs in particular individuals. As the psychiatrist Kay Redfield Jamieson remarks in *The Unquiet Mind*, 'People go mad in idiosyncratic ways.'[43] OCD is also now recognized as a heterogeneous disorder. Although a standard medical definition puts most emphasis on obsessions and compulsions, the previous section shows that mood problems, memory impairments, and indecisiveness are also prominent. Some patients highlight doubt as the major issue. For example, see Fletcher Wortmann's account in *Psychology Today*.[44] Up to 50% of patients with schizophrenia are also diagnosed with OCD,[45] so there is substantial overlap between the two conditions as well as considerable diversity within them.

Schizophrenia has positive and negative aspects. Cecilia McGough founded the non-profit organization Students with Schizophrenia,[46] her account of the condition is thought-provoking, she stresses the umbrella-like nature of schizophrenia.[47] Positive symptoms (also called psychosis) include hallucinations (seeing or hearing things without external stimulus) and delusions (false, fixed beliefs about reality). During normal REM dreaming we see and, sometimes, hear things that aren't there; indeed we inhabit an unreal, delusional world—although I'm asleep in my bed I think, for example, that I'm hanging onto the top of a double decker bus as it whirls around Edinburgh. I argue that this unreal delusional world isn't quite what it seems. When you hallucinate in dreaming you are looking at a visual pattern in your experience. You believe in this pattern because the associations are correct but the events didn't actually happen so you appear delusional. As mentioned earlier, Bleuler (1857–1939) the psychiatrist from whom the term schizophrenia originated, thought a loosening of associations was central to the condition, remaining present through the course of the condition.[48] As is clear, I think non-obvious or loose associations form dream images. Consequently, it's not hard to see that positive symptoms (a loosening of associations, hallucinations, and delusions) could be caused by a dream-like state of mind/brain intruding into wake. But because the intrusion is only partial, positive symptoms will differ from actual dreaming.

Dreaming is a private world. Mostly dream associations aren't recalled into consciousness during wake. Even if they are shared with others they don't cause confusion because they are 'just dreams'. But if very loose associations start to drive waking thought and conversations, other people are likely to be bewildered. Hallucinations are present in both dreaming and psychosis but dreaming is totally hallucinated, whereas, in psychosis, hallucinations only emerge from time to time and do not occupy the whole visual field. This would be expected in a hybrid de-differentiated state because the person is still processing external sensory data.

Delusions of body/mind control and persecution are common in schizophrenia[49] but not in dreaming. As we know during REM dreaming we are not aware of loss of top-down control so will not be concerned about inability to consciously control what we are doing. But in a de-differentiated hybrid state, with some ability to reflect on one's state of mind/brain, we are likely to recognize the loss of control. If you feel you don't control your own actions, then who does? You may well conclude your actions are being controlled by another, resulting in delusions of body/mind control and persecution.

Fear and anxiety are common in dreams. The delusion of control by others would be intensified through the fear and anxiety engendered by the intrusion of a dream-like state in wake. During normal dreaming fear and anxiety make sense in the context of the dream events. Dream emotions are tied to what is happening. But during wake, when fear and anxiety from the intrusion of a dream-like state don't make sense in terms of ongoing events, these emotions will fuel suspicions of concealed threats, promoting paranoia and delusions of persecution.

There are clear correspondences but also significant contrasts between dreaming and the positive symptoms of schizophrenia. These would flow from psychosis being a de-differentiated, hybrid state where only variable aspects of a dream-like state of mind/brain are incorporated into wake and this invasion is to a greater or lesser degree.

The negative symptoms of schizophrenia (social withdrawal, diminished emotional responses, poverty of thought and speech, loss of goal-directed action, and apathy) are generally accepted to be more incapacitating[50] and less curable[51] (being drug resistant) than positive symptoms. Negative implies loss. Bleuler argued that what is lost in schizophrenia is the sense of self—the experience of being a person and continuing to be the same person over time. From this perspective, the diversity of negative symptoms would all follow from this core deficit. How could this flow from an intrusion of a wake-like state into REM dreaming?

David Hartley (1705–1757), the English philosopher, first proposed that personally meaningful associations create a sense of self—this central principle of association works for the brain and the mind. Throughout this book I have emphasized the idea that REM dreams associate elements of different personal experiences to identify a personally meaningful pattern. Originally, this associative pattern aided survival so it was highly significant for the self! Memory is fundamental to a continuous sense of self. Chapter 5 proposes how REM dreaming creates associations between recent and remote memories. These associations are across time, enabling a sense of personal history and identity. They are also essential for memory retention and recollection. A more wake-like state during REM dreaming would disrupt the creation of these personally significant associations and so upset memory processes and the sense of self across time.

If dreaming projects into wake *and* a wake-like state projects into dreaming, what happens to memories? Hallucinations, caused by a dream-like state during wake, would be formed of dream associations. Hallucinations are very emotionally significant, so they will be remembered during wake. Consequently, during the dreaming that remains in people with psychosis, associative memories will be formed of what are already associations between memories rather than actual memories. In this way hallucinations would create delusions, i.e. fixed false beliefs about reality. All memory processes encoding, retention, and recollection (see Chapter 5) would be disrupted. Research into memory impairment in schizophrenia is consistent with this because it shows generalized dysfunction across a wide range of memory tasks.[52] As argued above, these profound memory problems may lie behind the negative symptoms of schizophrenia. Notably, Mark Solms and Oliver Turnbull, two neuropsychologists/psychoanalysts, found that people who do not dream become 'aspontaneous, inert and apathetic',[53] indicating that negative symptoms may emerge when REM dreaming is disrupted. As discussed earlier, negative symptoms are more debilitating than positive ones, so a wake-like state intruding into dreaming may be more problematic for mental health than a dreamlike state suffusing wake.

Bipolar disorder

Emil Kraepelin (1856–1926) was a German psychiatrist. He made a distinction between manic depression, now known as bipolar disorder, and what became known as schizophrenia—previously both were classified as psychosis. But, for some, the pendulum has swung back to thinking a single condition generates schizophrenia and bipolar disorder because their symptoms overlap, they can follow a similar deteriorating course, involve sleep problems, are difficult for psychiatrists to distinguish, partly share genetic profiles, and can both involve psychosis.[54] The loosening of associations that occurs in schizophrenia also happens in the manic periods of bipolar disorder.[55] Schizoaffective disorder is diagnosed when the overlap between schizophrenia and bipolar disorder is such that the conditions cannot be distinguished.

Like schizophrenia, bipolar disorder has positive and negative aspects. In bipolar disorder both facets (mania and depression) usually alternate across the course of the condition. Elation drives mania. This can be quite seductive. Patients feel the world is full of pleasure, promise and purpose, they are super-confident, everything seems to make sense.[56] But as the manic phase continues psychosis can take over. Kay Redfield Jamieson, a psychiatrist who has bipolar disorder, analyses her own experience:

> The most dreadful I had ever felt in my entire life was the first time I was psychotically manic. . . Although I had been building up to this for weeks and certainly knew something was seriously wrong, there was still a definite point when I knew I was insane. My thoughts were so fast that I couldn't remember the beginning of a sentence half way through. Fragments of ideas, images, sentences, raced around and around my head like the tigers in a children's story.[57]

In a pure dreaming state these fragments would be associated in a narrative, but in a hybrid state the fragments may fail to coalesce, remaining on the loose. Manic states switch into deep despondency as depression, the antithesis of purpose, promise, and pleasure, takes over.

Earlier in this chapter we discussed the possibility of autopoiesis as the brain's self-healing response to mental health conditions. Although bipolar disorder is a highly disturbing disorder it is not as severe as schizophrenia. Is the former an autopoietic response to the latter? The next section looks at neuromodulation in both conditions to explain this proposal.

Is Bipolar Disorder an Autopoietic Response to Schizophrenia?

You will recall that the brain is self-organizing and so, if perturbed through disorder, will organize to move out of the disordered realm back into the critical zone in-between order and disorder. This self-organizing occurs through neuromodulation.[58]

You may recall from Chapter 10 that during wake your mind/brain state is supported by two neurotransmitters (among others), serotonin and noradrenaline, but in REM sleep/dreaming these are more or less shut off. As we know, one result is that the brain region responsible for top-down control (the lateral prefrontal cortex) is deactivated. Without these two neurotransmitters and the lateral prefrontal cortex, the mind/brain cannot control its thoughts, engage in step-by-step reasoning, and remember what is happening from minute to minute. Another important neurotransmitter, acetylcholine, which is crucial for learning and memory, is present during both wake and REM sleep. But in REM sleep, without serotonin and noradrenaline, acetylcholine goes into overdrive. Dopamine is another neurotransmitter active during REM sleep and wake, but during wake it flows mainly through the cortex, whereas in REM sleep it flows primarily through the emotional, limbic system.

The main hypothesis on how schizophrenia occurs is that, during wake, more dopamine is transmitted through the limbic system and less through the cortex.[59] This is what you would expect if a dream-like state invaded wake. The dopamine hypothesis is long-standing, but other neurotransmitter imbalances are also suggested. Again during wake, in schizophrenia there is less serotonin and noradrenaline and more acetylcholine.[60] Post-mortem results also show less serotonin in cortical areas but more in limbic areas.[61] Again these patterns involving serotonin, noradrenaline, and acetylcholine would be anticipated if a dream-like state invaded wake.

If bipolar disorder is triggered by an autopoietic response to schizophrenia, then its manic phase may equate to self-organizing to reduce dream intrusion during wake through increasing serotonin and noradrenaline, reducing acetylcholine, and increasing cortical dopamine. Depression may result through autopoiesis to limit the intrusion of wake into dreaming through increasing acetylcholine, reducing serotonin and noradrenaline, and increasing limbic dopamine. Serotonin imbalances have long been implicated in bipolar disorder. Drugs that enhance serotonin are used to treat depression but can induce mania. This brief section cannot convey the complexity of research in this area. A recent review of 45 studies found increased serotonin and cortical dopamine in mania, with decreased serotonin, increased acetylcholine, and increased cortical dopamine in depression.[62] This review provides some support to the proposal that bipolar disorder may be an autopoietic response to schizophrenia—only excepting the finding that cortical dopamine is increased in depression.

Briefly. . .

You aren't mad when you dream—you are recognizing a non-obvious complex pattern in your experience. But if this pattern gets projected into wake and you don't recognize it as a dream, then you are delusional. What's happening is that you mistake a pattern in your experience for your experience as a result of the intrusion of a dream-like state into wake. But this is only one side of the de-differentiation equation. A wake-like state can also be projected into sleep/dreaming. This may ultimately be more detrimental because it would disrupt the ability to make the personally meaningful associations that underpin the sense of a self with identity and purpose. Although de-differentiation is consistent with the wide variety of mental health conditions observed, it also suggests that one fundamental process underlies them. This is certainly a challenge to conventional wisdom but recent evidence supports a common cause for all mental health conditions.[63] These data may support de-differentiation between waking and dreaming. For example, several sets of genes are expressed as shared biological factors that relate to the synapse and act across mental disorders.[64] As argued in this chapter de-differentiation would act across psychiatric disorders and originate at the level of the synapse. A review of 193 studies across six diagnostic classifications (schizophrenia, bipolar disorder, depression, addiction, OCD, and anxiety) found problems with a common brain area across the different diagnoses, which is likely to be expressed through a loss of top-down control.[65] Clearly a loss of top-down control would be the result if a dream-like state intruded into wake.

Finally, how can we understand madness from a non-medical perspective? Chapter 4 argued our brains were built to move about in the world. Finding our way in our minds is fundamentally the same as moving about in the world. If we wander about, we can get lost in the world. Chapter 10 argues mind wandering enables creativity but too much wandering would end in being lost mental space. Our language reflects this, think of "losing your mind" or even "going out of your mind". Madness means you don't know where you are in your own mind. Why would this mental disorientation result from de-differentiation? During wake your mind be-comes overwhelmed with diverse associations. Lorna Sage concludes her personal history, " … if everything in your life is connected to everything else that way mad-ness lies." [66] The intrusion of a wake-like state into REM sleep and dreaming, results in losing the ability to identify diverse patterns in experience and instantiate those patterns as landmark junctions in brain memory networks. Without landmarks to guide navigation in a mental space flooded with non-obvious associations, we would be lost in our own minds.

Next

The next and final chapter compares and contrasts my theory with those of other dream researchers and, in so doing, draws my ideas together.

Notes

1. See pp. 98–103 in Hobson, J. A. (2003). *Dreaming: An Introduction to the Science of Sleep*. Oxford University Press, New York; and p. 193 in Walker, M. (2018). *Why We Sleep*. Penguin, Random House, London.
2. Kendall, R., & Jablensky, A. (2003). Distinguishing between the validity and utility of psychiatric diagnoses. *American Journal of Psychiatry, 160*, 4–12.
3. Sauer-Zavala, S., Gutner, C. A., Farchione, T. J., Boettcher, H. T., Bullis, J. R., & Barlow, D. H. (2017). Current definitions of 'transdiagnostic' in treatment development: a search for consensus. *Behavior Therapy, 48*(1), 128–138.
4. Craddock, N., & Owen, M. J. (2005). The beginning of the end for the Kraepelinian di-chotomy? *British Journal of Psychiatry, 186*, 364–366.
5. Nuevo, R., Chatterji, S., Verdes, E., Naidoo, N., Arango, C., & Ayuso-Mateos, J. L. (2010). The continuum of psychotic symptoms in the general population: a cross-national study. *Schizophrenia Bulletin, 38*(3), 475–485.
6. Jamison, K. R. (1994). *Touched with Fire: Manic Depressive Illness and the Artistic Temperament*. Free Press, New York.
7. Jamison, K. R. (1989). Mood disorders and patterns of creativity in British writers and artists. *Psychiatry, 52*(2), 125–134.
8. Mood disorders. Available at https://report.nih.gov/NIHfactsheets/ViewFactSheet. aspx?csid=48
9. Ludwig, A. M. (1995). *The Price of Greatness: Resolving the Creativity and Madness Controversy*. Guilford Press, New York; and Ludwig, A. M. (1998). Method and mad-ness in the arts and sciences. *Creativity Research Journal, 11*(2), 93–101.
10. Andreasen, N. C. (2005). *The Creating Brain: The Neuroscience of Genius*. Dana Press, Vejle, Denmark.
11. Hudson, A. (2011). Poetry, the creative process and mental illness. *BBC News*. Available at: https://www.bbc.co.uk/news/entertainment-arts-12368624

12. Rybakowski, J. K., & Klonowska, P. (2010). Bipolar mood disorder, creativity and schizotypy: an experimental study. *Psychopathology*, *44*(5), 296–302; Santosa, C. M., Strong, C. M., Nowakowska, C., Wang, P. W., Rennicke, C. M., & Ketter, T. A. (2007). Enhanced creativity in bipolar disorder patients: a controlled study. *Journal of Affective Disorders*, *100*(1), 31–39; White, H. A., & Shah, P. (2011). Creative style and achievement in adults with attention-deficit/hyperactivity disorder. *Personality and Individual Differences*, *50*(5), 673–677; White, H. A. (2018). Thinking 'outside the box': unconstrained creative generation in adults with attention deficit hyperactivity disorder. *The Journal of Creative Behavior*, https://doi.org/10.1002/jocb.382; and van Heugten-van der Kloet, D., Cosgrave, J., Merckelbach, H., Haines, R., Golodetz, S., & Lynn, S. J. (2015). Imagining the impossible before breakfast: the relation between creativity, dissociation, and sleep. *Frontiers in Psychology*, *6*, 324.

13. MacCabe, J. H, Sariaslan, A., Almqvist, C., Lichtenstein, P., H. Larsson, H., & Kyaga, S. (2018). Artistic creativity and risk for schizophrenia, bipolar disorder and unipolar depression: a Swedish population-based case–control study and sib-pair analysis. *The British Journal of Psychiatry*, doi:10.1192/bjp.2018.23.

14. Being creative increases your risk of schizophrenia by 90 percent. Available at: https://www.iflscience.com/health-and-medicine/being-creative-increases-your-risk-of-schizophrenia-by-90-percent/

15. De Manzano, Ö., Cervenka, S., Karabanov, A., Farde, L., & Ullen, F. (2010). Thinking outside a less intact box: thalamic dopamine D2 receptor densities are negatively related to psychometric creativity in healthy individuals. *PloS One*, *5*(5), e10670.

16. Power, R. A., Steinberg, S., Bjornsdottir, G., Rietveld, C. A., Abdellaoui, A., Nivard, M. M., . . . & Cesarini, D. (2015). Polygenic risk scores for schizophrenia and bipolar disorder predict creativity. *Nature Neuroscience*, *18*(7), 953.

17. Alleyne, R. (2009). Fine line between genius and madness, scientists find. Available at: https://www.telegraph.co.uk/news/science/science-news/6243747/Fine-line-between-genius-and-madness-scientists-find.html

18. Guilford, J. P. (1967). *The Nature of Human Intelligence*. McGraw-Hill, New York.

19. Batey, M., & Furnham, A. (2006). Creativity, intelligence, and personality: a critical review of the scattered literature. *Genetic, Social, and General Psychology Monographs*, *132*(4), 355–429.

20. James, G. (2017). A messy desk is a sign of genius, according to science. Available at: https://www.inc.com/geoffrey-james/a-messy-desk-is-a-sign-of-genius-according-to-scie.html

21. See p. 169 in Goodwin, B. (1994). *How the Leopard Changed Its Spots: The Evolution of Complexity*. Weidenfeld & Nicolson, London.

22. See p. 169 in Goodwin, B. (1994). *How the Leopard Changed Its Spots: The Evolution of Complexity*. Weidenfeld & Nicolson, London.

23. Controversial mental health guide DSM-5 (2013). Available at: https://www.nhs.uk/news/mental-health/news-analysis-controversial-mental-health-guide-dsm-5/

24. Rosenberg, R. S. (2013). Abnormal is the new normal. Available at: https://slate.com/technology/2013/04/diagnostic-and-statistical-manual-fifth-edition-why-will-half-the-u-s-population-have-a-mental-illness.html

25. Adult attention-deficit/hyperactivity disorder. Available at: https://www.mayoclinic. org/diseases-conditions/adult-adhd/symptoms-causes/syc-20350878

26. Kirov, R., & Brand, S. (2014). Sleep problems and their effect in ADHD. *Expert Review of Neurotherapeutics, 14*(3), 287–299.

27. Niemantsverdriet, M. B., Slotema, C. W., Blom, J. D., Franken, I. H., Hoek, H. W., Sommer, I. E., & Van Der Gaag, M. (2017). Hallucinations in borderline personality disorder: prevalence, characteristics and associations with comorbid symptoms and disorders. *Scientific Reports, 7*(1), 13920.

28. Zanarini, M. C., Frankenburg, F. R., Reich, D. B., Fitzmaurice, G., Weinberg, I. (2008). The 10-year course of physically self-destructive acts reported by borderline patients and axis II comparison subjects. *Acta Psychiatrica Scandinavia*, 117, 177–184.

29. Salters-Pedneault, K. (2018). Do BPD symptoms decline with age? Available at: https://www.verywellmind.com/why-do-bpd-symptoms-decline-with-age-425211

30. Nakao, T., Nakagawa, A., Nakatani, E., Nabeyama, M., Sanematsu, H., Yoshiura, T., ... & Kuroki, T. (2009). Working memory dysfunction in obsessive–compulsive disorder: a neuropsychological and functional MRI study. *Journal of Psychiatric Research, 43*(8), 784–791.

31. Bayard, F., Thunell, C. N., Abé, C., Almeida, R., Banaschewski, T., Barker, G., ... & Desrivières, S. (2018). Distinct brain structure and behavior related to ADHD and conduct disorder traits. *Molecular Psychiatry*, 1.

32. Gillan, C. M., Apergis-Schoute, A. M., Morein-Zamir, S., Urcelay, G. P., Sule, A., Fineberg, N. A., ... & Robbins, T. W. (2015). Functional neuroimaging of avoidance habits in obsessive-compulsive disorder. *American Journal of Psychiatry, 172*(3), 284–293.

33. Thagard, P. (2018). How fear leads to anger. Available at: https://www.psychologytoday.com/gb/blog/hot-thought/201811/how-fear-leads-anger

34. Dresler, M., Wehrle, R., Spoormaker, V. I., Steiger, A., Holsboer, F., Czisch, M., & Hobson, J. A. (2015). Neural correlates of insight in dreaming and psychosis. *Sleep Medicine Reviews, 20*, 92–99.

35. Mota, N. B., Resende, A., Mota-Rolim, S. A., Copelli, M., & Ribeiro, S. (2016). Psychosis and the control of lucid dreaming. *Frontiers in Psychology, 7*, 294.

36. Zink, N., & Pietrowsky, R. (2013). Relationship between lucid dreaming, creativity and dream characteristics. *International Journal of Dream Research, 6*(2), 98–103.

37. Vyazovskiy, V. V., & Delogu, A. (2014). NREM and REM sleep complementary roles in recovery after wake. *The Neuroscientist, 20*(3), 203–219.

38. Savage, C. R., Baer, L., Keuthen, N. J., Brown, H. D., Rauch, S. L., & Jenike, M. A. (1999). Organizational strategies mediate nonverbal memory impairment in obsessive-compulsive disorder. *Biological Psychiatry, 45*(7), 905–916.

39. Cougle, J. R., Timpano, K. R., Sarawgi, S., Smith, C. M., & Fitch, K. E. (2013). A multimodal investigation of the roles of distress tolerance and emotional reactivity in obsessive-compulsive symptoms. *Anxiety, Stress & Coping, 26*(5), 478–492.

40. Oren, E., Dar, R., & Liberman, N. (2018). Obsessive–compulsive tendencies are related to a maximization strategy in making decisions. *Frontiers in Psychology, 9*, 778–803.

41. Aardema, F., O'Connor, K. P., Pélissier, M. C., & Lavoie, M. E. (2009). The quantification of doubt in obsessive-compulsive disorder. *International Journal of Cognitive Therapy, 2*(2), 188–205.

42. What is narcolepsy? Available at: https://narcolepsynetwork.org/what-is-narcolepsy/

43. See p. 90 in Jamison, K. R. (2015). *An Unquiet Mind*. Picador, London.

44. Wortmann, F. (2012). OCD: a sufferer's take on the 'doubting disorder'. *Psychology Today*, 4 May. Available at: https://www.psychologytoday.com/gb/blog/triggered/201205/ocd-sufferers-take-the-doubting-disorder

45. Berman, I., Merson, A., Viegner, B., Losonczy, M. F., Pappas, D., & Green, A. I. (1998). Obsessions and compulsions as a distinct cluster of symptoms in schizophrenia: a neuropsychological study. *The Journal of Nervous Mental Disorders*, *186*(3), 150–156.

46. Since 2020 this website has been entitled 'Students with psychosis'. Available at: https://sws.ngo/

47. Leary, A. (2019). This young scientist is out to prove people with schizophrenia aren't monsters. Available at: https://www.healthline.com/health/mental-health/student-takes-on-schizophrenia#1

48. Peralta, V., & Cuesta, M. J. (2011). Eugen Bleuler and the schizophrenias: 100 years after. *Schizophrenia Bulletin*, *37*(6), 1118–1120.

49. Appelbaum, P. S., Robbins, P. C., & Roth, L. H. (1999). Dimensional approach to delusions: comparison across types and diagnosis. *American Journal of Psychiatry*, 156, 1938–1943.

50. Andreasen, N. C. (1990). Positive and negative symptoms: historical and conceptual aspects. *Modern Problems Pharmacopsychiatry*, *24*, 1–42.

51. Erhart, S. M., Marder, S. R., & Carpenter, W. T. (2006). Treatment of schizophrenia, negative symptoms: future prospects. *Schizophrenia Bulletin*, *32*, 234–237.

52. Manoach, D. S., & Stickgold, R. (2009). Does abnormal sleep impair memory consolidation in schizophrenia? *Frontiers in Human Neuroscience*, *3*, 1–8.

53. See pp. 311–312 in Solms, M., & Turnbull, O. (2002). *The Brain and the Inner World*. Other Press, New York.

54. Craddock, N., O'Donovan, M. C., & Owen, M. J. (2006). Genes for schizophrenia and bipolar disorder? Implications for psychiatric nosology. *Schizophrenia Bulletin*, *32*, 9–16; and Craddock, N., & Owen, M. J. (2005). The beginning of the end for the Kraepelinian dichotomy? *British Journal of Psychiatry*, *186*, 364–366.

55. Solovay, M. R., Shenton, M. E., & Holzman, P. S. (1987). Comparative studies of thought disorder: mania and schizophrenia. *Archives General Psychiatry*, *44*, 13–20.

56. See pp. 9–10 in Mondimore, F. M. (1999). *Bipolar Disorder*. Johns Hopkins Press, Baltimore, MD.

57. See p. 82 in Jamison, K. R. (2015). *An Unquiet Mind*. Picador, London.

58. Singer, W. (1986). The brain as a self-organizing system. *European Archives of Psychiatry and Neurological Sciences*, *236*, 4–9.

59. Carlsson, A. (1988). The current status of the dopamine hypothesis of schizophrenia. *Neuropsychopharmacology*, *1*, 179–186.

60. Gottesmann, C. (2006). The dreaming sleep stage: a new neurobiological model of schizophrenia? *Neuroscience*, *140*, 1105–1115; and Sarter, M., Nelson, C. L., & Bruno, J. P. (2005). Cortical cholinergic transmission and cortical processing in schizophrenia. *Schizophrenia Bulletin*, *31*, 117–138.

61. Quednow, B. B., Geyer, M. A., & Halberstadt, A. L. (2010). Serotonin and schizophrenia. In Christian P. Müller & Barry L. Jacobs (Eds) *Handbook of Behavioral Neuroscience* (Vol. 21, pp. 585–620). Elsevier, Oxford.

62. Nikolaus, S., Müller, H. W., & Hautzel, H. (2017). Different patterns of dopaminergic and serotonergic dysfunction in manic, depressive and euthymic phases of bipolar disorder. *Nuklearmedizin, 56*(05), 191–200.

63. Jones, D. (2020). A radical idea suggests mental health conditions have a single cause. Available at: https://www.newscientist.com/article/mg24532660-500-a-radical-idea-suggests-mental-health-conditions-have-a-single-cause/

64. Hammerschlag, A. R., de Leeuw, C. A., Middeldorp, C. M., & Polderman, T. J. C. (2019). Synaptic and brain-expressed gene sets relate to the shared genetic risk across five psychiatric disorders. *Psychological Medicine*, 1–11. https://doi.org/10.1017/S0033291719001776

65. Goodkind, M., Eickhoff, S. B., Oathes, D. J., Jiang, Y., Chang, A., Jones-Hagata, L. B., ... & Grieve, S. M. (2015). Identification of a common neurobiological substrate for mental illness. *JAMA Psychiatry, 72*(4), 305–315.

66. Sage, L. (2000) *Bad Blood*. Harper Collins: London.

PART IV

DREAMS AS PATTERNS (IN BRIEF), OTHER DREAM THEORIES, AND FUTURES

12

Dreams as Patterns, Fit with Freud and Other Dream Theorists

Introduction

I began this book with this question: 'What is a dream?' Here I briefly summarize the answers my theory gives for rapid eye movement (REM) dreams.

1. A dream is a complex, non-obvious, associative pattern in the dreamer's experience. During dreaming the mind/brain is hyperassociative and divergent rather than predominately linear-logical and sequential, as in wake. So dreams identify a different type of complex pattern from those recognized during wake.
2. A dream reveals a patterned nexus of personally, rather than universally, meaningful associations.
3. A dream takes elements from different memories that, across evolutionary time, were associated with a place that held rewards (food, water, and potential mates) but also harboured dangers from predators and competitors.
4. A dream is represented in the brain as an omnidirectional junction, which works at an unconscious level, in the dreamer's memory networks.
5. Dreams originally had a survival function; unconsciously they now enable remembering, decision making, and prediction. They also reduce emotional reactivity during wake.
6. Dreaming can suffuse wake and wake can invade dreaming. So de-differentiated states are possible. In a mild form, de-differentiation can engender insight creativity; in a more severe and enduring mode it can result in mental disorders.

How does 'dreams as patterns' relate to other relevant dream theories? We begin with Sigmund Freud.

Sigmund Freud

He needs no introduction. Published in 1899, *The Interpretation of Dreams* got off to a slow start, selling only 600 copies in its first 8 years but, eventually, Freud's

What Do Dreams Do? Sue Llewellyn, Oxford University Press (2020). © Oxford University Press.
DOI: 10.1093/oso/9780198818953.001.0001.

ideas founded the practice of psychoanalysis, deeply influenced art and literature, and broke through into mass popular culture. We've all heard of Freudian slips, defence mechanisms, phallic symbols, and, most of all, the unconscious mind, but Freud has rather fallen out of favour with many dream researchers. His dream theory is thought to be untestable. I think some of his ideas are still relevant. Some certainly are to my dreams as patterns theory, because of Freud's strong focus on the associative nature of dreams.

Freud's dream theory

Freud thought dreams have a purpose. He thought all our dream content derives from our experience. He thought dreams are highly associative. I do too.

To get at Freud's idea of the purpose of dreaming you need to grasp his proposal for the nature of dreams. Freud believed dreams to be instinctive wish fulfilments, which often derive from early childhood experiences. These wishes, frequently sexual or aggressive, may flout cultural norms and our own principles. Consequently, they invoke conflict between our instinctive desires, in Freud's terms the 'id', and higher principles, in Freud's terms the 'superego'. This conflict leads to repression and disguise, in Freudian terminology. During wake, instinctive, unacceptable wishes are repressed (kept out of consciousness) but come back in dreams when primary, instinctive consciousness reigns. Even during dreams, Freud thought these instinctive wishes couldn't be openly expressed. The greater the emotional conflict the dream generates, the more heavily disguised the dream.

For Freud, dream association is disguise, through 'displacement' and 'condensation'. Displacement means the dream reduces psychic conflict by replacing any disturbing content with something merely associated with it. This disguises the conflict and renders the dream more acceptable to the dreamer. Condensation is also a form of disguise. It fuses several associated experiential elements into one image. Both these processes lead to Freud's distinction between manifest and latent dream content. If the dreamer recalls their dream, they remember the manifest disguised content. This is what the dream appears to be, after censorship through disguise. Freud thought this disguised manifest content symbolizes the latent content. The manifest content often depicts what Freud deemed trivial recent events because these trivia are associated in some way with the latent content. The true significance of the dream lies in its forbidden (by the superego) instinctive wishes. We can only reveal these wishes by unpicking the associative processes of displacement, condensation, and symbolism. For Freud, the purpose of dreams is to maintain sleep. Without the associative dreamwork, the unacceptable nature of the wishes would wake the dreamer.

Freud's dream theory is quite convoluted: instinctive wishes are repressed during wake but even in the instinctive dreamworld the censor is still active. If instinctive sexual and aggressive urges did become transparent in dreams, the dreamer would be shocked into waking! This theory is very much of its time within the liberal, Jewish middle class of fin-de-siècle Vienna. During the second half of the 19th century in Austria, sexual morality was even more oppressive than in Victorian England, yet at the same time, the middle class were aware of the work of Havelock Ellis and Richard von Krafft-Ebing, detailing the pervasive influence of sexuality on human behaviour.[1] Now, in the 21st century, Freud's idea on disguising sexual and aggressive urges through dream association doesn't convince. At least in the West, people are open about sex and even aggression. Fuelled by social media, we live in a confessional culture about our instinctive urges. The idea that they undergo an elaborate means of censorship, even during dreaming, seems far-fetched.

Comparing Freud's theory with mine

I think the original purpose of dreaming was survival. A dream portrays a non-obvious, associative pattern in experiences, usually involving other living creatures of emotional significance to the dreamer. The associations are non-obvious because many of the drivers of human and animal behaviour are non-obvious. Archetypically, across evolutionary time, we used this pattern to assess the likelihood of a predator at the waterhole when sensory data about the threat were ambiguous. The evolutionary purpose of dreaming was to identify this pattern and so increase the chances of obtaining rewards (archetypically, food, water, and sex) while avoiding predators and competitors. Freud's ideas aren't grounded in evolution—or only in so far as they recognize sexual and aggressive instincts.

We all desire rewards but still experience conflict in obtaining them. We don't risk death by predation at the waterhole but we do come into conflict with others or our own values in getting what we instinctively want. A reward–conflict dilemma can still play out in dreams. I think associating elements of experiences to identify a pattern produces bizarreness because the memory elements come from different experiences in time and place.

I don't think this is a strategy to disguise—the apparent disguise is merely a consequence of pattern identification. The mind/brain in wake isn't used to looking at a visual, associative pattern, particularly when the pattern is formed from non-obvious associations. So the pattern isn't recognized for what it is. Our logically sequential mind/brains in wake find it hard to decipher a dream in the sense of identifying the patterned memory elements and the associations. I agree with Freud on this: you have to interpret your dreams.

Freud famously said, 'The interpretation of dreams is the royal road to a knowledge of the unconscious activities of the mind'. He thought free association is the best way to interpret dreams and starting with associations to day residues often works well. I agree. But I don't think all dream associations reveal repressed desires and experiences in the unconscious. In Freud's view, dreams express the unconscious. Sometimes unconscious associations break through into wake generating

Freudian slips—where you say something that reveals your hidden wishes. In my view, dreams create, rather than express, the unconscious because, after constructing and experiencing dreams, we retain dream images at the unconscious level. Across evolutionary time, responses to threats and opportunities had to be unconscious to be fast to increase survival chances.

We now know the unconscious is much more extensive than Freud thought it to be. In particular, it isn't only a repository for repressed desires. You will recall from Chapter 4 that 95% of brain activity is unconscious; many of our actions, once mastered (walking, swimming, riding a bike) are unconscious and automated. Also many of our decisions, actions, and expectations, although not automated, in the sense of automatic, are based on unconscious information (see Chapters 6 and 7). We evolved amid many dangers. Unconscious responses make perfect sense—they are fast and efficient. Back in evolutionary time, conscious contemplation of options and possibilities was too slow. Speed, not repression, is the raison d'être for the unconscious.

Having said that, I think some dreams do spring from repressed wishes. Carl Jung coined the term 'big dream' for ones, which are particularly significant for the self. I illustrate with a big dream of mine: 'the museum'.

Illustrative Dream Report: 'The Museum'

Scene 1

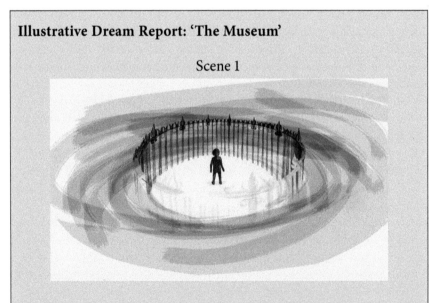

I'm standing by a fence. Only it's not a fence—it's railings. Fences are grey, flat, straight, and held together with wire. So this can't be a fence. These railings are tall, slender, black, and shiny, and gracefully curved in places too. We are all alone in a white circle, there is nothing else at all, and there is nothing beyond this ring. There's just me and the railings.

Scene 2

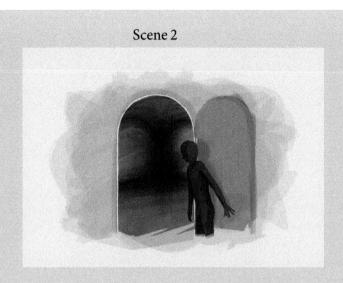

I'm in a building and I'm feeling driven. I'm on a search, but I don't know what I'm looking for. It's becoming lighter. Something is clearer—now I know what I'm supposed to be doing. I need to explore the rooms. I must make sure that I check each one. Actually the rooms are dark and empty so I don't really need to go inside, I can just peep in, which is fortunate because the rooms aren't right: the ceilings are curved and come right down to the floors. I suspect that the rooms contain a menacing presence. I'm becoming very frightened.

Scene 3

I'm in a corridor, now I'm free of the rooms. They are on my left but somehow checking them is no longer important. There is something even more significant. I'm rising quickly, the passage slopes up steeply in front of me and at the end there

is an opening with a brilliant light. The light at the end is so intense it's impossible to see what lies beyond. Everything is beginning to make sense; I must hurry up. I'm getting higher and higher, soon I'll be at the very top of the building, at the end of the corridor and I'll be in that light.

Scene 4

I'm falling. I'm terrified. I fell out of the building (or was I pushed out?). No, I did it myself because I was attracted to the light. Now I'm falling very quickly. Soon I'm going to hit the ground, head first. I came out of the building the wrong way—from the top rather than the bottom. But it's worse than that because now I've remembered the fence, but it's not just an ordinary fence—I knew that at the beginning— it's railings (and they are hard, high, spiky, and black) so I'm going to be impaled on my head and I'm going to die. . .

The dream became so scary it turned into a nightmare. I wake up. Although this dream was intensely frightening, at the point in Scene 3 where I rise towards the light I experience a moment of euphoria, a feeling of transcendence. Another feature of this dream is that the scenes progress from place to place. First I'm outside, surrounded by railings, then I'm inside a building, next I'm preparing to exit the building, finally I return to the beginning when I fall towards the railings. Chapter 5 argues that studies of many dream reports offer little evidence of dream scenes following a familiar route; rather dream scenes relate thematically. In one sense, however, This particular dream, does seem to echo the ancient tour in the home range. The tour began at base and returned there; this dream begins and ends at the railings.

The episodic memory sources for Scene 1

Recent episodic memory 1

I had this dream the night after a visit to the Natural History Museum in London with my two young sons (J and T). We had arranged to meet my sister D just inside the gate so we must have been hanging about by the railings surrounding the museum for a little while. Certainly long enough for me to notice them, although I don't remember thinking them particularly remarkable at the time.

Recent episodic memory 2

After the museum visit, later that day I had my ears pierced. I had been contemplating this for a while but, on the spur of the moment, I decided that I would go ahead. My sister D looked after J and T while I had my ears 'done'.

The episodic memory sources for Scene 2

Recent episodic memory 3

While we were in the museum we moved from room to room in the usual manner looking at the exhibits; there were arched entrances to the rooms. Some of the rooms were quite small and dark.

Remote episodic memory 1

I'm three, I'm small but I'm pretty solid and very stubborn. My mother is 33 and she is carrying a baby. My mother has had some bad luck over babies. My mother and father were married for 7 years before I was born; they were beginning to think that they couldn't have a baby. Prior to my birth my mother had a miscarriage. She also miscarried another baby between giving birth to me and the baby she is having now. At the time, women think that carrying heavy weights during pregnancy can bring on a miscarriage. My mother thinks this.

Late in the afternoon one winter's day my mother and I go down into the cellar to fill the scuttle with coal for the fire. Our cellar has several rooms: the front cellar; the back cellar; the room with the cold slab; and the coal heap room. While my mother is filling the scuttle I feel tired and get upset. Suddenly I'm not so sure about the new baby she is carrying. *I want her to carry me*. I want her to carry me through the cellar and up the cellar steps. She tells me that I must be a big girl and walk up the stairs. She has told me that she is carrying a new baby so she can't carry me. If she does she might have another miscarriage. The scene is set for a confrontation. I have a big tantrum. My mother leaves me in the cellar.

I am screaming. I cry for my mother to come and get me. She doesn't. I think about the two ways into the cellar and all the funny little dark cellar rooms. There is the 'back' scary entrance from the garden and there is the 'right' way out into the hall.

I've never been down here on my own before. Is it safe? Should I stand very still and wait for my mother to come and get me? Or should I look in all the little, dark cellar rooms to check they are safe? Has my mother left me down here to frighten me?

The episodic memory sources for Scene 3

Remote memory 2
Eventually I rush through the cellar, passing all the little dark cellar rooms with their funny sloping ceilings to stand at the bottom of the hall cellar steps. I look up at the light and scream. Finally my mother comes to get me. I am delivered. My mother picks me up. I rise up rapidly from the darkness into the light. I am safe again. But am I? What about the new baby?

Remote memory 3
The new baby is born. I am standing outside the hospital in the darkness. I am holding my auntie's hand. It's visiting time. My auntie has brought me to visit my mother and the new baby. My auntie points upwards 'Look at the light at that window, that's where your Mummy is with the new baby.' I feel very afraid. Is the new baby dead?

The episodic memory sources for Scene 4

Recent episodic memory 4
Having my ears pierced was slightly worrying—the woman who did it joked that the piercing instrument was like a gun. Guns can kill you. I wasn't sure how sore the piercing would be but I wanted to wear more glamorous drop earrings. So the possible pain and later discomfort seemed well worth it.

Remote memory 4
We're out of the cellar but my mother is very angry. She says I mustn't ask to be carried. Carrying heavy things—like me—means the new baby might come out too soon and too quickly. My mother told me the new baby is going to come, headfirst, out of her bottom. This seems like the wrong way to me. What if the new baby drops out very fast, hits its head on the floor, and dies because I've been carried? If that happens, it will all be my fault.

Remote memory 5
The new baby, my sister R, didn't die. She grew up.

My theory, Freud's, and the museum dream

Like me, Freud thought all dream material relates 'in some way' to remembered experience, 'That all the material composing the content of the dream derives in some way from our experience, and so is reproduced, remembered, in the dream—this at least we may count as undisputed knowledge' (p. 12 in the *Interpretation of Dreams*, all quotations in this section are from this book[2]). He believed recent events, 'day-residues', trigger dreams, 'I must first affirm the proposition that a reference to the events of the day just past is to be discovered in every dream. . . Knowing this fact, I can begin the dream-interpretation perhaps by first looking for the daytime experience which has set the dream off; in many cases, indeed, this is the shortest route' (p. 127). He also comments, 'If a single day has brought us two or more experiences suitable to initiate a dream, the dream ... obeys a compulsion to form a unity out of them' (p. 137). Recent events do seem trigger dreams. Chapter 8 reports research that dreams incorporate day-residues and other recent events from up to 7 days before the dream.

But, for Freud, the recent, manifest everyday material is not important it's only there because it triggers associations with the truly important stuff, the remote, latent content of dreams. Here's what Freud says on this, 'If I assess the meaning of the dream according to the latent content brought to light by the analysis—the only correct way of doing so—all of a sudden I come upon a new and important insight. The puzzle of the dream's preoccupation with worthless fragments of daily life dissolves before my eyes. . .' (p. 133).

For Freud, the museum visit and the ear piercing would be the 'worthless fragments of daily life'. These recent events are the manifest content. Residue of them only appears in the dream because they are associated with repressed material in the unconscious. Freud says, 'The Unconscious is the true reality of the psyche, its inner nature just as unknown to us as the reality of the external world, and just as imperfectly revealed by the data of consciousness as the external world is by the information received from our sensory organs' (p. 405). In my dream, the repressed material would be the traumatic events in the cellar and my fear of being blamed if the new baby falls out too soon and dies. Recent research shows REM sleep improves memory for material repressed during wake.[3] Also when people repress material, they dream more of their negative experiences.[4]

I agree that the museum visit and the ear piercing are associated with the cellar events but I don't agree that they are otherwise insignificant. Why is the natural history museum visit associated with the cellar we had when I was three? Both contain a complex of small rooms. Our word 'museum' derives from the Temple (or House) of the Muses in Alexandria, by the Nile Delta in ancient Egypt. This museum housed shrines for the nine muses, lecture halls, dissection rooms, botanical gardens, a zoo, and accommodation for visiting scholars.[5] In addition, the museum, like the cellar, has a right way to come out. After the trauma in the cellar I feared my mother would miscarry the new baby. It might die if it came out the wrong way from her bottom. But she didn't miscarry. The new baby, my sister R, grew up to became a curator at the Natural History Museum. So the cellar and the Natural History Museum are also associated through my sister R.

In my dream as pattern theory, the recent events in dreams aren't mere trivia. When I got my ears pierced, I had no previous comparator but I expected it to be painful. This seems worth it for the pleasure of wearing exotic earrings. The circle that surrounds me in Scene 1 may be associated with round hoop earrings; the railings themselves with long, stylish 'drop' ones. Also ear piercing is a transitional event to adulthood. Birth and death are the archetypical, often painful, transitions. Associations between ear piercing, birth, and death, as painful transitional events, may also have driven the formation of the museum dream.

Is the dream an instinctive wish fulfilment? It seems the antithesis. Do I really wish to fall headfirst from the Natural History Museum and die, my head impaled upside down on the railings? Can this dream be a wish?

At the time of the museum dream, I'm 33 years old. I'm grown up. The ear piercing is a transitional event to adulthood. I'm a mother. I have two small sons, J and T. But my own mother calls me 'little mother'. This annoys me intensely. I think the museum dream may be about escaping from the confines of my overly close relationship with my mother to transition to full adulthood. But this may entail a 'fall from grace' (the fall from the museum in the dream) because my mother would resist any wish to separate and I may lose my position as the favourite. In the museum dream, I relive a primal scene—the time in the cellar when I experienced a terrifying separation from my mother. I was left with the fear the new baby might fall from her body and die because I asked to be carried. But in the dream it's me who falls. Although I nearly die in the dream in the fall from her body, the dream could be a wish—a wish to make a full transition to adulthood and be free of my mother.

But a wish can come with a downside. I desired more freedom from my mother but I feared damaging separation, as happened in the cellar, and a fall from grace. I don't think all dreams are wish fulfilments but I do think many dreams play out reward–conflict or desire–danger dilemmas in interactions with personally significant others. This is hardly surprising if the origin of dreaming lies in obtaining rewards (food, water, and potential mates) from places visited by animal predators and human competitors.

Chapter 5 explained that once a dream identifies a pattern for a particular type of place, if you visit a new associated place, then your best predication of what will happen there is the associative pattern from the first place. Contemporarily, this means when you encounter a new place, you have unconscious expectations of what will happen based on a familiar place that is associated in some emotionally significant way. When I visited the Natural History Museum for the first time,

I think I made an unconscious association with the cellar of my childhood. For me, they were associated through my sister R and their complex of small dark rooms with curved ceilings.

Gaston Bachelard (1884–1962), a French philosopher, argued the house is a primal space from which we form expectations of other places we visit; he saw the cellar as the place of the unconscious and of nightmares.[6] So, some generally held, rather than purely personally experienced, associations with the cellar may also have played a part in the museum dream.

I started this chapter with Freud's theory because it addresses what I think is the most telling difference between consciousness in wakefulness and during dreaming: the hyperassociativity of dreams. By hyperassociativity, I mean dreams take elements of experiences that happened at different times and, sometimes, in different places, and associate them. In Freud's theory dream associations disguise, for me they reveal a pattern.

Perhaps the most significant difference between my dream theory and Freud's is he thinks the purpose of dreams is to protect sleep, whereas I ascribe many functions to dreaming: surviving, remembering, emoting, deciding, predicting, revealing, and creating. But all of these stem from making patterned associations.

Antti Revonsuo

Antti Revonsuo is a Finnish philosopher, neuroscientist, and psychologist at the University of Turku. He developed the Threat Simulation Theory (TST) of dreaming and, with others, a Social Simulation Theory (SST).

Revonsuo's dream theory

Revonsuo thinks dreams have a purpose. He thinks dreams evolved to aid our survival. He thinks dream content reflects the dangers our ancestors encountered. I do too.

Revonsuo argues dreams simulate the kind of threatening events encountered by early humans and, in so doing, rehearse skills in threat perception and threat avoidance. Clearly, his focus is on the evolutionary context within which dreaming developed. In his view, the purpose of dreaming is to increase the chances of early humans living long enough to reproduce and so enhance evolutionary fitness. By way of illustration, the museum dream is clearly threatening. The threat of falling is also one, which would have been fatal—if a predator was chasing you. Revonsuo recognizes not all dreams are threat simulations. His premise is that all dreams still have the capability to simulate threats. When the contemporary environment is safe, dreams will reflect current concerns, for example, work-related problems or issues with personal relationships, rather than the life-threatening events that were an everyday concern for early humans.

I agree with Revonsuo that any theory on the purpose of dreaming should focus on its original adaptive function within the hazardous environment inhabited by early humans. Clearly dreaming may have evolved since then to adapt to environmental changes. I also agree that dream content now reflects contemporary concerns rather than survival being the exclusive focus.

Comparing Revonsuo's theory with mine

Unlike Freud's and mine, Revonsuo's theory doesn't say anything about dream associations. He doesn't explain why, if dreams simulate the threats or concerns of wakefulness, the threat or concern isn't replayed exactly as it was experienced. Not all threats are the same, nor are concerns. The threat of a fall differs from being chased, for example, and threat perception and avoidance would take different forms in each. If the purpose of simulation is to rehearse threat perception and avoidance for a particular threat then it would seem necessary to reexperience the threat in the dream. In wake, I didn't fall headfirst through coming out the wrong way from an exit at the top of the museum. As I argued in the previous section, the threat seems to be created through associating my old fear of my sister R coming out the wrong way, being born too soon, and falling to her death with my fears of separation from my mother and with my anxieties about the ear piercing.

Also REM dreams don't replay experiences—they associate elements of different experiences. Chapter 3 points to Magdalena Fosse and colleagues at Harvard Medical School. They found memories of experiences were replayed in a scant 1–2% of dreams. Only in post-traumatic stress disorder (PTSD) is the trauma relived in a very similar way in dreams as it was in real life. One study found 50% of dreams in PTSD replicate the trauma.[7] But dreaming in PTSD isn't normal so a dream theory cannot be based solely on 50% of PTSD dreams. In addition, threat simulation to rehearse perception and avoidance is practised during wake. Experiencing a trauma leads, whenever the trauma is avoidable, to logical strategies to evade a repetition, so it's not clear what additional benefit would be gained from dreaming, which cannot devise logical strategies to avoid threats.

In contrast, my theory refers to the evidence for two different cognitive styles. In wake the style is logical, sequential reasoning. In REM sleep/dreaming the style is highly associative, diffuse connectivity. Both are likely to be useful in avoiding threats. During wake you can logically work out threat-avoidance strategies. But my theory argues that only REM sleep/dreaming can identify the non-obvious patterns in threat -related experiences that are retained as unconscious images to be used in wake to assess the likelihood of the threat when its presence is uncertain.

I agree with Revonsuo that dreams are necessary to avoid threats but I think they do so not through threat simulation and avoidance rehearsal but through identifying a pattern in the past behaviour of the threatening being. This pattern identification would also have worked to ensure a meeting with a mate. My theory is not only about avoiding threats but obtaining rewards. Reproductive success does not come only by evading predators!

The SST of dreaming is similar to the TST, albeit updated to reflect the importance of social interactions in the contemporary world. I agree that dreaming incorporates social experiences, but the same critique applies to SST as to TST. If the aim is to simulate, why associate elements of experiences to engender bizarre and, often impossible, scenarios? Why not simulate actual experiences? And why do this in dreaming when we can simulate perfectly well in wake?

Ernest Hartmann

Ernest Hartmann (1934–2013) was an Austrian-American psychiatrist and psychoanalyst who wrote several books on dreams and nightmares. He also worked on his own dreams and those of others. I do too.

Hartmann's dream theory

Hartmann thought the purpose of dreaming is to make new, emotional associations between our experiences. This integrates them into our memory systems, creating a meaningful, emotional basis for the self. I agree with this.

Hartmann emphasizes the loose nature of dream associations. He also points to the difference between the sequential, logical, focused associations we make in wake and the unfocused, more parallel, broader associations of dreaming (see Figure 2.1, which is taken from Hartmann, in Chapter 2). He argues that dream associations between experiences are creative; this means that dreams cannot simulate our experiences in wakefulness. A dream is always something new—never a replay—except in PTSD and, even then, Hartmann argues the dream, although similar to the traumatic experience, is not exactly the same.

Hartmann thinks central dream images important, defined, as 'A Central Image (contextualizing image) is a striking, arresting or compelling image—not simply a story—but an image, which stands out by virtue of being especially powerful, vivid, bizarre, or detailed.'[8] Arguing the power of this image reflects the strength of its emotional charge for the dreamer. By 'contextualizing' Hartmann means the image provides a 'picture context' for the dreamer's emotion. By way of illustration, in the museum dream the central image would be the fall from the museum towards my death through being impaled on the railings.

I think the strength of his account is to address the hyperassociativity of dreams, as Freud does, but without invoking the disguise explanation. Although I concur with Hartmann, his ideas are quite limited in scope. His main idea on the purpose of dreaming is the 'weaving in' or integration of new experiences with older associated ones in memory networks. But he doesn't offer an explanation of how this happens. Nor does he explain why integration requires loose or broad associations.

Comparing Hartmann's theory with mine

In contrast, my theory offers an evolutionary explanation for how dream associations integrate experiences. The evolutionary context for dream associations was the identification of probabilistic patterns in the behaviour of predators, competitors, and potential mates at landmark junctions. To identify the pattern, the dream construction integrates elements of different experiences. The behaviour of predators, competitors, and potential mates was an everyday concern for early humans because the landmark junctions held rewards but predators, competitors, and potential mates visited too. Contemporarily, assuming we are outside a war zone, our concerns are not about survival but about negotiating our personal and work-related issues with significant others.

I maintain these concerns still trigger the identification of patterns in our experiences. For example, in the museum dream, if my concern is to establish more distance from my mother, I also fear what this separation will bring because she left me alone in the cellar. The cellar is associated with the Natural History Museum in two non-obvious ways. Both are a complex of small rooms and relate to my sister R. These associations, along with the ear piercing, lead to the fear of coming out of the museum the wrong way, to fall and be impaled on my head on the railings.

These associations integrate (or in Hartmann's phrase weave in) the recent visit to the museum and the recent ear piercing with the remote cellar experiences. In terms of pattern identification, the associations are loose or non-obvious because the behaviour patterns of humans and animals are probabilistic, meaning tendencies rather than certainties characterize them. Will my mother react negatively to my seeking more independence? Will there be a fall from grace? Possibly but not definitely. My mother may surprise me. The unconscious image retained from the museum dream will make me wary of distancing myself from my mother but doesn't preclude it. Why would non-obvious associations be advantageous for integrating memories? Chapter 4 explains how non-obvious associations at landmark junctions make for stronger encoding and retention of memories because the episodic memories are more easily distinguished.

Hartmann thinks the non-obvious associations we make during REM dreaming create a meaningful basis for the self. In my view, these associations do underpin the self but they usually remain unconscious—my recollection and detailed unpicking of the associations in the museum dream is unusual. This book has outlined how unconscious associations drive the self who makes decisions, takes actions, anticipates, and creates. Conscious associations also form the conscious self—I like to think of myself as the sort of person who visits museums, for example.

Of those unconscious associations, which create the self, Hartmann's central image encompasses the most defining. For example, in the museum, the fall from the museum towards my death through impalement on the railings associates the cellar trauma, involving my mother and my sister R with my ear piercing and love of elegant earrings.

Are Dreams Just Noise, Nonsense or Epiphenomena?

Maybe dreams don't have any purpose. Maybe they're noise, nonsense, or just froth (more formally, epiphenomena).

Are dreams noise?

Back in 1977, Allan Hobson and Bob McCarley proposed an Activation-Synthesis theory. During REM dreaming, they say the brainstem (the most primitive, posterior part of the brain) generates random activation. This noise reaches the forebrain or cortex, which then synthesizes this input through access to memories, doing 'the best of a bad job in producing even partially coherent dream imagery from the relatively noisy signals sent up from the brainstem.'[9] This sounds as if Hobson and McCarley think dreams are just noise. Indeed, in this vein they present the Activation-Synthesis theory as a refutation of Freud's view that dreams are meaningful, albeit disguised, desires or wishes.

However, by 2003, Hobson comments that dreams are personally meaningful, instinctively emotional, and hyperassociative[10]—a position that is not so at variance with Freud. More recently still, Hobson argues dreaming is protoconsciousness—a preparation for waking consciousness[11], this idea is related to the simulation theories of Revonsuo in the sense that dreaming prepares the mind/brain for wakefulness. Clearly 'dreams as patterns' prepare for wakefulness too but my theory is more ambitious for the dreaming state in that these hyperassociative patterns are complementary to the linear-logical ones discerned during wake.

Are dreams nonsense?

A particularly interesting—to me—account of dreams as nonsense is the 1983 Crick and Mitchinson theory.[12] Like me, they think we retain memories of experiences in networks, which embed associations. They don't suggest landmark junctions but they do think memories in networks are liable to become superimposed, producing hyperassociations or mixtures of elements from different memories. Unlike me, they don't imagine these elements of different memories could identify a complex, non-obvious pattern in experience. Crick and Mitchinson think superimposed associations engender spurious memories, arguing that during REM sleep expels these false memories through a process they call 'reverse learning'. We dream of these spurious associations as we unlearn these nonsense memories.

It's not clear to me from this account whether Crick and Mitchinson think dreams, although nonsense, have a purpose. Could the process of reverse learning occur without dreaming? Of course, as should be clear by now, I don't think dreams are real memories but I don't think they are nonsense: they identify a pattern in experience. Crick and Mitchinson also mention the possibility that a defect in the process of reverse learning would mean spurious memories are retained, which may result in some forms of schizophrenia. What they term a spurious memory is, I think, a complex, non-obvious pattern in experience. But their account is somewhat analogous to mine in that I propose madness may result when you mistake a pattern in your experience for your experience.

Are dreams froth or, more formally, epiphenomena?

Epiphenomena are things that occur as a mere by-product of something else. In themselves, they have no function but the underlying generative processes do. In his 2001 book, Owen Flanagan, the philosopher and neurobiologist at Duke University, US, takes this position on dreams, arguing they are 'spandrels' of sleep—a spandrel is an architectural term for the triangle shapes that occur when making arches.[13] These spandrels have no significance in themselves, but are an inevitable consequence of building an arch. Similarly, Flanagan says dreams have no evolutionary adaptive significance. They just came along as a by-product of sleep. On the other hand, Flanagan argues that dreams can be self-expressive. Indeed, reflecting on one of his own dreams, he remarks they reveal aspects of the self, sometimes ones that the dreamer would rather not admit to. However, Flanagan argues this self-expression during dreams is always limited as compared with that in wake.

Theories that dreams are without function, just noise, nonsense, or epiphenomena, are now rather old, nevertheless they've been influential. They live on in the culturally prevalent notion of 'it's just a dream'.

Briefly...

After comparing the theories of Freud, Revonsuo, and Hartmann with my own, I conclude that much of Freud's now seems unconvincing but significant insights remain, as illustrated in my museum dream. The theories of Hartmann and Revonsuo are both important—I concur with Hartmann's ideas on association but they feel incomplete. I don't think Revonsuo's TST fits the available evidence; in particular it doesn't explain why dreams don't rehearse threats experienced in wake or, indeed, simulate possible threats in the way they would play out in the future. Of noise, nonsense, and epiphenomenon, I resonate most with Crick and Mitchinson. I agree dreams are false memories, in the sense that they didn't actually happen. But identifying a pattern from elements of different experiences is certainly not something to be expelled from memory networks.

Next

To conclude I speculate about the future of dreaming in 'What Dreams May Come?'

Notes

1. Historical context for the writings of Sigmund Freud. Available at: https://www.college.columbia.edu/core/content/writings-sigmund-freud/context
2. Freud, S. (1999). *The Interpretation of Dreams*, J. Crick (transl.). Oxford University Press, Oxford.
3. Fischer, S., Diekelmann, S., & Born, J. (2011). Sleep's role in the processing of unwanted memories. *Journal of Sleep Research*, *20*(2), 267–274.
4. Malinowski, J. (2017). High thought suppressors dream more of their negative waking-life experiences than low thought suppressors. *Dreaming*, *27*(4), 269.
5. Available at: http://brian-haughton.com/ancient-mysteries-articles/ancient-library-alexandria/
6. Bachelard, G. (2014). *The Poetics of Space*. Penguin, London.
7. Wittmann, L., Schredl, M., & Kramer, M. (2007). Dreaming in posttraumatic stress disorder: a critical review of phenomenology, psychophysiology and treatment. *Psychotherapy and Psychosomatics*, *76*(1), 25–39.
8. See p. 99 in Hartmann, E., Kunzendorf, R., Rosen, R., & Grace, N. G. (2001). Contextualizing images in dreams and daydreams. *Dreaming*, *11*(2), 97–104.
9. Hobson, J. A., & McCarley, R.W. (1977). The brain as a dream state generator: an activation-synthesis hypothesis of the dream process. *American Journal of Psychiatry*, *134*, 1335–1348.
10. See p. 4 and p. 113 in Hobson, J. A. (2003). *Dreaming: An Introduction to the Science of Sleep*. Oxford University Press, New York.

11. Hobson, J. A. (2009). REM sleep and dreaming: towards a theory of protoconsciousness. *Nature Reviews Neuroscience*, *10*(11), 803.

12. Crick, F., & Mitchison, G. (1983). The function of dream sleep. *Nature*, *304*(5922), 111–114; and Crick, F., & Mitchison, G. (1995). REM sleep and neural nets. *Behavioural Brain Research*, *69*(1–2), 147–155.

13. Flanagan, O. J. (2001). Dreaming Souls: Sleep, Dreams, and the Evolution of the Conscious Mind. Oxford University Press, Oxford.

Epilogue
What Dreams May Come?

We no longer dream to survive. Our lives are no longer contingent on making non-obvious associations to identify a pattern in the behaviour of predators, competitors, and potential mates as they move around to secure resources in the world. Has this changed our dreams? Has it had an impact on our minds/brains?

We no longer dream about predators and waterholes because we aren't concerned with them. We dream about other things—kite presents and sand-houses. That's okay because our contemporary world makes different demands on us. But are our dreams as good as they used to be? Are we as proficient at making non-obvious associations? One indicator would be dream bizarreness because non-obvious associations produce fantastic images. This is hard to assess. But I argue a dream-like state in wake makes us more creative. We can assess creativity.

We are becoming less creative. As measured by tests on divergent thinking, which reaches its zenith in dreaming, research in wake shows we are less able to come up with unique and non-obvious ideas, less imaginative, less adept at elaborating on ideas, and less funny.[1] We are less creative whenever customary patterns of thought and familiar ideas constrain our brains. Often-used patterns prevent us coming up with new patterns, new ideas.[2] Another pertinent research finding is: the fewer resources we have the more creative we are—affluence dulls the mind.[3]

Early humans possessed little to nothing, living like animals. They searched for food and water on daily tours in a very threatening environment. We were in the wild. Scarcity the norm. Our dreams were our survival kits. The more creative our dreams, the more likely we were to survive and reproduce. So creative genes were passed on. Now we don't have to be creative to survive. Many of us live in comfort and plenty. It's not surprising creativity is on the decline.

This book argues that the ability to dream—to detect non-obvious patterns in events—is not only critical for creativity but also for remembering, unconscious decision making, prediction, and insight. Undermining all these faculties is clearly concerning. On the other hand, while creativity declines, IQ scores are going up.[4] We understand sleep and dreams much better because we know much more. Can we use our intelligence in wake to boost our creativity during sleep, dreaming, and dream-like states in wake? Many of us have sleep trackers; the future will see sleep hackers and dream enhancers. I think dreaming and dream-like states identify

What Do Dreams Do? Sue Llewellyn, Oxford University Press (2020). © Oxford University Press.
DOI: 10.1093/oso/9780198818953.001.0001.

complex patterns. Can we boost our ability to identify complex patterns without survival as a driver? If we can, who knows what dreams will come.

Notes

1. Rettner, R. (2011) Are today's youth less creative and imaginative? Available at: https://www.livescience.com/15535-children-creative.html
2. King, P. (2016) Why our brains become less creative as we get older. Available at: https://www.forbes.com/sites/quora/2016/08/03/why-our-brains-become-less-creative-as-we-get-older/#27e801017955
3. DiSalvo, D. (2015) Study: The more stuff we have, the less creative we are. Available at: https://www.forbes.com/sites/daviddisalvo/2015/11/19/study-the-more-stuff-we-have-the-less-creative-we-are/#cacfe11505c0
4. Bronson, B. and Merryman, A. (2010) The creativity crisis. Available at: https://www.newsweek.com/creativity-crisis-74665

Name Index

Note: Figures are indicated by *f* following the page number

For the benefit of digital users, indexed terms that span two pages (e.g., 52–53) may, on occasion, appear on only one of those pages.

Subject Index

Note: Figures are indicated by *f* following the page number

For the benefit of digital users, indexed terms that span two pages (e.g., 52–53) may, on occasion, appear on only one of those pages.